ENTREPRENEURIAL
LITIGATION

ENTREPRENEURIAL LITIGATION

ITS RISE, FALL, AND FUTURE

JOHN C. COFFEE, JR.

HARVARD UNIVERSITY PRESS

Cambridge, Massachusetts   London, England

2015

LIBRARY OF CONGRESS CATALOGING-IN-PUBLICATION DATA
Coffee, John C., 1944–
Entrepreneurial litigation : its rise, fall, and future /
John C. Coffee, Jr.
pages   cm
Includes bibliographical references and index.
ISBN 978-0-674-73679-5 (alk. paper)
1. Class actions (Civil procedure)—United States.   I. Title.
KF8896.C64   2015
347.73'53—dc23   2014042252

This book is dedicated to my two favorite scholars:
Dr. Jane P. Coffee and Dr. Megan P. Coffee

CONTENTS

ENTREPRENEURIAL
LITIGATION

PART ONE

ENTREPRENEURIAL LITIGATION: A UNIQUELY AMERICAN CONCEPT

AMERICANS ARE DISTINCTIVE in many ways, but none more so than in the way they litigate. In much high-stakes litigation in the United States, the plaintiff's attorney both controls the litigation and finances it. Elsewhere, this pattern is unknown. Indeed, litigation is discouraged in most of the world—by rules that impede the financing of litigation and that force the loser to bear the often much larger legal costs of the winner. Above all, most legal systems find it unacceptable that a lawyer could represent a large group of individuals who had not specifically consented to the representation but who would nonetheless be bound by the outcome of the action commenced in their name. Yet, litigation in which attorneys represent and bind "involuntary" clients occurs on an everyday basis in class action practice in the United States, and the lawyer is paid a court-approved portion of the monetary recovery as his or her fee (without any need for client consent). Put simply, in group litigation in the United States, the lawyer often appears to be hiring the client, rather than the client hiring the lawyer.

All this did not happen overnight, and this book will trace the evolution of the laws and practices that give attorneys in the United States a unique level of control over their clients in group litigation. Indeed, the attorney's power over the client is such that when the plaintiff's attorney files a class action, any person included within the proposed class definition (which can include millions of persons) will be bound by the outcome of the case if the class is certified by the court—unless that class member takes affirmative action to opt out on a timely basis. Because most class members typically never learn of the action's pendency, they have no realistic means by which to escape. To the extent that (1) the attorney controls the litigation, (2) the client has a largely nominal role, and (3) the attorney is seeking to enforce a regulatory statute (such as the federal antitrust, environmental, or securities laws), the private attorney is taking on a public role and acting as a quasi-public servant. Such a plaintiff's attorney can be called a modern day "bounty hunter" (also an American invention) or, more politely, a "private attorney general." Whatever the name used, this attorney is a private actor, wielding a degree of public power, but motivated by powerful economic incentives, and yet subject to only limited accountability. Unsurprisingly, this combination of profit motive and public purpose has made the class action plaintiff's attorney increasingly controversial (and politically vulnerable) in recent years.

Indeed, if the invention and development of the class action was the dominant judicial innovation of the late twentieth century, its dismantling appears to be the major procedural project of the conservative majority of the contemporary Supreme Court in the twenty-first century. In a series of decisions over the last twenty years, the Court has closed the courthouse door to class actions across a range of substantive legal areas having little in common—for example, cases involving mass torts, employment discrimination, or antitrust claims. Only the securities class action has largely escaped judicial emasculation, but it too has been trimmed and its future remains uncertain. At the same time, the Court has limited plaintiff's attorney's fees, placed constitutional restrictions on the award of punitive damages, and made arbitration provisions in standard form contracts an insurmountable barrier to litigation in court.

What is driving the Court's majority, which normally believes in stare decisis and leaves legal change to Congress? Although its decisions are highly technical, a common denominator is the fear that, once a class is certified, the plaintiff's attorney will gain a degree of leverage that the Court's majority considers extortionate and that will compel defendants to settle, because defendants cannot gamble on the unpredictability of juries or safely await vindication on appeal.

Undoubtedly, a certified class under U.S. procedural rules does give the plaintiff's attorney great leverage, chiefly because the class will include all persons defined by the attorney to be within the class, unless the persons take affirmative action to exclude themselves. Because few class members opt out (or even know that an action in their name is pending), the plaintiff's attorney is empowered. But is this leverage "extortionate"? Here, two axiomatic ideas are locked today in mortal combat, because they represent the opposite sides of the same coin. On the one hand, small claimants often hold meritorious claims that they cannot afford to litigate. Such "negative value" claims (meaning that they cost more to assert individually than the plaintiff would recover, even if victory were certain) will be abandoned (and defendants will be enabled to exploit such claimants in the future), unless an attorney can aggregate these small claimants into an efficient procedural vehicle for common litigation. The plaintiff's attorney will do this only if the transaction costs that the attorney must bear to organize the class are exceeded by the attorney's expected fee award. The unique "opt out" class recognized by American procedure solves this problem by using as its default rule the inclusion of all putative class members unless they opt out. On the other hand, the "opt out" class confers great (and arguably extortionate) leverage on the plaintiff's attorney, because the merits of the underlying claim are largely irrelevant to the question of whether the class can be certified.

In short, the American-style "opt-out" class action, which automatically includes and binds all those who do not take affirmative action to escape it, both answers the plaintiff's key problem and creates the defendant's core dilemma. To liberals, the class action's benefits outweigh its costs, because it provides legal representation to dispersed and small claimants, who could never afford to sue on an individual basis. To conservatives, this solution creates an army of litigants under the command of a self-appointed general who will lead them into a combat for which they never volunteered. To the objective onlooker, it is clear that the plaintiff's attorney's clients in a class action are often "involuntary" (because they never expressly opted into the class). But this may be the only feasible solution that addresses the collective action problem inherent in the reality that most small claimants have too little at stake to justify individual action (either to sue or to opt out). At bottom, the issue is which do we value more: litigant autonomy or effective representation?

On closer inspection, the choice between these two values needs to be sensitive to context, and a uniform response might be overbroad. Some forms of class actions developed when claimants were small and held largely negative value claims, but the context has since changed. For example, in securities class actions, the vast majority of shares are held by institutional investors who typically hold claims that they can litigate themselves (and increasingly do). In this context, the degree to which "negative value" claimants benefit from the availability of the class action is unclear, as they may chiefly subsidize larger claimants by increasing the settlement value of the latter's claims.

The predicament of negative value claims has a global dimension. Today, Europe remains skeptical of the legitimacy of American-style class actions, but it (and other nations) are increasingly recognizing the need to develop new procedural forms to permit group representation. These nations agree that the central justification for such a group remedy is that it makes possible the vindication of claims with "negative value"—that is, claims that are legally meritorious but that will cost individual litigants far more to assert than any likely recovery. Aggregating such claims into an American-style class action may be an efficient means of reducing the transaction costs per litigant and thus obtaining some compensation for victims (as well as some deterrence for wrongdoers). Arguably, rough justice under U.S. rules may be better than no justice. But Europe still doubts that the goal of "access to justice" justifies the means of "involuntary" representation. Are there other alternatives? That question—how we should optimally design a private enforcement remedy for aggregate litigation—is one to which we shall return.

Complicating the European evaluation of the American approach to aggregate litigation is the fact that the U.S. approach goes beyond simply grouping small (and sometimes larger) claims into a procedural vehicle, called the class action, for their effective assertion. In addition, U.S. law also assumes that private enforcement of law is a necessary, or at least desirable, supplement to public enforcement of law. In the standard U.S. legal shorthand, the plaintiff's attorney pursuing a class or other form of group representation is deemed a "private attorney general," who necessarily supplements public enforcement (and also provides a safeguard against the "capture" or compromise of public enforcers). This idea, while distinct from the procedural issues surrounding the class action, evolved in unison with the modern class action, and it is difficult to discuss one without the other. A principal aim of this book is to examine the actual performance of the private attorney general across a variety of contexts. Has it lived up to its promise? When does it work well? When does it fail?

Even if Europe concedes the need for an aggregate litigation remedy, it remains deeply concerned that the American system converts the plaintiff's attorney from an agent serving clients into an entrepreneur who largely escapes client control. In reality, class actions and other representative actions for monetary damages in the United States are largely lawyer financed, lawyer controlled, and lawyer settled, subject to generally weak client control and only modest oversight by courts.

An economist would say that such a system is one with high "agency costs," because the lawyers, as agents, cannot be easily held accountable and can sometimes subordinate the client's interests to their own. But this economic language understates the full dimensions of the problem. Because no individual class member typically has a fraction of the economic stake at risk that the plaintiff's attorney has, the attorney's actions and decisions are seldom closely monitored by the class members. The attorney thus behaves more like a principal than an agent. In addition, large class actions inherently involve a continuing investment decision by the plaintiff's attorney, who in fact risks millions of dollars that the attorney advances to fund the litigation on a contingent fee basis. But if the prospects for a positive recovery fade, the action may be quietly abandoned or settled quickly and cheaply. For all these reasons, this book's starting point is to view the plaintiff's attorney in large class actions as less an agent than a risk-taking entrepreneur, with the class members serving as largely passive partners. This book will call such attorney-funded litigation "entrepreneurial litigation" to distinguish it from both other forms of high-stakes litigation, where the client retains control, and from "public interest" litigation (which is generally financed and conducted by organizations that raise funds from their supporters and sympathizers in the general public).

Obviously, this notion of the lawyer as an entrepreneur is normatively troubling to many, and it cannot be easily reconciled with traditional legal ethics, which views the attorney as an agent and insists that the client is entitled to make all significant litigation decisions. Given this distance between norm and reality, it is hardly surprising that scandals periodically erupt in the world of class and derivative actions, and plaintiff's attorneys have recently been criminally convicted for behavior that much evidence suggests was not uncommon in class actions. Does this mean that the class action should be abandoned? Clearly, curtailing class actions would deny "access to justice" to many individuals with meritorious (but "negative value") claims. Equally clear, it might leave the business community and other powerful interests underdeterred, because public enforcement of law is chronically underfunded. Private enforcement thus plays a failsafe function, arguably protecting society against the danger that important legal rules—whether relating to discrimination, the environment, or the antitrust and securities laws—may, from time to time, be quietly underenforced.

Given this problematic trade-off, this book will attempt a "warts and all" evaluation of the costs and benefits of the American system of entrepreneurial litigation. It will ask the following questions: How successful is this system? What reforms could curb its abuses without sacrificing the goal of access to justice for victims with negative value claims? It will not find any simple answers that work across the board. Rather, it will find that context counts and that the American system works better in some settings than in others. Above all, it will find it easier to justify the class action and entrepreneurial litigation generally in terms of the deterrence they generate than the compensation they garner. But in some areas, even this deterrence may be overstated.

Overall, it seems clear that the United States—rightly or wrongly—is retreating from its earlier, optimistic acceptance of entrepreneurial litigation. Indeed, in many areas of law, the class action has been progressively restricted or even shut down, as Congress and the courts have sometimes barred class actions, sometimes greatly tightened the rules on class certification, and sometimes allowed defendants to escape the judicial system entirely for arbitration systems that effectively foreclose the "negative value" claimant. For all these reasons, this book will argue that the class action needs to be strengthened in some settings and downsized in others.

Still, the focus of this book is not exclusively on the U.S. system of large-scale litigation. Europe and the rest of the world recognize the need to address aggregate litigation but continue to feel discomfort with the idea of the lawyer as entrepreneur. In particular, Europe is attracted to the idea of "litigation funding" by third parties. This approach (which began in Australia) seeks to secure litigation financing on an effectively contingent basis from risk-tolerant financial institutions (such as hedge funds). At the same time, the litigation funder can also (for another fee) insure class members against the danger that their adversaries' litigation costs will be shifted to them if the action is unsuccessful—thus solving the "loser pays" problem that would otherwise deter class members. Ideally, this makes the attorney a more objective professional, but this system is both costly and still unproven in the class action context.

This volume will consider whether a nonentrepreneurial alternative is feasible for Europe that can effectively litigate "negative value" claims. Here, it will draw comparisons with another U.S. innovation: public interest litigation conducted by not-for-profit organizations committed to a specific goal or agenda. In reality, the United States has long had two alternative systems—entrepreneurial litigation and public interest litigation—by which to handle aggregate litigation, and they have specialized in different areas. The rest of the world may prefer a hybrid of these two.

Lastly, this book will reconsider the relationship between public enforcement and private enforcement, and suggest that in many areas a hybrid of the two would be superior—at least so long as we can protect the private attorney general from political capture. If the private attorney general cannot carry the full responsibilities that its proponents originally assigned it, it can at least serve as a "failsafe" remedy that remains available when public enforcement is compromised. In this light, the final chapter will consider the possibility of a "Semiprivate Attorney General."

1

LITIGATION AND DEMOCRACY

GIVEN THAT THE AMERICAN SYSTEM of entrepreneurial litigation is distinctive, how and why did it develop? One cannot understand or reform a complex system without some insight into its origins and rationale. In particular, why did group litigation evolve in the United States and practically nowhere else? U.S. lawmakers delegated extraordinary discretion and power to lawyers. Why? At present, there is no satisfactory account that explains how this system coalesced. Although some work has been done on the individual elements of the American system—for example, the rise of the class action, the acceptance of the contingent fee, and the emergence of the unique "American rule" on fee shifting—the whole is greater than the sum of its parts. This volume seeks to fill some of that void.

In truth, the American system of entrepreneurial litigation has deep historical roots that extend back to the founding of the American Republic and that are closely entangled with core American political ideals. When Alexis de Tocqueville traveled through the United States in 1831, he marveled at the frequency with which political issues were taken to courts for their resolution.[1] This tendency to transform political issues into legal ones was at least partly explained, he recognized, by the ability of American courts to mediate these disputes in ways that led citizens to perceive courts as protecting their rights and interests. This legalization of political issues was possible because citizens in postcolonial America saw themselves as more protected by legal rights than by social class or political party. Difficult as it may be to believe today, they also saw the legal profession as the home of their natural leaders.[2] In contrast, in Europe, both the law and the courts were perceived by the ordinary citizen as agents of the state (and particularly the national government in its constant efforts to centralize power). If not actually oppressive, the courts were seen at least as guardians of a fairly rigid status quo. Instead, in the United States, the law—and ultimately the U.S. Constitution—guaranteed the citizen's liberty and property, and the courts and lawyers were its champions.

At least equally importantly, the process of American law was characteristically different. Robert Ferguson opens his book, *The Trial in American Life,* by noting that "Courtroom trials are central ceremonies in the American republic of laws."[3] True, but the American jury system was more than a symbol. Constitutionally enshrined,[4] it was recognized (at least in the nineteenth century) as an inherently democratic institution that made the law locally responsive and thus constituted one of the essential "checks and balances" in our system of constitutional governance. Indeed, in the early nineteenth century, the jury system was envisioned as virtually a fourth branch of government that protected citizens from overreaching by the executive branch.[5] Ideally, juries were expected to function something like a community legislature. To Tocqueville, the jury system insured "the sovereignty of the people."[6] Today, the jury system is but a shadow of its former self, but, as Tocqueville saw, it operated then in a strikingly different fashion from anything that European legal systems had seen.

Judges were also different in the United States. In Europe, judges were the appointees of the central government and were often charged with enforcing its policies against recalcitrant regions or provinces. In the United States, by the early to middle nineteenth century, the majority of state judges were popularly elected (and even where they were not elected, they were appointed by governors and legislatures that were politically accountable).[7] This combination of politically responsive state judiciaries and juries representing and reflecting the local community both decentralized political power and subjected it to a popular veto, thereby making the American legal system far more palatable to the common citizen.

A further consequence of this very different perception of the law in the United States—as the guardian of democracy and the rights of the common man—was a very different perception of the lawyer. As Tocqueville particularly emphasized, lawyers in the United States were the leaders of civil society and, in his view, its natural aristocrats. Because their perceived role was to protect the citizen from governmental abuse, lawyers occupied, and were accorded, a greater role in government in the United States than in Europe. This does not mean that there was not antilawyer sentiment (indeed, there often was), but lawyers dominated state governments and legislatures. From that position, as we will soon see, they predictably protected the interests of lawyers.

This differing view of the lawyer—as protector, not oppressor—helps explain why the United States quickly abandoned (probably by the mid-nineteenth century) the English rules against champerty, which would have precluded the development of any system of entrepreneurial litigation. Similarly, England's "loser pays" rule that required the loser in litigation to pay the winner's reasonable legal expenses was dropped even more quickly (if for somewhat different reasons). These developments are taken up in the next chapter, but their origins lie—at least in part—in a very different and uniquely American view of litigation. Law was perceived as the shield of democracy, and litigation as its engine—in effect, litigation, as implemented through juries and popularly elected judges, represented democracy in action.

In part because of this very different view (at least then) of the lawyer, American courts took four steps during the nineteenth century that laid the foundation for our contemporary system of entrepreneurial litigation:

1. They accepted the contingent fee as a necessary means by which the common citizen could finance and afford litigation;
2. They developed the "American rule" on fee shifting, as an alternative to the "loser pays" rule that prevailed in England and Europe. This rule effectively insulated the plaintiff, who otherwise would

have had to fear that an unsuccessful suit against a railroad or large corporation would result in the shifting of defendant's legal fees against the plaintiff in an amount that might dwarf the damages the plaintiff was seeking;

3. They extended the law of unjust enrichment so that a plaintiff who obtained a legal victory that benefited not simply himself but others similarly situated could ask a court to award legal fees out of the common fund so created in order that the others share equitably in the legal fees that benefited them.[8] This "common fund" doctrine established the basis under which, much later, the plaintiff's attorneys in a class action could ask a court to award them fees from the class recovery; and

4. They broadly recognized the legitimacy of the derivative action. Although the derivative action had antecedents in the equity practice of English courts, England had always tightly controlled the action and limited its availability.[9]

These legal steps did not occur in isolation, but were part and parcel of a larger conception of the citizen's role and rights. The first half of the nineteenth century was the Age of Jackson in the United States, a time that celebrated the common man and believed the individual capable of determining his own destiny. Inherently, the private citizen was seen as entitled to exercise self-help remedies (such as litigation). Equally important, there was little alternative to self-help and individual action, as the federal structure of the United States ensured that it had at that time only a relatively weak central government that was in no position to intervene or serve as the citizen's champion or protector.

In contrast, from at least the time of the French Revolution on in Europe, the state was the engine of change and the protector of rights. The masses might revolt, but they did not sue. Nor did public enforcers in Europe want potential competition from private enforcement; they preferred instead to hold monopoly control over enforcement. Not surprisingly, private enforcement of law grew deeper roots in the more fertile American soil, where citizens were allowed and expected to protect their own rights. These differing starting points had lasting consequences. A century later, the civil rights revolution began in the United States with the school desegregation cases. At least initially, these cases were brought by private litigants, assisted by private lawyers consciously acting as agents of social change. In Europe, a revolution starting from such a source and triumphing in court (rather than in the political process) would have been inconceivable. But, in the United States, *Brown v. Board of Education*, the famous 1954 school desegregation case that was actually four separate private suits, represents the culmination of a tradition that had long seen private enforcement as legitimate and necessary.[10] Without question, private enforcement accelerated the pace of social and legal change in the United States, on this and other occasions.[11]

A. THE REACTION TO ENTREPRENEURIAL EXCESSES

The seeds of entrepreneurial litigation, once sown, grew rapidly in the receptive U.S. soil—and in time produced a counterreaction. A good example is supplied by the fate of the derivative action. Following its recognition by the Supreme Court in 1856, the derivative action was quickly exploited by a new breed of opportunistic litigants—to the point that by the early 1900s courts in both New York and New Jersey began to use the term "strike suit" as a shorthand expression for a nuisance action brought to extort a settlement.[12] During the middle of the twentieth century, state legislatures and state courts began to curb the availability of the derivative action. Still, even in its key decision in 1949 upholding these efforts by states to curtail the derivative action, the Supreme Court acknowledged that the derivative action had been "long the chief regulator of corporate management."[13] Today, derivative actions play a much more marginal and downsized role. Studies have shown that the derivative action produced few litigated verdicts or large settlements, but even a weak deterrent may be better than none at all. In retrospect, the derivative action's principal success lay in the critical lawmaking role that it played, because its availability enabled courts to define the content and scope of fiduciary duties.

As discussed further in Chapter 3, the rise (and relative fall) of the derivative action demonstrates that a system of entrepreneurial litigation is prone to scandal and carries the seeds of its own destruction. Once discredited in the public's mind, it will predictably be curbed. This pattern has repeated itself. As will be seen, what happened to the derivative action in the mid-twentieth century has more recently reoccurred on a lesser scale (to this point) in the case of the class action.

B. THE PRIVATE ATTORNEY GENERAL CONCEPT

Congress, as well as the courts, laid the foundation in the nineteenth century for the United States' contemporary system of entrepreneurial litigation. During the Civil War, outraged by the behavior of corrupt war "profiteers," Congress passed the False Claims Act, which resurrected the medieval "qui tam" action that authorized private persons who had suffered no injury, themselves, to prosecute suits against those who had cheated the federal government and retain a share of any recovery as their reward. This was the original "private attorney general" statute in U.S. law (even though that term was not coined until nearly a century later in 1943)[14] because it both liberalized standing and explicitly used private attorneys to supplement public enforcement.

Later, in the nineteenth century, Congress passed several statutes that permitted the successful plaintiff to recover its legal fees from the defendant. Such "one-way" fee shifting (which is now authorized in the case of many statutes) is the key exception to the earlier described American rule, and it is intended to subsidize certain types of litigation based on the premise that they are socially desirable and need to be encouraged. An even more explicit form of "bounty hunting" was introduced by the Sherman Anti-Trust Act of 1890. To deter price-fixing and other antitrust violations, it authorized a treble damages penalty that went to the successful plaintiff—in effect a legal "bounty" over and above compensatory damages. Again, this essentially invited private litigants to serve as "private attorney generals" to supplement public law enforcement and to deter special forms of legal violations.

Thus, even if the term "private attorney general" had not yet been coined, the reality of private enforcement, incentivized by deliberately punitive damages, was already an established part of the litigation world in the United States by the early twentieth century. Private antitrust cases would later fuel the expansion of the class action in the 1960s, even before an expanded, more liberal class action role was adopted in 1966.

Of course, no one in the nineteenth century foresaw the possibility of class actions for enormous money damages or that thousands of persons might be included within the class. That came much later. But the groundwork for such a system had been laid in the nineteenth century as courts accepted a system of litigation financing under which the attorney (1) advanced or bore the costs of the litigation; (2) earned a fee and recovered these expenses only if successful; (3) escaped liability (if unsuccessful) for the defendant's legal expenses, at least absent special facts; and (4) represented persons (in addition to a usually nominal client) who had never retained the attorney or consented to the action. As the twig is bent, so grows the tree, and the young tree that was planted in the nineteenth century grew into the twentieth-century American system of entrepreneurial litigation. It did not fully flower, however, until the second half of the twentieth century when (1) the class action was expanded to include claims for money damages and (2) courts began to award attorney's fees to the plaintiff's attorney based on a percentage of the recovery obtained.

C. THE POLITICIZATION OF LITIGATION

The foregoing process was not a simple linear development. Each step was controversial and scandal plagued. Although a distinct plaintiff's bar began to develop by the end of the nineteenth century, its legitimacy was never accepted by many within the traditional bar. Even if the plaintiff's bar saw itself as private attorney generals, the defense bar (or at least its most vociferous elements) painted a very different portrait of the plaintiff's bar, characterizing them as disreputable "ambulance chasers" and "strike suiters."

These attacks had real consequences because they were part of a broader political strategy. If we look at the experience of both the derivative action and the class action, a pattern seems evident: liberal reform is followed by conservative reaction. As just noted, the derivative action arose in the nineteenth century, flowered in the early to mid-twentieth century, and then was cut back (both by legislation and court decision) from the mid-twentieth century on. Similarly, the securities class action became common in the 1970s and then exploded in the 1980s, facilitated by Supreme Court decisions that made it comparatively simple to certify such a class. But then a reaction set in, as an aroused business community successfully lobbied for protection from "frivolous" suits and succeeded in securing the passage of the Private Securities Litigation Reform Act (PSLRA) in 1995 (over the veto of then President William Clinton). Simultaneously, the judicial tide also shifted dramatically. After a series of "liberal" Supreme Court decisions had encouraged securities litigation, a steady series of "conservative" decisions cut back on the action's availability and tilted the balance of advantage significantly in the direction of the defendant. As a result, in recent years, the number of securities class actions has fallen sharply.

But conservative counterreaction is not necessarily the final stage. The "conservative" PSLRA was followed by the "liberal" Sarbanes-Oxley Act in 2002 and the "liberal" Dodd-Frank Act in 2010, each passed after much publicized financial scandals and consequent recessions. The political cycle may thus repeat, because the two major political parties in the United States have aligned themselves with the rival camps—Democrats with the plaintiff's bar; Republicans with the business community—and each is heavily financed by its chosen ally.

If the United States once viewed litigation optimistically as a socially desirable activity, that attitude has largely faded. Although radical change is not likely in the United States, two different visions of the plaintiff's attorney in class actions are today at war: (1) the vision of this attorney as a "private attorney general" and (2) the vision of the same attorney as a predatory, self-seeking opportunist. This book's position is that both views have some basis in fact. The "liberal" view of the plaintiff's attorney as a "private attorney general," who simply supplements public enforcement, significantly understates the reality and impact of our entrepreneurial system of private enforcement. Correspondingly, the "conservative" view of the plaintiff's attorney as a "strike suiter" seems increasingly dated after legislation (most notably the PSLRA) has substantially raised the bar for plaintiffs in order to protect defendants from "frivolous" litigation. No simple epithet—private attorney general or bounty hunter—

adequately captures the role of the plaintiff's attorney in high-stakes litigation. In truth, the plaintiff's attorney does not simply supplement public enforcement but extends and drives the law's development, sometimes pushing it in directions that public enforcers would not have gone. Entrepreneurial enforcement is inherently fast moving, adaptive, market driven, and opportunistic. And it is seldom constrained by the same principles of prosecutorial discretion that guide public enforcers.

Thus, a principal focus of this book will be whether the contemporary American system that delegates enormous discretion to the plaintiff's attorney needs to be (or can feasibly be) reformed and rehabilitated. Should greater client control be introduced—and, if so, how? Can the entrepreneurial zeal and motivation that the contemporary American system clearly produces be somehow reconciled with prosecutorial discretion and applied to public enforcement? Should public authorities play a greater gatekeeper role with regard to private enforcement of law? Finally, should Europe and other countries seeking to fashion a procedural mechanism for group litigation look to the United States or some other model? And, if so, what other models are feasible?

That is the road map for this book.

2

THE ORIGINS OF ENTREPRENEURIAL

LITIGATION

PRIVATE ENFORCEMENT OF LAW THROUGH CLASS and representative actions did not begin with the recognition of the class action for money damages in the mid-twentieth century. Rather, as earlier noted, it was shaped and directed by three doctrinal developments that occurred in the nineteenth century: (1) the acceptance of the contingency fee agreement, (2) the recognition of the "American rule" on fee shifting that exempted plaintiffs from the "loser pays" rule that largely prevailed in England and Europe, and (3) the development of a legal principle that one who creates or protects a "common fund" for persons besides himself could assess that fund for his own legal fees—thereby prorating the costs of the litigation equitably among all who shared in the fund or benefit. Underappreciated at first, this last legal principle created the economic engine that drove both the derivative action and later the class action.

Each of these developments occurred in a specific social and political context, and, particularly in the case of the contingent fee, was attended by legal controversy and the active opposition of many in the legal and business communities.

A. THE ACCEPTANCE AND CONSEQUENCES OF THE CONTINGENT FEE

From medieval times, England had forbidden anyone to provide legal assistance in return for a portion of the recovery sought. Both penal statutes and the common law doctrine of champerty enforced this prohibition.[1] The somewhat murky origins of the champerty doctrine apparently lay in efforts by rich landowners to subsidize plaintiffs in bringing suits challenging the titles of others to land in return for a portion of the recovery.[2] The underlying premise of the prohibition seems to have been that those funding such litigation were speculators who would encourage actions with a low probability of success to be brought, thereby oppressing legitimate landowners, in the hopes of sharing in an occasionally successful recovery. In this light, the champerty doctrine may be the first of many occasions on which those dubious of litigation closed down practices that gave the poor greater access to the courts on the theory that these practices encouraged the filing of frivolous actions.[3]

Based on this well-known English rule, early decisions in post–Revolutionary War state courts continued to hold contingency fee agreements to be void and unenforceable.[4] Nonetheless, evidence also suggests that contingent fee agreements were already quite common, probably because of the "scarcity of cash during the post-Colonial area."[5]

The legal tide began to shift in the second quarter of the nineteenth century, during which period at least a dozen state courts held contingent fee agreements to be enforceable.[6] Nonetheless, other courts (most notably in Massachusetts) continued to follow precedent and uphold the English rule.[7] These more doctrinally oriented courts insisted that only the legislature could repeal the English rule.

By 1850, the states were relatively evenly split on the enforceability of the contingency fee. Why had rapid doctrinal legal change occurred over this short, calm period? The best answer is the impact of the Age of Jackson on those courts accepting the contingent fee.[8] The Age of Jackson was an era of populism that celebrated the common man. Particularly those state courts on or near the frontier saw the need to simplify access to the courts for the common man (whereas Massachusetts, never a Jacksonian hotbed, insisted instead on fidelity to precedent). For example, in 1836, the Tennessee Supreme Court upheld a contingent fee agreement between a destitute woman and her attorney, describing the attorney's conduct in offering the agreement as "a grave and honorable duty of the profession."[9]

Not only were the frontier states more open to "access to justice" arguments, but their judges were more likely to be elected and thus politically accountable.[10] In some of these jurisdictions, the legislature resolved the issue in advance of the judiciary by repealing the common law doctrine of champerty. Early experience with the railroads and the first signs of industrialization convinced these legislatures that some corporations needed to be sued and that injured workers had no recourse but to rely on contingency fee agreements.

Still, a few courts in this era went beyond the politically powerful "access to justice" argument and noted that contingent fee agreements better aligned the interests of attorney and client.[11] Words like "efficiency" were not used in the mid-1850s, but a Virginia court noted in 1855 that contingent fee agreements "constituted a better guaranty for fidelity, energy and proper zeal from one's attorney than the fee certain."[12] After all, if the attorney were promised a fee certain, the attorney had an incentive to shirk and need not worry about the outcome; or if he were paid by the hour, he had an incentive to delay and collect an excessive fee (when the case might have been settled at an early point).

Although courts increasingly accepted the enforceability of the contingent fee (and this trend accelerated after the Civil War as the pace of industrialization increased), they were far from ready to confer broad discretion on the attorney and reluctant to accept any inroads on client control of the litigation. Thus, notwithstanding contrary provisions in the fee agreement, courts consistently held that the client could still settle with the adversary (over the attorney's objection).[13] Even if the client were breaching the fee agreement, public policy required that the client remain in control (and in any event settlements of disputes were favored).

Because the law is a profession that moves slowly, the actual use of contingency fee agreements appears to have developed more slowly than the law upholding their legality. Randolph Bergstrom has found that, even though New York courts had upheld contingency fees early in the nineteenth century, they were not much used prior to 1870, came into common use by 1890, and were pervasive by 1910.[14] By the last decades of the nineteenth century, the socioeconomic composition of tort plaintiffs had shifted so that the vast majority was composed of low-level office workers, domestics, and blue collar employees.[15] For these tort plaintiffs, it seems an obvious conclusion that they had no funds with which to hire a lawyer, and the contingent fee was their ticket of admission to the judicial system.

Despite the likely dependence of most plaintiffs on this system for financing litigation, the established bar generally resisted contingent fees. Throughout the last half of the nineteenth century, law journals and other legal periodicals frequently condemned both the contingent fee and the decline in legal ethics that it had occasioned.[16] Chief Justice Thomas Cooley of the Michigan Supreme Court was particularly critical, noting that the contingent fee system damaged the bar's reputation and created "antagonism" between "aggregated capital" and the "community in general."[17] It is difficult not to read between the lines here and recognize a growing polarization between established defense lawyers, representing corporations and railroads, and a new generation of plaintiff's lawyers, many of them immigrants or first-generation Americans, whose business model depended on the contingent fee.

Indeed, during the last decades of the nineteenth century, partnerships of personal injury lawyers, operating almost exclusively on contingent fees, began to appear in large eastern cities. These firms were the natural adversaries of the established firms that represented corporations, insurance companies, and railroads, and so predictably little love was lost between the two sides. But the business model of these new plaintiff firms was unique and different. Needing to operate on a high-volume basis, they hired a variety of agents to solicit victims of accidents. These agents—policemen, local low-level politicians, hospital staff, and ambulance drivers—contacted victims, sometimes literally chasing after the ambulance to solicit the victim and obtain his signature on a contingent fee retainer agreement.[18] Arguably, they were no more predatory than the agents of insurance companies, who also eagerly pursued the same victims to the hospital in the hopes of obtaining releases. But these practices gave rise to a new epithet—"ambulance chasers." These practices—real and alleged—horrified many, and eventually were outlawed by legislation in many jurisdictions.

Unseemly or even sordid as the practice of ambulance chasing may have been, it supplied the ammunition for those seeking to bar contingent fees altogether. It is thus an initial example of a phenomenon that will run like a leitmotif throughout this volume: new legal innovations—whether the contingent fee or the class action—that increase access to justice are often accompanied by scandals, as the new practitioners cross legal and ethical boundaries that earlier had seldom been transgressed. Appropriate as it may be to ban ambulance chasing and possibly the direct solicitation of victims, this abuse hardly justified restricting the contingent fee. But, as will be seen, scandals can produce overbroad reactions.

B. FROM "LOSER PAYS" TO THE AMERICAN RULE

As of the late colonial period, the law in most U.S. jurisdictions did not differ from that in England on the allocation of litigation costs: the winner in a lawsuit could seek its reasonable expenses, including attorney's fees, from the loser. Legal shorthand calls this a "loser pays" rule. This rule was partly common law but mainly statutory, as legislation in most of the colonies regulated both attorney's fees generally and, more specifically, the fees that could be taxed to a "loser" in a civil case.

Relatively quickly after the American Revolution, this English or "loser pays" rule gave way to a new rule under which each side generally bore its own legal costs. This became known as the "American rule." It would be tempting to conclude that this shift (which came much more rapidly than the acceptance of contingent fees) was the product of the same liberal belief in "access to the courts" and the need to avoid deterring meritorious litigation by financially strained plaintiffs. But the actual history is more complex.

The reality is that all legal fees were closely regulated by statute prior to the Revolution, and afterward the bar lobbied hard for the deregulation of attorney's fees.[19] Why were attorney's fees prescribed by statute? One answer is that, in the eighteenth century, the legislature directly regulated much of the economy, but, in addition, fee schedules in the United States were a substitute for the British practice under which a barrister could never sue a client for a fee and had to be content with whatever the client was willing to pay.[20] That gentleman's rule was never applied to the more rough-and-tumble law practice in the colonies (which also never distinguished the solicitor from the barrister). These new statutes, enacted shortly after the Revolutionary War, still required some modest cost recovery from "losers." But courts soon became aware that there was a vast gap between the usual fees that attorneys charged and the much smaller amount that could be shifted under this remaining "loser pays" rule.[21] Yet, neither courts nor the bar pressed for a realistic schedule of fees that could be shifted to the loser.

Why not? Basically, the bar did not want to depend on suing (or seeking to enforce a judgment against) the loser (who might be judgment-proof). Lawyers preferred to be paid by their clients, in part because they knew that legislative fee schedules would always remain low and in part because many "losers" would be judgment-proof. Payment by clients would result in higher fees with less delay. Finally, the bar was aware that under a "loser pays" system, some decisions had refused to allow trial lawyers to recover more from their clients than the statutory fee provided in the fee-shifting schedule.[22] Apart from all these practical reasons, an ideological rationale came to dominate the debate: the bar's position that legal fees should be determined by private contract became, as the nineteenth century wore on, increasingly consistent with the free market, laissez-faire ideology of that era.

Courts picked up this contractarian theme and began to generalize this new "American rule" under which each side bore its own legal expenses without fee shifting. As early as 1796, the Supreme Court announced that "The general principle of the United States is in opposition to [fee shifting]."[23]

By the 1840s, American courts were regularly upholding fee contracts, even though the fee was well above any amount that could be shifted.[24] Legislation soon followed. In 1848, the Field Code of Civil Procedure was enacted in New York, and it expressly struck down all provisions "establishing or regulating the costs or fees of attorneys" and provided that "hereafter the measure of such compensation shall be left to the agreement, express or implied, of the parties."[25]

This acceptance of private contracting had an important further consequence: if freedom of contract was to be accepted as the governing principle (as it increasingly was in nineteenth-century America), then there was little ground for prohibiting contingent fee agreements, which were also private contracts. The legitimization of the contingent fee may thus owe as much to the free market ideology that crested in the late nineteenth century as to the populism of the Age of Jackson that peaked in the first half of the nineteenth century.

At its high-water mark in the late nineteenth century, the American rule became so firmly enshrined in American jurisprudence that the Supreme Court even struck down as unconstitutional a modest Texas statute that required certain defendants to pay a $10 attorney's fee to a plaintiff who established a claim not exceeding $50 against a railroad for injury to livestock, unpaid wages, or other damages.[26] Such a statute was typical of the Granger movement, which had succeeded in passing antirailroad legislation in many farmer-dominated states. To a conservative Court, the small amount of the fee was unimportant, because, once legitimized in principle, $10 today could grow into $10,000 later. The divided Court did not find fee shifting unconstitutional, but rather focused on the fact that the statute singled out railroads as the lone defendant required to pay the $10 fee. This feature, it ruled, involved a suspect classification that could not survive the Constitution's Equal Protection Clause.

Still, even in the late nineteenth century, fee shifting against the loser never truly died. Even the Field Code, which was adopted by Congress in 1853, provided for very modest attorney's fees (generally not to exceed $20) that could be recovered from the losing side.[27] Congress, like the Field Code, itself, simply struck a political compromise that was intellectually unprincipled: some fee shifting was required but nothing like the full costs of the winning side. This paralleled what state legislatures had also done in the period directly following the American Revolution.

Fee shifting made a legislative comeback late in the nineteenth century but only in the case of special forms of litigation that Congress wished to encourage. In voting rights legislation (adopted in 1870), in the Interstate Commerce Act (adopted in 1877), and in the Sherman Anti-Trust Act of 1890, Congress authorized successful plaintiffs to recover their legal expenses in addition to their damages.[28] Congress, of course, had no obligation to be intellectually consistent, and these statutes were aimed at disfavored behaviors.

Most of these statutes provided only for "one-way" fee shifting in favor of successful plaintiffs. They were deliberately one sided, because these new statutes were an outgrowth of the Populist movement, which arose as a protest against the power of railroads and large corporations. As a result, no attempt was made to revive the English rule, because Congress had no general theory about litigation or cost recovery. Rather, Congress clearly wanted from time to time to favor one side over the other with respect to a variety of topical issues.

Begun in the nineteenth century, this pattern of subsidizing the successful plaintiff through fee shifting accelerated in the twentieth century—to the point that commentators began to speculate whether the American rule was dying.[29] In fact, the American rule was never directly challenged (as Congress made no attempt to change the litigation rules for tort or contract litigation), but simply riddled with exceptions. Most of the civil rights and environmental legislation passed after 1960 provided for "one way" fee shifting in favor of a successful plaintiff.[30] In 1976, Congress went further in enacting the Civil Rights Attorney's Fee Awards Act and extended "one way" fee shifting to a broad area of litigation based on a clearly articulated policy of social engineering.[31]

But still, the American rule did not die. Indeed, in 1975, in *Alyeska Pipeline Service Co. v. Wilderness Society*,[32] the Supreme Court broadly reaffirmed the American rule in a case where an environmental group had successfully sued to block the issuance of oil pipeline permits in Alaska. Although the district court awarded the successful plaintiff attorney's fees based on its asserted equitable power, the Supreme Court reversed, finding that the American rule governed, unless it had been legislatively overruled in a special context. The newly conservative Court did not argue the case for the American rule as efficient or otherwise desirable, but simply blanched at the idea of allowing district courts to shift fees on a case-by-case basis based on a broad equitable power.

The bottom line then is that the U.S. law today lacks the formal neutrality of either the English rule or the American rule (neither of which necessarily favors either side in the litigation). Instead, it is characterized by a general pattern under which the plaintiff is almost entirely insulated from fee shifting against it, while being encouraged by a host of special, context-specific statutes that shift fees only in the plaintiff's favor (when it is successful). The American rule survives, but with statutory exceptions that make it resemble a Swiss cheese.[33] Whatever the intent, the effect of such a compromise is to subsidize a system of entrepreneurial litigation.

C. THE "COMMON FUND" DOCTRINE

In 1881, in *Trustees v. Greenough*,[34] the Supreme Court held that a party who created or preserved a fund was entitled under principles of unjust enrichment to recoup the reasonable fees and expenses that party incurred in protecting the fund by taxing the fund for those fees and expenses (which thereby prorated the costs among all the fund's beneficiaries). Because this decision relied on the law of unjust enrichment, it was arguably also a product of the Court's new reliance on a contract law rationale as the basis for fee awards. From this perspective, fees were not being shifted to the defendant (a prospect that worried the Court in that era) but simply imposed on all the plaintiff's lawyer's clients (including the "involuntary" ones).[35]

The rationale of *Trustees v. Greenough* was criticized both contemporaneously[36] and more recently.[37] But its full implications were not then perceived because the class action had not yet developed. The decision's logic clearly implied that an individual plaintiff in a class or derivative action could retain an attorney and enter into a fee agreement (presumably on a contingent fee basis) that would be paid out of the class recovery (if any). Absent such a rule, a successful plaintiff's attorney in a class action might have won the litigation but would have no client able or willing to pay it.

Although the *Greenough* decision was articulated in terms of contract law, some observers believe the Court was more concerned with developing a rationale for fee awards in railroad receiverships (which was both the context of the *Greenough* action and then a major and controversial new specialty for federal courts).[38] Four years later, in *Central Railroad & Banking Co. of Georgia v. Pettus*,[39] the Court returned to this topic in another railroad insolvency case, and now it permitted the plaintiff's attorneys to recover a fee from the common fund that was actually greater than the fee their plaintiff client had agreed to pay them. *Pettus* thus extended *Greenough*, both by allowing the plaintiff's law firm to make its own application for fees to the court and by permitting the court to consider not just the benefit to the individual client, but to all others with an interest in the common fund, in determining the reasonable level of compensation.[40] The implications of *Pettus* for future class action fee awards are difficult to overstate.

The principle established by *Greenough* and *Pettus* lay largely dormant (outside of the bankruptcy context) until the emergence of the derivative action in the early twentieth century. Because the derivative action seeks to force the defendants to pay a recovery to the corporation (which is largely a bystander to the suit), this corporate recovery could be regarded as a common fund before the court, and plaintiff's attorneys could apply under *Pettus* for a reasonable fee. The next step was a settlement based not on monetary damages, but rather on injunctive or equitable relief. Plaintiff's attorneys convinced courts, beginning in the early 1930s, that such relief constituted a "common benefit," which should be treated the same as a "common fund," so that the plaintiff's attorney's fees could be taxed to the corporation.[41] But, as will be seen, nonpecuniary relief can be cosmetic and illusory. If nonpecuniary relief will be rewarded generously, then both plaintiff's attorneys and defendants have incentives to structure such a settlement (so that the defendants escape personal liability and the plaintiff's attorneys can avoid litigation risk).

The era of the Great Depression was the golden age of the derivative suit, probably because it was a time when corporate managers were not held in high regard and anti-business sentiment was strong. Academics during this period urged courts to set plaintiff's fees in derivative actions so as to incentivize attorneys to undertake socially desirable litigation.[42] In particular, courts and commentators began to move to the idea that the plaintiff's attorney's fee should be based on a percentage of the recovery obtained.[43] This reform had a variety of impacts: (1) it simplified the court's task in awarding fees, (2) it eliminated the attorney's incentive to delay the litigation until more attorney time could be expended, and (3) it incentivized the plaintiff's bar to behave as bounty hunters.[44]

Although fees based on a percentage of the recovery may well make more sense than fees based on the time expended (which is the principal alternative), such a formula does have one well-recognized deficiency: it incentivizes plaintiff's counsel to settle early and perhaps prematurely (in terms of the interest of the class). To the plaintiff's attorney, early settlements mean less delay in the eventual receipt of compensation by the contingent fee-paid attorney and less risk that must be borne (because the longer the case is in court, the more time that imaginative defendants have to devise new defenses and motions). As will be seen, the tendency toward early and cheap settlements in class and derivative actions has persisted since their outset, and the source of this problem probably lies in legal rules formulated many decades ago.

D. A SUMMARY

None of the foregoing three legal doctrines was unreasonable, but the cumulative impact of their recognition changed the fundamental relationship between lawyers and their clients in plaintiff's litigation in the United States. While the contingent fee enabled lower-income Americans to undertake litigation, it also made it possible for the plaintiff's attorney to contract for a substantial share of any recovery—and thereby made the plaintiff's attorney a co-venturer with the client. The substitution of the American rule for the English rule on fee shifting did not by itself encourage litigation (indeed, the case can be made that the English rule better encourages plaintiffs to bring meritorious litigation), but it did invite a particular type of litigation. If we assume a cost asymmetry between plaintiffs and defendants (with defendants paying more in legal fees), then the American rule is preferable from the plaintiff's perspective, because the plaintiff escapes the prospect of truly punitive fee shifting. Particularly with respect to "negative-value" claims, the adoption of the American rule in the nineteenth century did two things at once: (1) it encouraged underfinanced plaintiffs (and the contingent fee-paid lawyers representing them) to sue corporations, railroads, and other business entities that would predictably incur higher legal expenses; and (2) it invited plaintiffs to bring an action that had less than a probability of success (whereas the English rule tends to discourage such litigation).

Although the individual litigant may have little incentive to bring an action with a low probability of success, the plaintiff's attorney who is handling a portfolio of similar cases faces a very different decision calculus. Consider here the difference between depending on the outcome of a single coin flip versus the outcome of 1,000 coin flips; the latter can be safely predicted (as roughly 50/50) and relied upon. Knowing that he will win half his cases (or even only 40 percent), the plaintiff's attorney with a portfolio of cases can focus on the discounted value of these actions and make a more objective economic calculation. So long as this attorney can accurately predict his or her rate of success and keep his or her total litigation costs within the projected payoff from the winning cases, the attorney will profit.[45] This attorney is also freed from the tendency to be risk averse when one has to depend on a single outcome. Thus, under the American rule, the plaintiff's attorney could deliberately economize on his or her litigation expenditures (even if it reduced the prospect for success) because the attorney knew that greater legal costs would be incurred by the corporate defendant. This litigation cost differential could induce a defendant to settle even in a case that it was likely to win, because winning was more expensive than settling (at least when costs would not be shifted to the loser).[46] In effect, the American rule enables the plaintiff's attorney to exploit any significant differential in litigation costs. Defendants will characterize this plaintiff's attorney as bringing "nuisance actions," but these actions are not necessarily weak or frivolous. The real point is that the plaintiff's attorney in the United States can exploit a litigation cost differential because the attorney is freed from the risk of cost shifting against the loser.

The foregoing elements were not the only factors that tilted the balance of advantage in the direction of the plaintiff under the U.S. legal system. The right to a jury trial and the availability of punitive damages in the United States also distinguished it from Europe and implied that there was greater uncertainty and higher variance in the U.S. legal system (whereas the dominant role of judges in civil law systems in Europe implied greater predictability as to the outcome). Still, the foregoing factors predisposed the United States toward a particular style of litigation, as a combination of factors—the easy availability of attorney financing, weak client control, the absence of a "loser pays" rule, and the prospect of attorney's fees from a common fund to the successful plaintiff's attorney—collectively made litigation against corporate entities more attractive in the United States than in England or Europe. And all of this occurred well before the advent of the modern class action in the twentieth century.

This brief account still leaves one question unanswered: why did entrepreneurial litigation not develop at a later point in Europe and the United Kingdom? If the United States was more democratic and populist in the nineteenth century, this can explain why private enforcement of law developed first in the United States, but not why Europe and the United Kingdom never followed. After all, in the latter half of the twentieth century, socialist governments prevailed for decades in most of the major European nations and the United Kingdom. Why was no effort undertaken then to design a vehicle for aggregate litigation or to permit litigation to be financed through contingent fees?

Here, the best answer must rely on a form of American exceptionalism. The United States was different (and unique) in that it believed in litigation, the role of the courts as an agent of social change, and individual action through private enforcement. Socialist governments were not sympathetic to such ideas, believing instead that the welfare of the common man was best protected by the state through political action and regulatory oversight. Private enforcement of law was not a relevant tool in the Socialist toolbox, in large part because the state saw itself as the champion of the masses. Indeed, not only were courts not seen as the champions of reform, they were suspected as likely obstacles to such reform.

Beyond this point, the United States was also a more pluralistic society in which public enforcers may have found it easier to cede some responsibility to private enforcers (an idea resisted in more monolithic societies). In any event, only in the United States did a deep respect for the role of law and for courts as the guardian of the citizen's liberties combine with the idea that private enforcement of law served as a safeguard against political capture of public enforcement. Letting citizens sue was a regulatory answer that uniquely resonated in the United States, because ultimately the United States believed much more in the individual citizen's capacity to fend for himself.

PART TWO

THE RISE OF THE
ENTREPRENEURIAL LITIGATOR

So FAR, WE HAVE EXAMINED only legal doctrine. The doctrinal rules identified to this point may have created logical incentives for a particular style of litigation that we are calling "entrepreneurial litigation," but history, far better than logic, explains the development of legal institutions. In this part, our focus will now shift from legal rules to social institutions and actual practices. How did actual attorneys respond to the incentives inherent in the United States' legal rules, and how did they exploit those rules? How in turn did courts and legislatures react to this new development—the appearance of the entrepreneurial plaintiff's attorney? Part Two examines in successive chapters (1) derivative litigation, which, while judicially recognized in the mid-nineteenth century, only became common in the twentieth century; (2) class action litigation in federal court, with special attention to securities class actions; (3) merger class actions, which for special reasons are litigated almost entirely in state courts; and (4) mass tort class litigation. Although these contexts are very different, they all share several common characteristics: (1) weak client control; (2) active competition among plaintiff's attorneys to win control of the case; (3) indefinite legal rules governing how control of the litigation should be allocated; and (4) a tendency for collusive settlements (based on differing factors, but usually involving the exchange of a weak recovery for a lucrative fee award).

This part intends not simply a legal history of how these rules developed, but a sociolegal history of how participants responded to them. Each of the following four chapters looks at a different population of lawyers (with some overlap among them) who responded rapidly to changing economic incentives. Each also shows a different, if related, vulnerability associated with the private attorney general model.

3

THE DERIVATIVE ACTION

ALTHOUGH THE SUPREME COURT RECOGNIZED the availability of
the derivative action in 1855,[1] little happened in direct response. The
reason was simple: there were then few, if any, public corporations with
dispersed ownership. Until the 1890s, most corporations had a controlling shareholder or a control group and few public shareholders.[2] Then,
a merger wave in the 1890s, coupled with a technological revolution that
forced companies in new industries (automobiles, steel, telephone, and
electric utilities in particular) to raise more capital and grow in scale,
resulted in a sudden increase in the number of corporations that had
public shareholders and were in effect manager controlled. Between 1900
and the early 1920s, dispersed ownership became pervasive, and ownership and control separated in the publicly held company in the United
States (as Adolf Berle and Gardiner Means recognized a decade later).[3]

With this transition, dispersed, public shareholders held the majority
of the stock in large corporations but were less able to monitor, negotiate with, or otherwise control their managers, who were now relatively
free from the oversight of a controlling shareholder or controlling family.
The derivative action was the only legal remedy then available to shareholders, and in the first decades of the twentieth century its use
increased.

In principle, a derivative action is really two actions: first, there is an action brought in equity to allow the shareholder to supplant the board of directors and sue in the corporation's name, and, second, if the court permits the action to proceed, there is the suit in law to obtain a recovery on behalf of the corporation against those defendants who typically are alleged to have breached their fiduciary duties to the corporation. It is thus an extraordinary remedy, which requires that the court permit the plaintiff to displace the corporation's board and sue in the corporation's name. Courts will not do this readily, and so the barrier to success is high. Nonetheless, it gives the plaintiff a legal means by which to challenge and delay major corporate transactions, even if the ultimate outcome will seldom be a plaintiff's victory.

During the first decades of the twentieth century, the transactions that were most frequently attacked by plaintiffs were reorganizations and mergers. During this era, the procedures for both were complex, cumbersome, and sometimes uncertain. But many corporations often had a strong interest in effecting such major transactions to achieve economies of scope and scale. Against this backdrop, one individual—now virtually forgotten—achieved notoriety and a certain celebrity status for his ability to challenge these transactions, usually on procedural grounds.

Clarence H. Venner was not a lawyer, but he became a professional litigant in campaigns that he orchestrated against public corporations. During the first decades of the twentieth century, he sued (among many others) American Telephone & Telegraph, the United States Steel Corporation, J. P. Morgan & Company, Bethlehem Steel, New York Life Insurance Company, and most of the major railroads of the day.[4] All told, he conducted "at least 23 campaigns against such defendants . . . [which] involved at least 40 separate actions and have left over 100 cases in the reports."[5] Venner did not just sue a corporation; he mounted a full scale litigation offensive. For example, his campaign against the New York Central "extended over 14 years, involved 12 suits in 4 jurisdictions, employed 4 nominal plaintiffs, left 29 cases in the reports, and reached the United States Supreme Court 5 times."[6]

Venner seldom won the suits he brought (by one account he lost thirty-four reported cases and won five),[7] but he was hardly quixotic. Often, he sold his stock interest to the defendant corporation, which preferred to buy him out, rather than continue to litigate interminably. For example, he settled his action against the Greater Northern Railway and its formidable president, James J. Hill, by selling his 980 shares, which he had acquired for $188,587, for $513,000.[8] Similarly, Union Pacific Railroad purchased bonds that Venner held having a face value of $30,000 for $300,000—in return for Venner withdrawing his suit against the railroad.[9]

Tactically, Venner often sought to delay or challenge important corporate transactions. His tactics hardly won him judicial favor. In 1913, a New York Supreme Court described him in a reported decision as "an artificer of litigation and a menace to corporate society."[10] In 1917, a New Jersey court referred to him as "a professional agitator."[11] On another occasion, a New Jersey court agreed that Venner's requests as a shareholder for information from a corporation had been improperly rebuffed by the corporation, but added, "Some allowances must be made, however, for the weakness of human nature. I can conceive of no monster of the jungle . . . that could [so] unsettle the nerves of a corporation director . . . as the appearance of Mr. Venner in search of information."[12]

Still, Venner's cases were seldom "frivolous" in the sense that they lacked any legal merit. He researched them carefully and often found some arguable procedural error or some element of self-dealing in a reorganization plan. Nor was he simply a "one share shareholder" suing on behalf of an attorney, who was running the action. Venner held substantial stakes (at least for his day). His game plan was usually to search for a legal flaw in a complex reorganization or merger and, based on it, seek to hold up a transaction that was critical to the corporation.[13] Because delay would be costly to the corporation, it might seek to buy him out at a premium.

His suits were arguably "nuisance" actions, in that they were brought for an ulterior purpose, but not "frivolous," in the sense that they lacked all merit. He had his defenders. Jerome Frank, a noted legal scholar and judge (who coined the term "private attorney general") once suggested that Venner deserved a treatise written in his honor.[14] A biographer has likened him to a legal Robin Hood and described him as the corporate law equivalent of "a policeman on a beat"—except that "he would sell his nightstick—at a price."[15]

This last characterization needs emphasis. Venner might often identify a violation of corporate law procedures that a company had engaged in, but rather than press his derivative action to its conclusion, he would typically reach a private settlement, selling his shares back to the company or its controlling shareholder and dropping his suit. Other minority shareholders were thus left out in the cold (as Judge Frank duly noted).

Venner was unique for his day in that he actually owned an appreciable stake in the corporations whose managements he battled, and he conducted litigation as a multifront war, bringing actions in different jurisdictions and maintaining his campaigns for years at a time. He died in 1933, just as the Great Depression (and the anti-business sentiment that it produced) provoked the full flowering of the derivative action. During this era, judges were probably more prepared to question managerial decisions than at any time before or since.[16]

With the Great Depression, the derivative action entered its heyday, fueled by public dissatisfaction with the banks and brokerage firms that had inflated the 1920s stock market bubble. Early on, the derivative action found its true champion and master craftsman. That man was Abraham L. Pomerantz, who in his lifetime became known as the "Father of the Shareholder Suit." The very opposite of Clarence Venner, who was a wealthy and conservative investor, Pomerantz was born poor and Jewish in Brooklyn, with strong political associations on the Left. As a lawyer, however, he sought to do both good and well. Starting out as a personal injury lawyer in Brooklyn, he filed his first real derivative action as a young lawyer in 1934 against Charles E. Mitchell, the former chairman and chief executive of National City Bank, and his fellow directors. By then, Mitchell had become a leading symbol of the financial chicanery that had characterized the "bubble era" of the 1920s, and his activities at National City Bank were thought to have so antagonized Congress that the Glass-Steagall Act was passed in response in 1934 to separate commercial and investment banking prophylactically. Even given his unpopularity, Mitchell and his fellow directors were no easy target for a young lawyer. Still, Pomerantz focused on very large bonuses paid to Mitchell and other National City's executives and pursued his prey doggedly. Eventually, he recovered $1,800,000 for the bank's shareholders, for which he received a court-awarded fee of $450,000. At that time, both the recovery and the fee were unprecedented.

A lawyer's lawyer, who obsessively mastered all the details of even the most complex case, Pomerantz followed up his initial success with celebrated victories over other symbols of corporate excess, including American Tobacco Co.'s President George Washington Hill, from whom Pomerantz recovered a bonus paid to Hill of $2 million (and won a fee of $500,000), and William Randolph Hearst, who Pomerantz forced to repay Hearst Consolidated Publishers, Inc. some $5 million, on the theory that it had overpaid Hearst in buying some of his papers from him (this time, Pomerantz's fee was $800,000).[17] To Depression-era America, Pomerantz probably seemed the personal scourge of capitalism's robber barons—a Robin Hood operating within the law (and very well paid for so doing).

His success may have owed much to the temper of the times, as corporate executives, particularly when engaged in self-dealing transactions, were attractive targets in an era that considered corporate executives to be "economic royalists." But this argument can be pushed too far. Because no contemporary approached his level of success, a simple political theory that the Depression (and the public dismay toward business that it generated) enabled him to win his cases cannot truly explain his unique level of success. Similarly, others might explain Pomerantz by beginning with the fact that he was Jewish. They would explain that he became a plaintiff's attorney because he was excluded from the "elite" firms at Wall Street by the then reigning anti-Semitism. But this same era saw the development of major Jewish corporate law firms, and Jewish lawyers did not naturally gravitate to the plaintiff's side. A committed Socialist, Pomerantz seems unlikely to have been content defending major corporations in such a firm. Ultimately, what was most distinctive about Pomerantz was his ideological commitment and the meticulous professionalism with which he researched and prepared his cases.[18] In so doing, he won the respect of the established bar, which fought him fiercely but respected him (and virtually only him among the plaintiff's attorneys of his era).

Pomerantz's craftsmanship (and probably also his ideology) had an economic consequence: because he invested great time and effort in the preparation of his cases, he could not bring many cases. Both because of that and his prickly independence, his firm stayed small. Even as late as 1969, after he had become an iconic legend who regularly testified before Congress, his firm still had only six lawyers.[19] The consummate craftsman, he did not mass produce cases, and his firm only expanded marginally, even after the advent of the class action changed law firm practice.[20] For these reasons, other plaintiff's firms eventually overtook his, as we shall see.

Although Pomerantz's prominence and high recoveries motivated others to imitate him, few, if any, of his contemporaries ever approached his level of success. The plaintiff's bar then consisted of solo practitioners and very small firms. Economically, they lacked the financial resources to carry a derivative action for an extended period, gambling on the hope of an eventual, but uncertain, contingent fee. Even more importantly, they did not have the size or scale to diversify their risk by developing a portfolio of similar cases so that they were not dependent on the outcome of a single case. As a result, most plaintiff's attorneys needed to settle quickly and cheaply, exploiting the fact that defendants would be forced to spend even more in litigation costs if protracted litigation ensued. The term "strike suits" developed to characterize such litigation that was brought largely on its nuisance value and cost differentials favoring the plaintiffs. Those attorneys most eager for settlement became known as "pilgrims" (because they favored early settlements). Pomerantz's level of preparation and research (plus his raw talent) stood out in stark contrast to the lesser level of professionalism that the typical derivative action evidenced in its hasty preparation and conclusory pleadings.

The best evidence about the actual practice in derivative actions during this era comes from a controversial study commissioned by the corporate community. In the early 1940s, the Chamber of Commerce of the State of New York (a private body) responded to what it saw as extortionate litigation by underwriting a study, conducted by Franklin Wood, a respected practitioner, of derivative actions filed in New York between 1932 and 1942.[21] All told, Wood and his staff identified some 1,400 derivative actions filed in state and federal courts over that ten-year period—clearly showing that derivative actions were an active source of litigation.

Wood minced no words in broadly stating his bottom-line conclusion: derivative actions were filed, he wrote, by nominal shareholders "having no real financial interest in the corporation," and it was obvious to him that "the only one likely to profit substantially in the event of success is the [plaintiff's] attorney."[22] Specifically, Wood found that (1) a small group of plaintiff's attorneys brought most of the actions;[23] (2) these attorneys principally contested among themselves for the role of "general" counsel, resulting in the filing of numerous duplicative and largely overlapping complaints with similar allegations;[24] (3) few cases resulted in a litigated outcome; (4) settlements were easy to negotiate because the costs were generally picked up by the corporation's insurer;[25] and (5) the plaintiff's attorneys received substantial legal fees by virtue of the settlement.[26] Wood also computed that the typical settlement was for less than 3 percent of the damages alleged in the complaint.[27]

Wood's factual description of derivative actions seems accurate, although his normative conclusions were more debatable. Several key elements of Wood's portrait bear special attention because they appear to have persisted. In particular, when we survey class action practice in Chapter 4, we will again encounter (1) nominal plaintiffs owning only a trivial number of shares, (2) a small group of plaintiff's attorneys who are repeat players and who compete for control of the case, which is usually "up for grabs," (3) modest recoveries (under 3 percent of the stock market loss), and (4) high plaintiff's attorney's fees. Although the plaintiff's preferred vehicle for litigation changed in the 1970s from the derivative action to the class action, much of this pattern has largely remained the same.

Indeed, the weak client control described by Wood actually grew worse. In subsequent decades, the plaintiffs in derivative actions became professionals, who were used by the principal plaintiff's law firms on a high-volume basis. Three names—Harry Lewis, William L. Weinberger, and, more recently, Alan Kahn—stand out as legendary figures in this regard, as they have served as plaintiffs in many hundreds of actions (with Harry Lewis being estimated to have alone brought between 300 and 400 actions).[28] Indeed, Delaware decisions have described these plaintiffs as "quasi mythical" figures in terms of their willingness to litigate on behalf of their fellow shareholders.[29] Although federal legislation today restricts professional plaintiffs from appearing in securities class actions, the professional plaintiff continues to dominate derivative actions (where institutional investors appear as plaintiffs in only about a third of the cases).[30] Much as plaintiff law firms find the professional plaintiff convenient, their use necessarily implies that the plaintiff's attorney is not monitored by a client and is thus an agent that is effectively unaccountable to any principal.

Wood's data and factual conclusions have stood up over time, but his policy conclusions were fiercely challenged then and now. Wood's critics asserted that, in dismissing the deterrent value of the derivative action, Wood understated the rate of plaintiff's success (i.e., cases in which some recovery was obtained), which they computed to be around 44 percent, and thus comparable (or better) to the rate of plaintiff's success in other forms of commercial litigation.[31] There is legitimate room for debate here, but, even if some recovery was secured in many cases, this does not establish that derivative actions produced, on average, a net recovery (once the legal fees and expenses of both sides are deducted). In addition, if the source of the recovery is directors and officers (D&O) insurance, the corporation may have already paid for (or will ultimately return) that recovery in the form of higher premiums for D&O insurance. For the time being, it need only be concluded that little evidence supports the derivative action ever having played a significant compensatory role.

The Wood report was intended to have a political impact, and it did. In 1944 (two years after its publication), the New York legislature and newly elected Republican Governor Thomas Dewey amended New York's corporation laws to require a "securities for expenses" bond as a precondition to filing a derivative action in certain cases. Specifically, unless the plaintiff or plaintiffs held either $50,000 of the defendant company's stock or 5 percent of that stock, such a bond was required to compensate the company for its expenses in successfully defending the action. In effect, this restored the English rule (i.e., the loser pays the winner's legal fees) for derivative actions (because the plaintiff's attorney's fees are paid by the corporation if the action is successful, and the bond would mean that plaintiffs would compensate the company if the action was unsuccessful). The New York "security for expenses" bond was a tailor-made response to Wood's critique, as it applied only when the plaintiff held a merely nominal stock ownership (i.e., under both $50,000 and 5 percent). A number of other states enacted similar legislation,[32] and the Supreme Court held in 1949 that these state procedural statutes applied in federal court as well to corporations incorporated in these states (thus departing from a long history of seeking to keep federal procedural law uniform).[33] All told, a counterreaction set in during the era after World War II, reflecting both the more conservative political mood in the 1950s and the public's sense that the entrepreneurial lawyers bringing derivative actions had overreached.

Yet, curiously, the New York "security for expenses" statute had relatively little impact. Plaintiff's attorneys quickly found an effective response to it by seeking a shareholder list to solicit other shareholders to join their suit in order to escape the bond requirement.[34] Not wishing adverse publicity, most corporations usually agreed to withdraw their demand for a bond to avoid such a solicitation. The New York statute also had an unintended consequence: it spurred a number of plaintiff's attorneys to sue instead in Delaware (the preferred jurisdiction of incorporation for large public corporations) because Delaware had not enacted a similar securities for expenses statute (probably because Delaware was happy to attract litigation away from New York). The result was regulatory arbitrage, as the key actors—that is, the plaintiff's attorneys—shifted to the less regulated system. This pattern has also persisted, as we will see when we review the modern history of the class action. Ironically, plaintiff's attorneys are today fleeing Delaware to bring class actions in merger cases in states with less-developed procedures or more-lenient judicial scrutiny.[35]

The essential elements of the Wood report have been largely confirmed by later studies. An eight-year study that followed 531 derivative and class action suits brought against officers and directors of public corporations from 1971 to 1978 found that 70 percent of these actions settled, while in less than 1 percent did plaintiffs win a litigated judgment.[36] Although plaintiffs did obtain some form of relief in 75 percent of these cases, no effort was made to distinguish monetary from nonmonetary recoveries or compare the size of the recovery to the damages originally sought. Another academic study reviewing the prior empirical research underscores the likelihood that the relief was often cosmetic, finding that "one-third of the total reported settlements involved no monetary relief" and that "significant attorneys fees" had been recovered in a number of cases in which the relief consisted only of "procedural changes."[37] A particularly thorough study, by Yale Law Professor Roberta Romano, followed a random sample of 535 public corporations from the late 1960s to 1987.[38] Her study found that only 19 percent of the corporations surveyed experienced a derivative action, but a few encountered repetitive litigation. Again, the high rate of settlement stood out, with eighty-three of the 128 derivative actions identified settling over this period (or roughly 65 percent). In only 55 percent of these settlements (forty-six out of eighty-three) was there any monetary recovery; thus, in only 36 percent of all cases surveyed (128) did the corporation recover any money. In another 30 percent (twenty-five out of eighty-three), the settlement was principally based on nonmonetary structural relief. Still, in over 90 percent of the settlements, a fee award was made to the plaintiff's attorneys. In those cases where the settlement fund could be valued (thirty-nine out of eighty-three), the average recovery was $9 million, but the median recovery was only $2 million, suggesting high variance.

The most recent empirical study of derivative actions, which focused on all derivative actions filed in federal court between 2005 and 2006, found the dismissal rate to be distinctly higher, with over two-thirds of these cases being dismissed.[39] Meaningful financial recoveries were even rarer, however, with cosmetic corporate governance reforms constituting the most common form of settlement and only one case in the entire sample producing a monetary recovery at trial. Still, even if most derivative actions are dismissed, the attorney's fees on the minority that do settle can make such litigation attractive to those plaintiff's attorneys that can minimize their litigation costs. A high dismissal rate thus implies the need for cost minimization and a consequent low investment in any individual case by the plaintiff's attorney.

What do these studies prove? Although Wood and others saw a consistent pattern of small monetary recoveries and high attorney's fees as evidence that derivative actions were frivolous and extortionate, this evidence may better demonstrate a pattern of implicit collusion under which the individual defendants (i.e., corporate officers and directors) used the corporate treasury to buy off the plaintiff's attorney with a lucrative fee award. A unique feature of the derivative action is that the successful plaintiff's attorney's fees are paid by the corporation (and not out of any recovery by the shareholders) on the theory that the individual share-holder who brought the action benefited all the other shareholders and so was entitled to repayment of his reasonable expenses under "unjust enrichment" principles. Even in cases where there is no monetary re-covery, a fee award to the plaintiff's attorneys can (and usually will) be approved by the court if it concludes that the shareholder who sued suc-cessfully conferred a "substantial benefit" on the corporation. This is a variant on the "common fund" theory discussed in Chapter 2, but the underlying reality is that courts understand that settlements depend on fee awards. Desiring settlements in derivative cases (and recognizing that the corporation wants to resolve the dispute), most courts will approve fee awards that are a necessary concomitant of settlement, even when they may harbor severe doubts about the merits of the case.

As a result, the corporation picks up the costs of both sides—if the action settles. Thus, when corporate officials are sued in a derivative ac-tion, they may initially seek its dismissal at the outset on a variety of grounds (and often they succeed). But if those efforts fail, then their prac-tical choice is to either (1) reach a settlement in which defendants pay a monetary settlement (probably primarily funded out of D&O insurance policies on which the corporation had paid the premiums) or (2) struc-ture a nonmonetary settlement involving structural relief or additional disclosures, with the fee award coming in all of these cases from the cor-poration. Viewed in this light, the low rate of litigated decisions may then simply reflect the obvious preference of defendant officers and directors (and their insurers) to settle based on governance reforms rather than based on their own money. Plaintiff's attorneys are content with this pref-erence so long as their fees are also paid by the corporation. Even if the risk of personal liability is low, defendants see no need today to run even a small risk.

Correspondingly, plaintiff's attorneys are at least as eager to settle be-cause they face a forbiddingly high barrier under the traditional "de-mand" rule that governs derivative actions. In virtually all jurisdictions, a plaintiff seeking to bring a derivative action must either (1) allege that the plaintiff has made a demand on the corporation's board of directors to take the requested relief (i.e., typically to sue the corporate officers) or (2) provide the reasons why such a demand would be futile.[40] Making demand on the board typically concedes that the board is entitled to resolve the dispute, and thus plaintiffs typically spurn this option and instead seek to show that demand was "futile."[41] Even if all the directors are sued, this is still not enough under the case law to make demand "futile." Rather, to excuse demand, a plaintiff must plead particularized facts showing that the board is "incapable of exercising its power and authority to pursue derivative claims directly."[42] This is a very high standard and one that inclines plaintiff's attorneys to settle—at least if their fees are paid by the corporation. As a result, even though a derivative action will generally be dismissed, both sides may prefer settlement to a litigated outcome, because settlement avoids all risk and allows the costs to be passed back to the subject corporation. Such a system is ideal for lawyers but less so for shareholders. Under it, the private attorney general often looks less like a vigilant watchdog and more like a well-fed lapdog.

The 1942 Wood report also found that plaintiff's attorneys spent much of their time fighting among themselves for control of the action (and thus filed duplicative complaints). As will be seen in Chapter 4, this same problem also arose in securities class actions (where it has been more satisfactorily addressed). Given that derivative actions have a high settlement rate and presumptive fee awards to plaintiffs if the parties settle, they naturally attract a surplus of attorneys willing to bring them. Yet, no legal rule clearly specified which plaintiff's attorney out of this crowd would be selected to run the case. For many years, the de facto practice in Delaware was for the court to appoint the first attorney to file the action, but Delaware has more recently abandoned this rule. Elsewhere, the court might appoint the attorney who was supported by the largest number of plaintiffs, or the attorney elected by the other attorneys in the case, or the attorney who the court decided was the most qualified. No selection rule was followed uniformly anywhere.

As a result, in the absence of any authoritative legal rule entitling one attorney to priority, uncertainty and a degree of anarchy prevailed. Law and economics scholars view this vacuum as a "common pool" problem.[43] As will be seen, it can produce not only fierce competition among the plaintiff's attorneys and wasted judicial resources, but, more importantly, crippling disincentives that discourage any attorney from expending funds or time on the case—at least until the selection of lead counsel is resolved. Common pool problems arise regularly in entrepreneurial litigation, and, at their worst, can result in cheap settlements that harm investors because the plaintiff's attorney settles prematurely, often out of a fear that others will settle the same action before him.

This skeptical assessment does not imply that derivative actions are necessarily frivolous. Weak actions can usually be dismissed, and derivative cases that settle usually either have colorable claims of self-dealing or challenge an important corporate transaction (such as a merger) where defendants cannot accept any risk of delay. The key point here is more that the process of settlement is dysfunctional, both because (1) cosmetic and nonpecuniary settlements enable plaintiff's attorneys to obtain an acceptable return at low risk and (2) courts are prepared to accept weak settlements rather than spend the time and effort to screen them out.

Since its peak in post-Depression America, derivative actions have declined in frequency and importance. Rarely do they today produce favorable judgments or settlements with significant monetary recoveries.[44] Multiple reasons explain their decline, but probably the two most important causes have been (1) the rise of independent boards of directors (on which the vast majority of directors have no insider status or other conflict of interest) and (2) the development of the class action into a more attractive vehicle for entrepreneurial litigation.

With regard to the former explanation, a court is far less likely to "excuse demand" on the board as "futile" when the board is independent. Courts universally recognize that boards are better at business decision making than they are and will defer to them, unless the board appears conflicted. Back in the heyday of Abraham Pomerantz, few corporations had majority independent boards, and thus the demand rule was less of an obstacle. But this began to change in the 1960s. As Figure 3.1 shows,[45] the percentage of insider-dominated boards declined throughout the 1970s, and then, over the next two decades, the percentage of "affiliated" directors (i.e., directors with other economic affiliations with the company) also fell sharply. By the 1990s, the typical board of a public corporation was highly independent, with only a few inside members. This development truly sounded the "death knell" of the derivative action.

The second factor driving the eclipse of the derivative action was the rise of the class action. Although some important antitrust and securities

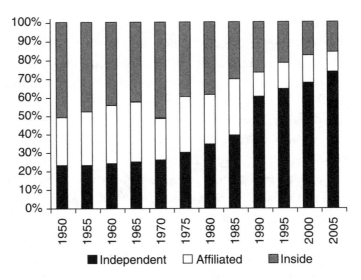

FIGURE 3.1: Board Composition, 1950–2005

class actions can be traced back to the late 1950s and even earlier, the explosive growth of the class action begins with the revision of Rule 23 of the Federal Rules of Civil Procedure in 1966 to facilitate class actions. Class actions offered much higher potential damages and (at least initially) lower procedural and pleading barriers (i.e., they were not subject to anything like the "demand rule" for derivative actions). To understand this point about higher damages, imagine that a chief executive of a public company is revealed to have engaged in an illicit, under-the-table transaction by which he gained a $1 million benefit at the expense of his shareholders. Imagine further that, on public disclosure of this transaction, the company's market price falls 20 percent for a total stock market decline of $100 million (as shareholders expect they may be victimized by management again in the future). In a derivative action, a plaintiff can seek to recover for the corporation the $1 million illicit gain (subject to the still serious obstacle of the demand rule), but in a class action the plaintiff shareholders can seek to recover $100 million for themselves (and from the corporation as well as the CEO). This disparity quickly motivated the plaintiff's bar, which largely moved to federal court in the 1970s.

Today, the conventional wisdom is that the derivative action has become an outdated relic, obsolete, unimportant, and used (and usable) only in pathological cases where the corporation's board has lost all credibility.[46] Considerable evidence supports this assessment. For example, in Delaware, relatively few derivative actions have been filed in its Court of Chancery in recent years, with the annual number ranging between twenty-two and fifty-two. As Table 3.1 shows, year after year, derivative actions in Delaware are vastly outnumbered by class actions filed in Delaware.[47] If we add up the columns in the table, class actions exceed derivative actions by an over 6-to-1 margin, and that margin seems to be increasing.

Yet, perhaps surprisingly, other studies show that derivative actions are brought in federal court with greater frequency, and, in federal court, their number may be increasing. The most recent survey found that over 180 actions were filed during a one-year period between 2005 and 2006.[48] Surprisingly, these federal actions are principally directed against large public companies with independent boards (not smaller private companies without independent boards). Although most of them are dismissed, many do settle[49]—generally for largely cosmetic corporate governance reforms and the payment of the plaintiff's attorney's fees (with the average plaintiff's fee award being around $1 million in the above-noted study of 2005 to 2006 derivative filings).[50]

All this seems counterintuitive. One would expect derivative actions to focus on smaller, private firms that lack independent boards and to be filed in state court (where the case load pressure is greater and judicial oversight less intense). In addition, if derivative actions produce, on average, no discernible benefit for shareholders, it seems puzzling that they are becoming more common, at least in federal court.

What explains this? As usual, there are multiple answers. The derivative action does flicker to life from time to time because of "episodic" scandals (i.e., many companies engaging in the same type of misconduct

Table 3.1   Delaware class and derivative actions, 2008–2012

Year	Class actions	Derivative actions
2008	83	22
2009	138	33
2010	251	30
2011	342	38
2012	318	52

at the same time). The two recent examples of such "episodic" misbehavior were stock option backdating and "market timing" at certain mutual funds.[51] In both cases, publicly held entities appear to have decided that because "everyone else was doing it," there was safety in numbers. Both types of misbehaviors were more easily attacked through derivative actions than securities class actions.[52] Both episodes appear to have been short lived but gave rise to a flurry of derivative actions for a brief period.

Still, these two short-lived episodes do not account for the puzzling persistence of derivative actions in federal court. Here, the answer that better explains the resurgence (at least in federal court) of derivative actions is also one that reveals inherent deficiencies in the private attorney general concept. This answer begins with a curious procedural fact that exposes the real dynamics in derivative litigation. Today, to the extent that derivative actions persist, they are increasingly the tail to a larger litigation dog. That is, in the majority of derivative actions brought today in federal court against public companies, the derivative action is filed as a "tagalong action" in the wake of an earlier securities class action.[53] Typically, after a series of securities class actions are filed and consolidated in one court, some plaintiff's law firm files a parallel derivative action (generally on behalf of a small shareholder) that largely repeats the same charges but seeks a recovery from corporate officers and directors in favor of the corporation. Why does this happen? Multiple reasons can be given. Sometimes, in cases involving large class action settlements, the defendant settling the securities class action may want to settle a parallel derivative action that raises the same basic allegations in order to assure itself that every conceivable claim has been resolved, including the potential derivative claims.[54] Or, it may just want to wrap up all the loose ends in a global settlement. Because the parallel derivative action is typically settled on a nonpecuniary basis (with no monetary payment by the defendants to the corporation), the settlement adds little to the defendant's overall settlement cost (basically, the only additional cost is that of the plaintiff's attorney's fees). From this perspective, the derivative settlement provides a useful and low-cost insurance policy against the claims being relitigated under a different guise. So understood, the derivative action appears a fairly toothless tiger, with little deterrent threat.[55]

But the defendant's desire for iron-clad protection against further litigation explains only part of this "tagalong" phenomenon. Above all, tagalong actions essentially involve plaintiff's attorneys seeking to find a niche in a highly competitive legal market—in effect, a legal crevice through which they can become involved in a large, lucrative litigation and claim a fee. As discussed in Chapter 4, smaller plaintiff's law firms have been excluded from the world of large securities class actions by federal legislation that effectively gave control of this litigation to the largest institutional investor willing to take on the role of "lead plaintiff."[56] Because these large institutional investors generally have established relations with a major plaintiff's law firm, the smaller plaintiff's firm cannot obtain a sufficiently large client to win control of the securities class action. But, they can file a parallel derivative action (often in the same court). In effect, denied entry at the front door of the litigation, the smaller firms reappear at the back door and typically earn modest fees if the case settles. In a major securities class action, the expense of settling a parallel derivative action is probably only a rounding error for defendants.

Reinforcing this interpretation is the fact that the plaintiff's bar in derivative actions is highly concentrated and consists largely of smaller firms. The most recent empirical study finds that some ten plaintiff's law firms appeared in nearly 75 percent of the derivative actions filed against public companies.[57] Yet, there was little overlap between these firms and the firms that dominated securities class action practice.[58] This reflects specialization, as the larger plaintiff's firms fund and litigate the more expensive securities class actions (and earn much larger fees), while the smaller firms survive on the scraps they leave behind by filing "tagalong" derivative actions. But no litigation opportunity goes unexploited in the intensely competitive contemporary legal marketplace.

What then do we learn from this brief review of the derivative action? The derivative action represents the initial American experience with the "private attorney general" concept. As late as 1949, the Supreme Court described the derivative action as the "chief regulator of corporate management."[59] For a time, that seems accurate, as the derivative action did sustain a specialized bar of plaintiff's attorneys, provided the forum in which much American corporate law was made, and yielded some notable victories for plaintiffs. But that day is now largely over. Today, the derivative action serves more as a Full Employment Act for plaintiff's attorneys in smaller firms by creating additional claims that they can litigate, more or less enabling them to play the jackal to the class action lawyer's lion.

Attractive and idealistic as the private attorney general concept may sound, it has a darker side. Ideally, the private attorney general should perform as a heroic Lone Ranger, who, motivated by profit, rescues clients who cannot sue on their own. In reality, however, a single private attorney general seldom appears to rescue the aggrieved client; rather, a surplus of private enforcers appears, and to achieve a settlement, all or most of these volunteers must be paid for their largely superfluous services. The result is confusion, delay, and excess costs—a scenario resembling Charles Dickens's nineteenth-century novel *Bleak House* (where the litigation ended only when the lawyers had consumed the entire estate with their fees).

To be fair, some plaintiff's attorneys—most notably Abe Pomerantz, but others also—lived up to the ideals of the private attorney general concept. More generally, however, the private attorney general in practice has proven less than incorruptible. At the era's outset, Clarence Venner frequently "sold his nightstick," and, more recently, plaintiff's attorneys have been regularly seduced into accepting cosmetic settlements involving only corporate governance reforms or additional disclosures in return for generous fee awards. Inherently, the derivative action is more susceptible to collusion than other representative actions because the costs of both sides can be fully shifted to the corporation in whose name the action is brought.[60] The great vulnerability in the attorney general concept is then that the two active participants—defendant's and plaintiff's counsel—can collude to advance their interests to the detriment of those clients supposedly served. Often, this does not happen at first, but over time protocols develop, as both sides find that de facto collusion is the course of least resistance. This pattern began with derivative actions in the United States, but it has been repeated in a host of other contexts, as we will see.

In rebuttal, plaintiff's attorneys can respond that they were forced to compromise and accept modest settlements because of the high and forbidding standards imposed by the demand rule and the other procedural obstacles placed on the derivative action. Yet, these obstacles were erected by courts and legislatures in response to plaintiff's attorneys' early success and apparent overreaching. At a minimum, the legislative counterreaction to the derivative suit indicates that political support was lacking for a thorough-going implementation of the private attorney general concept.

Arguably, the derivative action may have also largely outlived its usefulness, as the rise of independent boards of directors curbed many of the abuses that Abe Pomerantz once litigated. Or, one may explain the derivative action's decline by concluding that plaintiff's attorneys discredited themselves. To the extent that they exploited the nuisance value inherent in the derivative action, they eventually lost public support, as their behavior appeared more that of a self-interested private actor than that of a dedicated public servant. Finally, there is an even more cynical possibility: lawyers on both sides, and the legal system generally, may have erected an illusory Potemkin Village that benefits only lawyers. That is, plaintiff's attorneys sue in the name of protecting shareholders; defense attorneys resist in the name of protecting the corporation, but all the costs are borne by shareholders who end up being worse off as a result of a costly litigation system for protecting shareholders that has no real parallel in other Western legal systems.

For the time being, no choice need be made among these alternative possibilities. But, if the private attorney general concept contemplates the harnessing of the entrepreneurial spirit to serve the public interest, experience with the derivative action suggests that this union is a dysfunctional one. The profit motive tends to dominate the troubled marriage between entrepreneurship and idealism.

4

THE EMERGENCE OF THE CLASS ACTION

THE ORIGINS OF THE CLASS ACTION can be traced back to medieval times,[1] but it was not originally designed to enable a collection of unrelated individuals to assert a claim for money damages against a common defendant. That transition took centuries—and continues. Moreover, the modern history of the class action shows that each step forward has been accompanied by at least a half step backward. Politics and the class action have been inextricably interwoven for the last half century.

Although the English equity courts had developed a class action procedure as early as the seventeenth century, their cases tended to involve closely knit groups (such as a church congregation suing to protect its right to continue to use its traditional cemetery, or a group of heirs seeking to resist actions by a defendant that would deprive them of their patrimony). In such cases, the preexisting relationships within the class largely eliminated any issue as to whether the class representative could adequately represent the absent class members. In the brief space of a half century, the class action evolved in the United States from this modest starting point to become an engine for group litigation that permitted widely dispersed shareholders, each relying on different information or none at all, to sue their corporation or its agents for fraud and to obtain multibillion dollar recoveries. Chapter 6 will examine the parallel development of the class action in the mass tort context to enable victims (and potential victims) injured by dangerous products (tobacco, asbestos, or silicone gel breast implants) to sue their producers for bankrupting amounts. These developments depended on the class action as its procedural vehicle, generated controversy, and elicited a judicial and legislative counterreaction (which ultimately largely ended the mass tort class action).

History thus matters, and a brief tour of the class action's development is necessary. After the American Revolution, U.S. legal scholars (most notably, Justice Joseph Story) recognized that the class action was part of the legal inheritance that U.S. courts had received from England.[2] Although he was an enthusiastic proponent of the class action, Justice Story was much less clear about the purpose of this procedure. Generally, he and his contemporaries in the nineteenth century saw the class action as a means of avoiding duplicative litigation, which would have resulted if each class member was compelled to sue individually.[3] In their view, the class action's virtue was judicial economy, as it reduced the total volume of litigation.[4] Totally missed by this narrow perspective was an alternative and more radical role for the class action, namely, to facilitate litigation that otherwise would not have been brought. The class action did this by allowing small claimants to aggregate their claims. So viewed, the class action empowered persons who otherwise lacked access to the courts. Economically, it enabled "negative value" claims to be litigated, and politically it gave a legal voice to the unrepresented.

Because the nineteenth-century legal mind did not understand that there could be a case for encouraging litigation, this broader vision of the class action's role did not emerge until a justly famous 1941 law review article by Harry Kalven, Jr., and Maurice Rosenfield: "The Contemporary Function of the Class Action Suit."[5] In their view, the class action needed to be redesigned not only to enable "negative value" claims to be litigated, but to encourage private attorney generals to supplement governmental regulation and enforcement. As they saw it, the class representatives and their attorneys could ferret out wrongdoing and compel the return of ill-gotten gains that overworked (or conflicted) regulators might miss. In this light, the class action was not merely a procedural device, but also a political tool by which to restrike the balance of power between the powerful and the dispossessed. They were the first to recognize that the class action could be the procedural mechanism by which to arm and finance the private attorney general. In a time of ferment, they articulated a Republican vision of citizens organizing to counterbalance corporate power, which vision has inspired and animated many. But, as this chapter will stress, courts, legislators, and the draftsmen of the Federal Rules of Civil Procedure have always stopped well short of adopting their model. Although fragments of their vision eventually found their way into Federal Rules of Civil Procedure 23 (which is discussed in the section below), both courts and Congress have continued to balance competing considerations: the need to enable "negative value" claims to be asserted against the interests of judicial economy. As a result, the Kalven and Rosenfield private attorney general model has received at most an equivocal implementation.

A. THE EVOLUTION OF RULE 23

Noble as their vision was, Kalven and Rosenfield wrote in 1941, several years after the drafters of the Federal Rules of Civil Procedure had already produced their first unified set of federal procedural rules in 1938—and thus Kalven and Rosenfield had no influence on those rules. The 1938 promulgation of the Federal Rules of Civil Procedure was the major achievement in American civil procedure during the twentieth century, and its drafters were themselves liberal reformers but on a more modest, incremental scale.[6] Class actions were far from the focus of the 1938 rules, which instead concentrated more on simplifying pleading rules and establishing a system of civil discovery that entitled litigants to the disclosure of much more information from their adversary than could have been obtained in any other legal system. Still, these new Federal Rules took a nineteenth-century Supreme Court Equity Rule on class actions and generalized it to apply to all federal litigation. From that acorn grew a sizable oak.

The drafters of the 1938 rules had to be cautious because they were subject to special constraints. Although Congress had instructed them to produce uniform procedural rules for the federal courts, Congress also directed them that their uniform rules could not "modify or abridge" substantive rights.[7] As a result, the drafters needed to present their work product as largely codifying existing precedents and practices. Nonetheless, the drafters of the 1938 Federal Rules of Civil Procedure did not simply restate the prior precedents on class actions in a faithful codification. Across the board, they attempted to simplify and streamline civil procedure to enable greater access by ordinary citizens to the courts. In the particular case of the class action, they sought to liberalize its availability, but this expansion was accompanied by much confusion and opacity as they struggled to present it as a codification. To stay within the role allotted to them by Congress and not abridge any substantive rights, the drafters needed to reconcile their new rule with the tangled judicial history on class actions. Purporting to reflect all the elements of that history, they divided class actions into three fairly murky categories, which became known in legal shorthand as "true," "hybrid" and "spurious" class actions. The "true" class action consisted of those familiar cases in which one individual in a recognized, preexisting group (for example, an unincorporated church congregation) seeks to represent all the group's members in litigation for their common good.[8] The drafters described these cases as involving a "joint or common right," which was something more than simply a common interest.

"Hybrid" class actions involved another area where there had been much experience: suits by creditors to force an entity into receivership. As a practical matter, the passage of the federal bankruptcy laws trivialized this category, leaving its remaining role to be that of perplexing law students in first-year civil procedure classes for the next generation.

The final category in their new rule was the "spurious" class action, and here the draftsmen did indeed push the envelope.[9] The class members in a "spurious" class did not need to share any preexisting relationship among themselves (or even to know each other), but simply needed to share common facts or interests. But the "spurious" class action did not intend the aggregation of thousands of persons into a united action for money damages. The actual intent of the draftsmen is far from clear, but they appear to have seen the "spurious" class action as a "permissive" joinder device, rather than as a mandatory aggregation. Clearly, they did not intend that absent class members would be bound by the outcome of a "spurious" class action.[10] Their goal was probably more to liberalize joinder by creating a form of "opt-in" class for those plaintiffs who wanted to use it. In all likelihood, the draftsmen saw the "spurious" class action as an experiment and left it to the discretion of individual judges to strike proper balances on the facts before them.

However vague and fuzzy the original concept of the "spurious" class action was, the judicial reaction to it is more important than the original intent. On its face, it did offer an apparent mechanism by which unrelated individuals could pursue a money judgment for each individual class member against a common defendant. Plaintiff's attorneys took up this invitation (including Abe Pomerantz, who showed great interest in the "spurious" class action) from the late 1940s on. For years, they experienced mixed results, but did achieve some early success in both securities and antitrust cases.[11]

Then, a major scandal broke in 1960 that focused national attention on corporate misconduct. The Department of Justice discovered blatant price fixing in the heavy electrical equipment industry (particularly with regard to steam turbines). The details were lurid: executives at General Electric, Westinghouse, and other industry giants had met in rural motels and allocated bids by the phases of the moon.[12] This became headline news, prompted a public morality crisis, and elicited a flood of private litigation for damages by injured parties. The Department of Justice indicted and convicted the major corporate participants, and several corporate officers actually went to prison. All this activity opened the doors for private litigation, and antitrust cases soared (see Table 4.1).[13] Above all, the table shows both the impact of public enforcement on private litigation and the speed with which the plaintiff's bar could mobilize to exploit an opportunity. Following the 1960 indictments of G.E. and the other corporate conspirators, the number of private cases involving the electrical equipment industry skyrocketed from thirty-seven in 1961 to 1,739 in 1962. Plaintiff's attorneys appear to have rushed to respond to both (1) the incentives created by the treble damage provisions of the federal antitrust laws and (2) the fact that convicted defendants are estopped from denying guilt in the follow-on civil cases. In all likelihood, plaintiff's attorneys sensed they were "shooting fish in a barrel."

Table 4.1   Antitrust cases commenced, fiscal years, 1960–1972

Fiscal year	Total	Government cases		Private cases	
		Civil	Criminal	Electrical equipment industry	Other
1960	315	60	27	—	228
1961	441	42	21	37	341
1962	2,079	41	33	1,739	266
1963	457	52	25	97	283
1964	446	59	24	46	317
1965	521	38	11	29	443
1966	770	36	12	278	444
1967	598	39	16	7	536
1968	718	48	11	—	659
1969	797	43	14	—	740
1970	933	52	4	—	877
1971	1,515	60	10	—	1,445
1972	1,393	80	14	—	1,299

The litigation proved, however, less simple. These private actions were virtually all individual suits, not class actions, and they were typically brought by public utilities or other private power generators (for example, hospitals); thus, they were hardly "negative value" claims asserted by individuals of modest wealth. Collectively, they amounted to a then unprecedented litigation explosion. Over 2,000 cases were soon pending in twenty-five district courts, and the possibility of inconsistent rulings, repetitive depositions, and resulting chaos loomed.[14] Historically, this was probably the first occasion on which an army of plaintiff's attorneys mobilized and perfected many of the techniques that later became standard in entrepreneurial litigation.

This crisis produced two direct consequences. First, the Chief Justice and the U.S. Judicial Conference appointed a coordinating committee of nine federal judges to monitor this litigation and minimize the risk of inconsistent rulings. With the enactment several years later of special legislation requested by the Judicial Conference, this committee matured into the Judicial Panel on Multidistrict Litigation (JPML), a judicial body authorized to transfer similar cases to a single court for pretrial purposes to achieve consistent rulings and to minimize inefficient

duplication.[15] Although the primary goal was to avoid inefficient duplication (such as forcing the defendant's chief executive officer to give
depositions in thirty-odd overlapping cases involving the same facts),
this provision had an unanticipated and important consequence—
without which entrepreneurial litigation might never have matured:
namely, it reduced the prospect for competition and collusion among
rival teams of plaintiff's attorneys. When different teams of plaintiff's
attorneys are in competition, defendants can exploit their vulnerability.
Each team knows that the first team to reach a settlement blocks the
others and ends the litigation, and the team offering the cheapest settlement should be the logical choice of the defendants to settle with. The
more the contenders, the more a race to the bottom becomes likely. With
the JPML, however, plaintiff's attorneys in one federal court no longer
had to fear that their claims would be settled cheaply in another federal
court, as all were before the same judge. Ironically, the JPML was the
solution to a problem that had not yet been recognized but soon would
appear at the state level. Protected from the poaching of their cases by
other plaintiff's attorneys, class action attorneys in federal court could
now invest time and resources in their cases, with less fear of being
undercut in another forum.[16]

Second, the plaintiff's attorneys in these cases learned to network—
to share information and depositions, and to develop a common strategy.
The electrical equipment cases of the 1960s produced the flowering of
the plaintiff's antitrust bar—well before the advent of the modern class
action. So viewed, entrepreneurial litigation was not dependent on the
class action but actually preceded it. Still, the heavy electrical equipment
cases demonstrated to many the need for a modernized class action procedure as an alternative to hundreds of individual suits.

In overview, the bottom line here may be that legal change is more
typically precipitated by scandal and crisis than by long-term policy formulation. These private antitrust cases forced the federal judiciary to im-
provise and generated important legislation. As a direct result of the electrical equipment cases, the plaintiff's bar came to master a new legal
technology: private antitrust litigation. Even after the Department of Justice concluded its electrical equipment prosecutions in the mid-1960s,
the number of private antitrust actions continued to increase well into

the 1970s. Having acquired new skills in the electrical equipment cases in the early 1960s, plaintiff's attorneys began to apply those skills to other antitrust cases that were not preceded by a governmental action. Some firms reoriented their practice to specialize in antitrust cases and ultimately antitrust class actions. The leaders in this legal pioneering were plaintiff's lawyers based in Philadelphia—most notably, Harold Kohn and David Berger—and a tradition of aggressive antitrust enforcement begun by them continues in Philadelphia to this day.[17] As the twig is bent, so grows the tree.

In contrast to the rapid development of private antitrust litigation, securities litigation moved at a slower pace. Some class actions were certified during this era but generally only in cases arising under the express statutory provisions of the Securities Act of 1933.[18] An important barrier slowed developments in the securities field. Not until the late 1960s did appellate courts recognize a private cause of action under Rule 10b-5 that was generally applicable to open market trading.[19] Procedure could not outrace substance, and so securities actions developed more slowly than antitrust class actions (where the federal antitrust laws had long codified an express private action for treble damages).

By the early 1960s, it would have been fair to conclude that no one really knew the boundaries of the "spurious" class action, despite over twenty years of practice under the Federal Rules of Civil Procedure. What was clear, however, was a structural unfairness that prejudiced defendants. The "spurious" class action could give significant relief to plaintiffs but less so to defendants. If the action was successful, class members could opt in, but, if it was unsuccessful, they would not, meaning that only the actual plaintiffs bringing the case were bound by the defeat—in effect, the "spurious" class action was a one-way street. Alone, these problems surrounding the "spurious" class action might have justified revision of Rule 23 (and many did recognize the need for a procedural vehicle to enable a class action for money damages), but that need was not the cause of the next major round of rule changes to the Federal Rules.

An even stronger force crested in the 1960s that dwarfed all other pressures for the reform of Rule 23. This driving political force was the Civil Rights Movement. The principal civil rights organizations had been relying on the class action to desegregate schools and combat racial discrimination and had encountered problems. In particular, they often used the "spurious" class action as their preferred procedural means for seeking injunctive relief. But the "spurious" class action was an imperfect vehicle for this purpose because it left many important issues undecided.[20] For example, did civil rights plaintiffs have to provide notice to everyone within the class at the time of class certification (which could be expensive)? Although federal courts could clearly order the admission of specific students to a school, more troubling questions surrounded whether they could order class-wide relief, redrawing school boundaries at the request of a small number of plaintiffs who sought to represent a much broader class. Did absent parties in school desegregation have the right to opt out from the litigation, so that they were not bound by the court's decree? Facing these and other questions, civil rights organizations wanted a stronger procedural remedy that could better enable them to obtain broad injunctive and declaratory relief.

At least partially in response, the Federal Rules Committee, which was charged with recommending changes to the Federal Rules of Civil Procedure, undertook a special project in the mid-1960s to rewrite Rule 23 on class actions. In due course, they fashioned an entirely new Rule 23, which was approved by the Supreme Court in 1966. Harvard Law School Professor Benjamin Kaplan served as Reporter for this project and was its key draftsman, assisted by his then young protégé, Arthur Miller, later also a Professor at Harvard Law School. Although it would overstate to say that the new rule was designed primarily to facilitate civil rights litigation, the intended impact of the proposed new rule on civil rights cases was probably the leading consideration that shaped the revised Rule 23.

Once again, the drafters subdivided all class actions into three categories: Rule 23(b)(1), Rule 23(b)(2), and Rule 23(b)(3). Only the last two of these categories have relevance from our perspective. The centerpiece of their new structure was Rule 23(b)(2), which authorized "appropriate final injunctive relief or corresponding declaratory relief with respect to the class as a whole," at least if the defendants had "acted or refused to act on grounds generally applicable to the class." Thus, if a Mississippi school board had refused to integrate, relief could be ordered for the class as a whole, meaning that the court could adopt a comprehensive plan to integrate the school system, not just allow the named plaintiffs to attend the school. Possibly the most important feature of Rule 23(b)(2) was what it did not say. It did not require special (and expensive) notice to all class members, did not permit class members to opt out, and did not contain any of the more restrictive conditions that were uniquely made applicable to Rule 23(b)(3) classes. A plaintiff wishing to rely on Rule 23(b)(2) would have to satisfy the requirements of Rule 23(a) (which applied to all class actions), but these provisions basically only required that the class representative have his or her interests aligned with the class that he or she proposed to represent and be capable of adequately representing their interests. These conditions in Rule 23(a) largely stated the minimal requirements of due process. Life was thus simplified for the ideologically or politically motivated plaintiff in suits brought by the NAACP, the ACLU, or later the Sierra Club.

In contrast, Rule 23(b)(3) specified far more restrictive requirements for plaintiffs seeking a money judgment in commercial litigation.[21] Although the draftsmen of the 1966 revision were aware of the Kalven and Rosenfield article and its model for class litigation, they were clearly not willing to grant a free-ranging commission to private attorney generals to do justice through class actions. At the time, new Rule 23(b)(3) seemed even-handed, because it bound absent class members, not just those who opted in—thus ending the "one-way" street that had long offended defense attorneys. In addition, under Rule 23(b)(3), before a class for money damages could be certified, the class would not only have to meet the standard requirements of Rule 23(a), but would also have to satisfy the following three new basic requirements as well.

First, the court would have to find "that the questions of law or fact common to the members of the class predominate over any questions affecting only individual members." In legal shorthand, this has become known as the "predominance requirement," and it is today the principal obstacle to class certification in large-stakes class litigation.

Second, the court must find "that a class action is superior to other available methods for the fair and efficient adjudication of the controversy." This has become known as the "superiority requirement," and it reads as a virtual invitation to plaintiffs to use the class action to resolve "negative value" claims.

Third, the court must consider "the difficulties likely to be encountered in the management of a class action." This "manageability" requirement allowed the court to decline certification, even if the merits clearly favor the plaintiffs, if the burden on the court appears to be excessive or inefficient. In a formal note to the rule, the draftsmen indicated that certification of a complex mass torts dispute would rarely be appropriate.

Viewed in terms of Kalven and Rosenfield's vision, Rule 23(b)(3) reflects at most a very qualified and incomplete acceptance of their model. To be sure, Rule 23(b)(3) does advance the cause of group litigation to the extent that (1) it does not require a "joint and common" right to be held by class members (as the 1938 version of Rule 23 generally did), but only that class members share common facts and interests, and (2) it gives rise to a judgment binding on the absent parties. Still, Rule 23(b)(3) places its primary emphasis on considerations of judicial economy. In determining whether a class is to be certified, the predominance test looks to whether the court can resolve sufficient common issues so that the court can advance most of the way to a final judgment. If it cannot, it should not proceed, even though it might resolve important issues as to the legality of the defendant's conduct. This focus on predominance (and thus judicial efficiency) would not be the guiding criterion if one started instead from Kalven and Rosenfield's premises. The drafters might have instead looked to whether the private attorney general had identified serious issues of public policy or shown a probability that significant legal violations had occurred. From the Kalven and Rosenfield perspective, "superiority" would logically have been the primary criterion for class certification and might even have alone made a class action mandatory, at least if it could be shown that no practical alternative existed by which class members could assert "negative value" claims.

Instead, Rule 23(b)(3) balances superiority against feasibility and requires in all instances that the common issues that can be resolved "predominate" over the individual issues that will remain. Ultimately, this phrasing gives a priority to the value of judicial economy over that of empowerment of victims of wrongdoing. To illustrate, assume plaintiffs seek to bring a securities class action against a corporate issuer and can clearly show that it made materially misleading statements. This is a "common" issue for purposes of Rule 23(b)(3), but numerous potential "individual" issues remain: (1) Did the individual class members rely on the misleading statement (or did they even learn of it)? (2) Did they already know the true facts? (3) Did they suffer very different and hard to compute damages? (4) Did they recklessly fail to check out easily available sources that would have revealed the truth to them? A proponent of Kalven and Rosenfield's model would not have let these questions interfere with class certification and instead might have recognized them only as damage setoff issues.

Correspondingly, in a mass tort case, it might be clear that the defendant's product was unreasonably dangerous (a "common issue"), but the defendant might still respond that many class members had used their product recklessly in ways unintended by the defendant (these contributory negligence issues would be "individual issues"). At least as of the 1966 date on which Rule 23 was adopted, it was uncertain how courts would strike the balance in deciding whether such an action could be certified under the new language of Rule 23.

Nonetheless, what was clear was that the new Rule 23(b)(3) would bind absent parties, and thus it greatly enhanced the litigative power of plaintiff's attorneys, as they now represented everyone in a class who did not opt out. In turn, by settling with plaintiff's attorneys in the class action, defendants could forestall and preclude other individual litigation, again unless the individual plaintiff formally opted out of the class. The settlement process thus took on new importance.

The response to new Rule 23 was immediate and predictable: class action filings soared. Within a few years, the Judicial Conference of the United States noted "growing concern" about the number of class actions and undertook a study.[22] That study found that, as of June 30, 1972, there were some 3,148 class actions then pending in federal court, up nearly 20 percent from the preceding year.[23] Of these, 1,369 (or 43.5 percent) were civil rights class actions. That was expected, because Rule 23(b)(2) had been framed to encourage them. But another 20 percent of the class actions then pending were securities and commodities class actions, and still another 10 percent were antitrust class actions.[24] These new class actions for money judgments reflected entrepreneurial plaintiff's attorneys beginning to respond to the new incentives (both Rule 23 and federal court decisions in the late 1960s finding that a private cause of action under Rule 10b-5 could be asserted in open market trading cases).

A new landscape of legal specialization was also emerging. The 1972 study found that the two leading locations for class actions were the Southern District of New York (which had seen 151 class actions filed in fiscal 1972) and the Eastern District of Philadelphia (which saw 116 new filings in the same year).[25] Securities class actions tended to be filed in New York, while Philadelphia's plaintiff's bar concentrated on antitrust class actions. Still, the dawn was just breaking.

B. SECURITIES CLASS ACTIONS AND THE RISE OF MILBERG, WEISS

Even with the groundwork laid for securities class actions, the plaintiff's bar did not rush to exploit this new opportunity. Obstacles remained. New Rule 23 required that notice be given to the class (which plaintiffs would have to pay for unless there was an early settlement), and defendants could procrastinate, forcing the plaintiff's attorney to absorb costs and defer its fees. The early signals were mixed. In the one major securities class action that went to trial during the 1960s, *Escott v. Bar Chris Construction Corp.,*[26] plaintiffs filed their case in 1962 and only won at trial in 1968. Although the decision established significant legal principles, specifying the due diligence standards for underwriters, directors, and accountants, it was no more than a modest economic success for the plaintiff's attorneys. And it was based on a strict liability statute (Section 11 of the Securities Act of 1933) that gave all the procedural advantages to plaintiffs, requiring the defendants in effect to prove that they were not negligent. Thus, it was a relatively easy case to win (but even then it took a six-year battle).

In contrast, Rule 10b-5 placed more of the burden on the plaintiffs and represented a greater challenge. Although Rule 10b-5 was promulgated by the Securities and Exchange Commission (SEC), its content was largely filled in by judge-made common law. Well into the 1980s, much of that law was unclear: Did the plaintiff have to prove fraud or only a negligent misstatement? Did the plaintiff have to show individual reliance by each class member? Who had the burden on loss causation? These were major uncertainties. Before most of the plaintiff's bar would risk their time and money on class actions grounded on Rule 10b-5, they needed to see a major plaintiff's victory based on it. That victory was achieved in 1973 by a young lawyer named Melvin Weiss. Trained as an accountant, Weiss was no stranger to financial statements and accountants' work papers. Weiss convinced his senior partner, Lawrence Milberg, to bankroll his pursuit of Dolly Madison Industries, a typical 1960s conglomerate that had acquired more than thirty companies through acquisitions during an eighteen-month buying spree—all allegedly based on inflated financial statements.[27] Dolly Madison was representative of many acquisition-minded conglomerates of that era that used their inflated stock price to make acquisitions and bent (or broke) accounting rules to maintain a high stock price. From a financial standpoint, Weiss's deeper pocketed target was Dolly Madison's outside public accountant, Touche Ross & Co., one of the then "Big Eight" accounting firms.

Following the usual strategy of defendants, the case was delayed in order to maximize the economic pressure on the plaintiff's attorneys. Eventually, the case went to trial in 1973, and on the eve of the verdict, Touche Ross settled for $2 million (which resulted in a $500,000 fee for Weiss's firm).[28] At the time, that was a celebrated victory—David defeating Goliath.

Just as Abe Pomerantz had built his reputation on litigation victories won at a young age, so did Mel Weiss exploit the Dolly Madison case. His victory gave him instant credibility and a leadership position within the plaintiff's bar, which lacked any experienced leader in securities litigation at this stage. Other victories followed, and Weiss aggressively sought to be named lead counsel in large securities class actions. But at this point, the styles and careers of Weiss and Pomerantz diverged. If Pomerantz was a legal scholar and perfectionist, Weiss was more a negotiator and politician. Unlike Pomerantz who meticulously prepared a few cases and kept his firm small, Weiss wanted to grow Milberg, Weiss. To develop a high-volume practice, Weiss pursued two independent strategies. First, he effectively hired "professional" plaintiffs, nominal clients with small holdings in a large number of companies, effectively making them "in-house" clients, so that his law firm would always have easy access to clients with standing to sue. Lawyers hiring clients (rather than the reverse) are the hallmark of the entrepreneurial plaintiff's firm, because it reverses the usual principal/agent relationship. This practice was not lawful, but it could be effectively disguised.

Second, at or before the time major corporate law firms opened branches, Milberg, Weiss opened a permanent West Coast office in the 1970s, headed by the equally redoubtable Bill Lerach. Now a national law firm, Milberg, Weiss was uniquely positioned to exploit stock price drops at companies on either coast. In particular, Milberg, Weiss monitored the young start-up companies of Silicon Valley, which typically had highly volatile stock prices. If such a firm's stock price fell significantly over a one- or two-day period, Milberg was able to file an action before the local federal courthouse closed for business.

Weiss's desire for growth and larger scale was grounded on a strong economic logic for two distinct reasons. First, although securities class actions were easy to bring, they faced a high mortality rate. To sue, all one really needed was a plaintiff with standing, as a minimally adequate complaint could be filed within hours of a significant stock price drop at a Silicon Valley company. But judges reacted differently to these actions, and predictably many would be later dismissed on a variety of grounds. Thus, developing a large portfolio of cases permitted efficient diversification. If a small firm pursued a Pomerantz-like strategy of investing heavily in a few (but well chosen) cases, a single defeat could produce a cash flow crisis. Associates, secretaries, and the rent still had to be paid in the short term. But a large portfolio of cases (even if they were, on average, somewhat weaker on the merits) assured economic stability for the larger firm. Early settlement (even at a discounted price) enabled the large firm to manage its cash flow and avoid crises.

In retrospect, if Pomerantz was the consummate craftsman, Mel Weiss was the Henry Ford of representative litigation, who perfected the technology of mass production. The polar opposite of Pomerantz, Weiss placed class actions on the assembly line.

Second, Weiss recognized not only that a firm needed to manage a portfolio of cases to control risk, but also that the real challenge in resolving securities class actions lay less in convincing the defendant to settle than in winning control of the case from other plaintiff's firms. Winning control required teamwork and advance preparation. To illustrate, suppose the stock price of XYZ Corp. falls 25 percent over two days, after unexpectedly poor financial results are announced. Assume further that ten securities class actions are thereafter filed by different law firms and are eventually consolidated in the Southern District of New York before one judge. Everything now depends on whom that judge appoints as class counsel. That law firm will control the case and receive the lion's share of the fee award if the case settles.

Which counsel would the court choose? Once, the conventional wisdom was that the court would presumptively favor the counsel in the first action to be filed. For this reason, it paid to have an "in-house" professional client, so that law firm's filing of the complaint need not be delayed by the need to wait for an actual client to retain the law firm. This conventional wisdom that the first to file would win was probably somewhat overstated, but it did motivate a race to the courthouse. Another (and complementary) explanation is that a larger plaintiff's law firm with multiple "in-house" professional clients could file several (but identical) actions in different courts. When all these actions were eventually consolidated, the law firm might have four different lawyers representing four different nominal clients. Milberg, Weiss was skilled at this. Typically, all the counsel filing parallel class actions would meet to discuss their common strategy and organize their case. At this point, a miniature political convention might ensue, with the law firms electing a proposed class counsel and then asking the judge to ratify their choice. Other things being equal, the judge was likely to accept their candidate. In this political convention, it was better to have four votes than only one, and so it made sense to file multiple actions with different "in-house" clients.[29]

Such a brokered deal allowed all the participating firms (or at least those voting for the winner) to demand something in return—typically, a right to participate in the litigation and share in the fees (if the case were settled). Although this process stacked the deck in favor of the law firm that filed multiple actions, the even clearer consequence of brokered deals was egregious overstaffing of the case. Every plaintiff's firm that filed a complaint could negotiate for a piece of the action as its price for joining in the coalition backing the winning class counsel. To gain their votes, class counsel was compelled to accept featherbedding and find a role for less able counsel; such log-rolling practices necessarily implied higher legal fees to the class. Whether by filing first, by filing multiple actions, or by brokering deals over who would participate in the action, Milberg, Weiss usually dominated the organization of the plaintiff's team when multiple firms contested for the position of class counsel. It ran the network, because it uniquely had the money, expertise, and contacts, and courts also preferred a law firm that knew what it was doing in a specialized field.

Securities complaints in this era became a slapdash affair, shaped by the need to file quickly. Thus, plaintiff's attorneys wrote brief skeletal complaints, filled with largely conclusory and highly generalized allegations. ("Defendants omitted to state material facts relating to this transaction in their SEC filings.") Often, complaints in one case were obvious mark-ups from the complaint in a prior case, sometimes with the earlier defendant's name still appearing in some paragraphs by mistake.

Nonetheless, despite the ease of filing, the number of securities class actions did not rise steadily throughout the 1970s; rather, they seem to have peaked in 1974 and then declined for the rest of the decade.[30] This was partly the product of a depressed stock market, which had few peaks and valleys during this period (thus reducing the supply of sudden "stock drops" off which the plaintiff's bar made their livelihood). In addition, the Supreme Court ruled in 1974 that plaintiffs had to pay the costs of sending class action notice to class members.[31] This was an added financial hurdle, which discouraged smaller firms. Ultimately, although it added to the pressures on plaintiff's attorneys to settle, plaintiff's firms soon found that, if they did settle, the settlement agreement could shift these costs to the defendant by agreement.

In contrast to the cost of notice (which only drove down the settlement value), one major legal obstacle did hang over securities litigation in this period, much like Banquo's ghost. This was the problem of proving individual reliance. At common law, reliance was a standard and necessary element of a fraud cause of action, and the plaintiff had to demonstrate his or her reasonable reliance on the defendant's misrepresentation or omission. But if reliance had to be shown by each class member in a class action, this would give rise to numerous individual factual determinations, which would in turn likely prevent the so-called common issues from predominating over the individual issues. If so, the class could not be certified under the "predominance" requirement of Rule 23(b)(3).

To answer this problem of showing reliance, plaintiff's attorneys fashioned an innovative and intellectually original theory that relieved them from the need to prove individual reliance—the "Fraud-on-the-Market Doctrine." Under this theory, an efficient market is presumed to reflect all material information about a company. Thus, because the stock's price in an efficient market should incorporate all material information (including false information), the buyer of the security can be presumed to have relied on the accuracy of all publically disclosed material information. If a material misrepresentation or omission is made by the defendant, it will distort the market price and injure those plaintiffs who purchased the stock prior to corrective disclosure, because they relied (it is assumed) on the stock's price to be accurate. The practical impact of this theory that the plaintiff relies on the accuracy of the market price is that materiality subsumes reliance. Under it, the plaintiff need only allege a material misrepresentation or omission and show that the security traded in an efficient market, and reliance then drops out of the picture.

The first appellate decision to adopt this simplified approach and hold that direct proof of reliance was not necessary was the Ninth Circuit's decision in 1975 in *Blackie v. Barrack*.[32] Not surprisingly, the case was won by Milberg, Weiss and argued by Mel Weiss.[33] Not all circuits accepted this doctrine, but the Second Circuit agreed with the Ninth Circuit in 1981.[34] Once the two major circuits on both coasts had adopted the Fraud-on-the Market Doctrine, securities class actions became easily certifiable, at least in the jurisdictions where plaintiff's attorneys most wanted to file. Eventually, in 1988, the Supreme Court also bought into the Fraud-on-the-Market Doctrine.[35] In overview, with these victories, the securities class action became substantially easier to certify than antitrust or consumer fraud class actions. Uniquely, in securities cases, the balance of advantage now favored the plaintiff.

The ease and predictability of class certification attracted other plaintiff's attorneys into this field, but the new entrants had to recognize the

already oligopolistic position of Milberg, Weiss and seek to join its network. Facing reduced legal barriers and enjoying market power, Milberg,
Weiss perfected a new style of plaintiff's litigation in the 1980s. In the
wake of a sudden stock price drop at a public company, many suits might
be quickly filed, but Milberg would organize the network of firms and
emerge as at least co-counsel for the class. Unlike many of its rivals, Milberg also invested in its cases, advancing funds for discovery and experts,
seeking documents by the millions, and actively taking depositions. Early
in his career, Mel Weiss had learned that such investments paid off in
larger settlements, and, almost alone at this time, Milberg, Weiss could
afford to make such investments.

Equally important, the costs in securities litigation are inherently
asymmetric, with a significant cost differential favoring the plaintiffs.
Typically, the defendants needed to retain multiple law firms to represent multiple defendants and thus incurred costs that were a multiple of
the plaintiff's side. Defense counsel is also paid monthly and at usually
higher hourly rates. Defendants could also expect that their senior executives would be pursued and deposed (often by the notoriously difficult Bill Lerach) and that the process would be time consuming, expensive, and painful for them. This was particularly true if the Milberg, Weiss
lawyers could find any evidence that senior executives of the company
had sold stock in the period before the adverse news was released. Given
all these factors, defendants generally found discretion to be the better
part of valor and settled. Trials were rare events. The scale of Milberg's
success was epic. All told, from the mid-1990s through its breakup in
2006, it maintained a dominant market share, serving as either lead or
co-lead counsel in 50 percent of securities class actions, and, even more
impressively, it recovered over $45 billion in recoveries for its plaintiff
classes.[36]

To defendants, however, the process resembled extortion. Although
Mel Weiss was generally liked and respected by his adversaries on the
defendants' side in New York (who thought he settled early and "reasonably"), Bill Lerach was viewed entirely differently in California. Often
abrasive and characteristically arrogant, he did not settle easily and held
out for settlements that his adversaries considered excessive. This may
have been in the interests of the class, but it contrasted sharply with the

style of the "pilgrim" plaintiff's attorneys on the East Coast, who believed in early settlements that economized on the costs for both sides. Lerach's aggressive style gave rise to a new verb: "Lerached"—meaning a litigation assault, based on a stock price drop at a company with a characteristically volatile stock price and facilitated by a cost differential favoring the plaintiffs. The outcome was typically a multimillion dollar settlement. The 1980s and early 1990s were the salad days for Milberg, Weiss, and by some estimates Lerach alone amassed a personal fortune of over $700 million.[37] No other lawyers in any field in the United States attained comparable wealth.

Well before Bill Lerach had become a symbolic name in Silicon Valley, the Supreme Court had begun to curb the reach of Rule 10b-5, criticizing the quality of the claims asserted under it. In 1975, Justice Rehnquist wrote broadly in the *Blue Chip Stamps* case that

> There has been widespread recognition that litigation under Rule 10b-5 presents a danger of vexatiousness different in degree and kind from that which accompanies litigation in general. . . . The first of these concerns is that in the field of federal securities laws governing disclosure of information even a complaint which by objective standards may have very little chance of success at trial has a settlement value to the plaintiff out of any proportion to its prospect of success at trial. . . . The very pendency of the lawsuit may frustrate or delay normal business activity of the defendant which is totally unrelated to the lawsuit.[38]

Justice Rehnquist's claim was not supported by any serious empirical evidence, but it reflected the corporate bar's view (and was consistent with much anecdotal information).

Eventually, because so many companies were sued by him, Lerach's very success spawned a predictable political reaction. In the 1990s, a prominent Silicon Valley venture capitalist raised more than $40 million to fund a statewide voter initiative, known popularly as the "Get Lerach Initiative," to limit the ability of plaintiff's attorneys to use state courts.[39] That effort failed, but it clearly identified who Silicon Valley saw as its enemy. During the early 1990s, a nationwide political coalition, with its roots in Silicon Valley, formed to seek federal legislation curbing securities litigation. Support for such "reform" came from two groups that were particularly threatened by securities litigation and had both ample resources and the ability to organize for political action: (1) the accounting industry (which was highly concentrated) and (2) the young, high-tech companies of Silicon Valley (whose volatile stock prices uniquely exposed them to litigation). The two groups organized to seek corrective legislation at the federal level, and their opportunity arrived after the 1994 congressional election turned into a Republican landslide that yielded Republican majorities in both Houses of Congress.

Elected on a campaign platform (known as the "Contract With America") that promised to curb securities litigation, the new Republican majority in the House set to work with a clear and very specific agenda: to curb Milberg, Weiss. The legislation that they produced—known as the Private Securities Litigation Reform Act of 1995 (or the PSLRA)—did a number of things, but it was aimed, like a rifle shot, at Milberg, Weiss. First, the PSLRA created a "safe harbor for forward-looking statements" that promised virtual immunity to issuers for their forecasts, projections, and estimates. This responded to frequent suits triggered by a company's failure to meet projected earnings or other targets. Second, the PSLRA threatened to shift fees against the plaintiff's attorney in cases they lost (once again, the English "loser pays" rule). Third, it replaced joint and several liability among defendants with a system of proportionate liability that protected those liable only as secondary participants. In particular, this sheltered the accountants, who had been otherwise potentially liable for the entire decline in the market capitalization of an issuer whose financial statements they certified. But, above all, the PSLRA changed the pleading rules for securities litigation. No longer could plaintiffs file conclusory pleadings that vaguely alleged material misrepresentations and omissions. Instead, to avoid a motion to dismiss, the plaintiffs had to plead "with particularity" facts giving rise to a "strong inference" of fraud. More importantly, they had to do this before they could obtain discovery.

This was a dramatic change and arguably a justified response to the hasty and unsubstantiated pleading that had characterized securities litigation. The PSLRA's new pleading requirement created something of a "Catch-22" dilemma for the plaintiff's bar. To plead with particularity, plaintiff's attorneys normally relied on civil discovery, but now it would be necessary to plead a factually detailed complaint in order to obtain discovery. Seemingly, this put the cart before the horse. But, its purpose was clear: plaintiffs would no longer be able to file their complaint within hours after a stock price drop but would have now to research it in detail before filing. Over time, the better plaintiff's attorneys learned to do this by a variety of means: interviewing the defendant's employees, hiring private detectives, and tracking stock sales by insiders. Nevertheless, the PSLRA slowed the pace and raised the costs of securities litigation for plaintiffs.

The net result was an irony. Although the PSLRA was intended to end Milberg, Weiss's oligopoly, it instead reinforced it. Smaller, boutique-sized plaintiff's firms could not afford the new costs of factual investigation or the prospect of fee shifting against them if they lost. After the PSLRA, Milberg, Weiss's market share of securities class actions actually rose.

The PSLRA also imposed one other change that had a profound impact on Milberg, Weiss. It established a presumption that a securities class action should be organized and run by the plaintiff who both volunteered for this role and had the largest stake in the action. This change was designed to end both the de facto control of securities class actions by the first to file and the use of professional "in-house" plaintiffs. Effectively, it shifted control over the action to institutional investors, who were invited by the PSLRA to become the "lead plaintiff" and choose the class counsel.

At first, it was not at all clear that institutional investors would respond to this invitation. Again, a transitional learning process was necessary. But, for a variety of reasons, public pension funds (and only they at first) began to volunteer for the "lead plaintiff" role. This transition produced internal tension within Milberg, Weiss. At least at first, the New York office, dominated by Mel Weiss, wished to continue to rely on their traditional system of using individual plaintiffs. To obtain lead plaintiff status, their plan was to aggregate many individual plaintiffs in the hopes that their collective holdings would give them sufficient losses to win the competition for lead plaintiff. But even a hundred or more individual plaintiffs could not collectively hold the level of stock that a state pension fund would typically hold in a company in its portfolio.

Meanwhile, on the West Coast, the more innovative Bill Lerach began to develop relationships with major public pension funds, such as CalPERS, and was able to use these California pension funds to gain control of securities class actions. Other plaintiff's law firms—most notably the Bernstein, Litowitz, Berger & Grossmann firm in New York City— formed their own alliances with major pension funds (such as the New York State Common Retirement Fund and the New York City pension fund). Because Mel Weiss had lagged behind, the New York office of Milberg, Weiss found itself for the first time facing real competition from rival firms for the control of large class actions.

Milberg, Weiss's competitors had perceived early on the potential in the PSLRA's "lead plaintiff" provision. State and municipal comptrollers ran public pension funds, but had relatively little access to political contributions (as least in comparison to governors and senators). By making generous donations to a comptroller's campaign fund, plaintiff's law firms in effect gained the right to rent the pension fund and use it as their lead plaintiff in securities litigation. This exchange of political contributions in return for selection as class counsel became known as "pay to play"—that is, a plaintiff's firm had to pay if it was to play with the pension fund's assets in securities litigation. Some pension funds were relatively insulated from these conflicts of interest because they were not administered by elected officials, but other funds were eager to play for pay. In truth, many public officials had a dual motivation, because, as elected officials, they also enjoyed the publicity associated with suing wrongdoers, such as Enron or WorldCom, and serving as the champion of the small investor.

The seriousness of this conflict can be debated, but the impact of "pay to play" again squeezed out the smaller boutique and start-up litigation firms. They could not afford the costs of large political contributions, and so they were unable to compete with more established (but not necessarily more skilled) larger firms. Smaller firms thus stayed on the sidelines or represented smaller clients in lesser cases where the major pension funds were not interested.

Of the new rivals that challenged Milberg, Weiss, the most successful was Bernstein, Litowitz, Berger & Grossmann. It was an experienced plaintiff's firm that started out in employment discrimination and civil rights litigation, and it had some skilled attorneys. Equally important, it had developed good relations with New York State's comptroller and thus New York's pension fund. This relationship (plus substantial political contributions) helped it to win control of the WorldCom securities class action, with Milberg, Weiss losing that battle to win control of an obviously lucrative class action.

But Bill Lerach was not a man to concede defeat graciously. Unlike Mel Weiss, Bill Lerach had actively recruited California's public pension funds, and he sought to use them to win control of the WorldCom litigation. Because the New York State pension funds had an even larger investment in WorldCom, Lerach lost out to Bernstein, Litowitz. In response, Lerach then took an unprecedented step: he induced some forty-one California funds to opt out of the WorldCom class action and agree to sue the WorldCom defendants in individual actions in state court (with him as their counsel). This was feasible only because of the large stakes that the California funds held. Traditionally, retail investors could not afford to opt out, as they held only "negative value" claims. In contrast, the California pension funds could easily afford individual suits because their losses in WorldCom ran into the billions of dollars.

Their decision to opt out at Lerach's urging led to bitter fights both between the two contending law firms and within Milberg, Weiss. Over the long run, Lerach's new tactic (i.e., opting out with your institutional client if you lost the battle for control of the class action) became the dominant strategy of many other plaintiff's law firms with large institutional clients. Tactically, it was a "no brainer," as counsel for the opt-outs earned some fees, rather than none. But, over the short run, it provoked a crisis, as the New York State pension funds objected to Mel Weiss that Bill Lerach was jeopardizing their class action. Opting out complicated the settlement of the class action, as the defendant did not want to pay twice (once in the class action and later in the individual, opt-out actions brought by large funds). To Mel Weiss, Lerach's decision to opt out was treasonous—a rejection of the class action procedures that Milberg, Weiss had perfected and profited from.

Others have concluded that Lerach's decision to opt out in WorldCom essentially "broke" the Milberg firm and made its dissolution inevitable.[40] Perhaps it did, but an eventual Milberg, Weiss breakup was virtually inevitable. The styles of Lerach and Weiss were simply irreconcilable. Weiss was a "settler" who wanted to play within the rules of the game, while Lerach was an angry iconoclast who did not need to be accepted by the established bar and preferred to pressure his adversary for a record settlement, rather than agree to an early one. The negotiations to dissolve the firm began in 2003, and the formal announcement of their separation into an East Coast firm (which kept the name "Milberg, Weiss") and a West Coast firm (which became known as "Lerach, Coughlin") was made in May 2004.[41]

Milberg, Weiss's troubles only began with its dissolution. Also in 2003–2004, a long-standing federal criminal investigation of Milberg, Weiss and its partners intensified. The government had found that "referral" fees as large as $250,000 had been paid by Milberg, Weiss to attorneys who had done no real work on the case.[42] Closer investigation found that Milberg had retained some individuals to serve as "in-house" plaintiffs, promising them, in some cases, a percentage of the overall class recovery. Although the investigation began in Los Angeles, it quickly moved back to New York, where the key figure was David Bershad, Mel Weiss's longtime deputy who handled the firm's finances. Eventually, the prosecutors were able to show that Mr. Bershad administered an extraordinary, multimillion dollar cash slush fund from a safe in his office, which was used to deal with and/or buy off objectors, other plaintiff's firms, professional experts, and others who needed to be paid off. Although other plaintiff's firms had probably also compensated their plaintiffs, the Milberg, Weiss story involved an unprecedented scale and a unique level of hubris. The tabloids could not get enough of the lurid details about these well-known lawyer-entrepreneurs. Because the pattern was pervasive, the government also took the unusual step of indicting the firm as a whole. Ultimately, four of the "name" partners of Milberg, Weiss—Weiss, Lerach, Bershad, and Schulman—went to prison.

But even if their behavior was sleazy and the pattern of misconduct long-standing, the question remains: who was really injured by the payments to professional plaintiffs? Defenders of Milberg, Weiss argue that no one was and that a Republican administration was pursuing a vendetta against the firm. They point to the likelihood that in most of the class actions where Milberg, Weiss appeared, other law firms were also seeking the role of class counsel (or would have sought that role if Milberg, Weiss had not preempted them). Thus, defendants suffered little real injury from these payments because the action would still have been brought, absent any payment, by some other law firm. That answer, however, ignores other victims. Indeed, the clearest victims were the other plaintiff's law firms that arguably had valuable cases stolen from them by Milberg, Weiss. To be sure, other plaintiff's law firms were not Congress's intended beneficiaries when it enacted the PSLRA to prohibit any payments to a plaintiff for serving in that role. Rather, Congress was aiming at Milberg, Weiss—and ultimately it succeeded. Beyond specific victims, there is an injury to the judicial system. Payments to a professional plaintiff encouraged and ensured perjury, because defendants were certain to question the plaintiff under oath about any economic relationships with the plaintiff's law firm.

Milberg, Weiss's fate underlines again the anomalous position of the entrepreneurial attorney. Effectively, the firm was destroyed because its attorneys hired their clients. Yet, such subordination of the client to the attorney is virtually inherent in most cases involving "negative value" claims because the client is generally "rationally apathetic" about the small loss. Milberg, Weiss went beyond soliciting clients to actually retaining them in ways that would necessitate perjurous testimony by these clients when questioned by defense counsel. The real irony was that Milberg, Weiss was convicted for a practice that had already become obsolete. By the time of his conviction, even Mel Weiss had recognized that "in-house" individual plaintiffs were a thing of the past, as dated as the horse and buggy in the era of the automobile. Institutional lead plaintiffs had rendered them obsolete and were a positive step in responding to weak client control.

C. THE CONTEMPORARY SECURITIES CLASS ACTION

The passage of the PSLRA in 1995 interrupted what had been a steady growth in securities class action filings, and their number dropped in 1996. But the PSLRA's impact was more like a road bump than a barrier. Plaintiff's law firms experimented with a variety of ways to outflank it.

Their initial response was to move their cases from federal court to state court, generally filing them in California in the case of Silicon Valley companies. This approach was a classic attempt at regulatory arbitrage. Just as plaintiff's law firms had moved from New York to Delaware when New York enacted a "security for expenses" statute in the 1940s, so did they now move to state courts, which they saw as a less regulated environment. For a brief time, this tactic seemed to work. But the same political coalition that had pushed the PSLRA through Congress quickly in 1995 responded with new legislation in 1998: the Securities Litigation Uniform Standards Act (or SLUSA). SLUSA denied plaintiffs the right to bring a securities class action in state court, forcing them to litigate in federal court where the PSLRA governed.

Compelled to sue in federal court, class action plaintiff's attorneys found that it no longer mattered who filed first, because the case eventually went to the investor with the largest stake in the action. No longer needing to rush, plaintiff's attorneys learned to investigate their cases before they filed them. This investigation often involved interviewing corporate employees and hiring private detective firms to gather information. Complaints grew from the ten- to fifteen-page length of the early 1990s to 150-page massive documents, whose length alone was intended to convince the court that the pleadings were adequately particularized. The technique that best enabled plaintiffs to raise a "strong inference" of fraud was to follow the stock trading by the corporation's insiders. If plaintiffs could show that insiders were dumping their shares in large quantities in the weeks before the adverse news was released by the corporation, this seeming pattern of insider trading went far to create the requisite "strong inference" of fraud.

Overall, these changes made securities class actions less easy to file and more costly to prosecute. But, in turn, this may have made plaintiff's firms less prepared to settle cheaply. The more they invested in preparing and prosecuting an action, the more they had to demand as a settlement, simply to break even. Since the PSLRA, the number of securities class action filings and settlements has fluctuated, but over the last decade there has been a steady decline in the number of securities class action settlements. In 2012, the number of securities class action settlements fell to fifty-three, a fourteen-year low.[43] This decline has been counterbalanced, however, by a corresponding increase in the size of the average settlement.[44] For example, the ten largest securities class action settlements now each exceed $1 billion (see Table 4.2).

Because the size of the settlement is principally a function of the size of the estimated damages, damages (and thus settlement size) tend to be greatest in the years following the collapse of a "bubble" when a number of large corporations fail. As a result, the total amount paid out annually in securities class actions reveals an apex-like pattern that peaked with the settlement of Enron, WorldCom, and Tyco in the 2005–2007 period. Figure 4.1 (prepared by Cornerstone Research) shows the total

Table 4.2   List of the ten largest securities class action settlements

Case name	Settlement amount
1. *In re Enron Corp. Sec. Litig.*, No. H-01-3624 (S.D. Tex.)	$7.227 billion
2. *In re WorldCom, Inc. Sec. Litig.*, No. 02-cv-3288 (S.D.N.Y.)	$6.133 billion (combined)
3. *In re Bank of Am. Corp. Secs., Derivative, and ERISA Litig.*, 2013 U.S. Dist. LEXIS 57463 (S.D.N.Y. April 11, 2013)	$4.250 billion
4. *In re Tyco Int'l Ltd., Sec. Litig.*, No. 02-1335 (D.N.H.)	$3.2 billion
5. *In re Cendent Corp. Sec. Litig.*, No. 98-cv-1664 (D.N.J.)	$3.186 billion
6. *In re AOL Time Warner, Inc. Sec. & "Erisa" Litig.*, No. 02 Civ. 5575 (S.D.N.Y.)	$2.5 billion
7. *In re Nortel Networks Corp. Sec. Litig.*, ("Nortel I"), No. 01-cv-1855 (S.D.N.Y.)	$1.142 billion
8. *In re Royal Ahold N.V. Sec. & ERISA Litig.*, No. 03-MD-1539 (D.Md.)	$1.1 billion
9. *In re Nortel Networks Corp. Sec. Litig.*, ("Nortel II"), No. 04-cv-2115 (S.D.N.Y.)	$1.074 billion
10. *In re McKesson HBOC, Inc. Sec. Litig.*, No. 99-cv-20743 (N.D. Cal.)	$1.042 billion (combined)

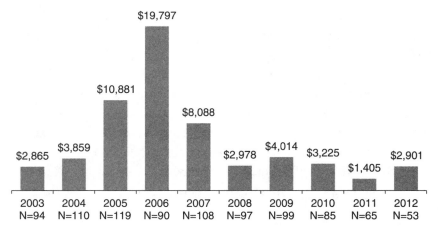

FIGURE 4.1: Total Settlement Amounts (Billions), 2003–2012

settlement dollars recovered between 2003 and 2012 in securities class actions and highlights the extraordinary apex in the years 2005–2007.[45]

The WorldCom, Enron, and Tyco International settlements (each among the largest securities class action settlements) were approved by courts, respectively, in 2005, 2006, and 2007. As a result of this concentration of cases, the amounts paid in securities class actions rose from $2.9 billion in 2003 to $19.8 billion in 2006 and then fell back to $2.9 billion in 2012.[46] Although both the aggregate settlement amount and the number of settlements rose again in 2013 (largely as a result of the settlement of several "mega" mortgage-backed securities cases remaining from the 2008 crash),[47] the 2006 peak does not seem likely to be matched in the foreseeable future.[48] Thus, in terms of its macroeconomic impact on corporate defendants, the securities class action may already be past its peak (as evidenced by the fact that the even greater 2008 financial crisis produced only lesser recoveries).

Still, even if the number of securities class action settlements and the annual aggregate amount paid by the defendants in them has been declining over recent years, the size of the average settlement is increasing.[49] This reflects the growing significance of the "megasettlement," which can be defined for present purposes as a settlement in excess of $100 million. In 2013, such megasettlements accounted for 84 percent of total settlement dollars paid in securities class action settlements in that year.[50]

Although this was an increase over the prior year, 2013 was by no means a record year (megasettlements accounted for 95 percent of all settlement dollars in 2006).[51] The key point here is that securities class actions are increasingly being litigated on two separate tracks, and the plaintiff's bar is dividing into separate camps. On the "megatrack," a large institutional investor will act as lead plaintiff and retain a major plaintiff's law firm to serve as class counsel in a case, seeking perhaps $1 billion or more in damages and settling for over $100 million. But because the median securities class action settlement in 2013 was only $6.5 million,[52] there have to be many smaller cases to bring the median down to this level. These smaller cases are litigated at a quicker pace,[53] with smaller institutions or individuals serving as lead plaintiff and smaller boutique law firms handling the case. On this lesser track, plaintiff's counsel will rely heavily on a litigation cost differential favoring it that makes it cheaper for defendants to settle than to fight. Defendants will characterize these actions as nuisance suits, but neither side can probably justify significant investment in litigating them.

Reflecting this growing division of securities class actions into two litigation tracks, the plaintiff's bar in securities cases is becoming increasingly concentrated. A 2011 Cornerstone Research study found that three plaintiff's law firms accounted for 58 percent of the securities class action settlements in that year.[54] This seems a predictable consequence of the "lead plaintiff" provision of the PSLRA, which has raised the barriers to entry for new firms. Smaller law firms cannot attract the larger public pension funds and lack the financial resources to compete at "pay to play" or to carry contingent fee cases for a significant duration. They are thus left to pursue those smaller cases that do not interest the largest institutional investors (and to pursue merger-related cases in state court, as Chapter 5 will discuss).

Prospectively, securities class actions face a somewhat diminished but relatively secure future, subject to one serious threat discussed at the end of this chapter. The survival of the Fraud-on-the-Market Doctrine had for several years seemed in doubt. Indeed, in 2013 and 2014, the doctrine lived a "cliffhanger" existence, as the Court twice reconsidered it. First, in *Amgen v. Connecticut Retirement Plans and Trust Funds*,[55] the Supreme Court called the doctrine into question, and four justices expressly announced their dissatisfaction with it. Then, in 2014, the Court did formally reconsider the doctrine in *Halliburton Co. v. Erica P. John Fund, Inc.*, but, with the entire bar on the edge of its seats, upheld it, by a 6-to-3 margin.[56] Still, the Court narrowed the doctrine, giving the defendant the ability to demonstrate at the class certification hearing that the allegedly false statement had no "price impact."[57] In so doing, the Court relied less on arguments about economics and market efficiency and more on the rule of stare decisis. Under the revised doctrine, the burden will be on the defendant to show that the corrective disclosure did not produce an adverse price impact. It is premature to predict how much this change will tilt the balance of advantage in the defendant's favor, but it seems unlikely to prevent class certification in most cases.

Empirically, the majority of securities class actions today survive pretrial motions to dismiss or motions for summary judgment and are thereafter settled.[58] Even if something like 40 percent are eventually dismissed or discontinued, the majority that survives seem more than sufficient to compensate plaintiff's attorneys (or at least those firms large enough to maintain a diversified portfolio of cases). More cases may be dismissed after the *Halliburton* II decision (which will also drive up the cost of securities litigation to plaintiff's attorneys by featuring a battle of experts and associated discovery at the class certification hearing), but the securities class action is not truly endangered, so long as settlement remains the most likely outcome.

Still, change is occurring, along a variety of dimensions: (1) big cases are pushing out smaller cases; that is, although the number of settlements has recently declined, the average size of the settlement has grown; (2) the plaintiff's bar in these cases is rapidly consolidating, with only a few large firms handling the megaclass action; and (3) institutional investors appear to be fleeing the class action in droves by opting out. These developments are interconnected, and the most important is the third: the new pattern of opting out by institutional investors. This pattern was highly controversial when Bill Lerach initiated it in *WorldCom*, but it has since become the prevalent approach. At a minimum, it indicates that larger institutions do not truly need the class action. Indeed, some plaintiff's firms (most notably, the Grant & Eisenhofer firm) now specialize in representing institutions in opt-out actions.

The force driving this pattern of institutional opting out is the broad perception that opt-outs seem to settle their cases on markedly superior terms to the class—and by a dramatic margin.[59] Class action plaintiffs recover on average somewhere between roughly 2 percent to 3 percent of their estimated losses in securities class actions that settle,[60] but the opt-outs may recover as much as the majority of their losses.[61] There are a variety of reasons why opt-outs outperform the class, but the key implication of this pattern is this: the securities class action may be returning to its original role of serving "negative value" claimants.

For the foreseeable future, the class will continue to be headed by an institutional lead plaintiff, who will perform this role either as a public service or because of "pay to play" contributions (or both). But the majority of institutional investors (or at least those with sizable losses) are increasingly likely to opt out of the class, leaving behind a residual class membership that would be economically unable or unwilling to sue on an individual basis. Defendants vociferously resist the growing number of opt-outs (which exposes defendants to multiple recoveries) and have attempted a variety of tactics.[62] But opting out is the rational strategy for the institution with a large block of stock, and defendant's only practical recourse has been to demand a renegotiation of the class action settlement with the plaintiff's attorneys in the class action to reflect the opt-outs.[63]

This development raises a policy issue. Because opting out may reduce the size of the class settlement, it initially appears that this development pits the interests of one group of plaintiffs (the institutional opt-outs) against the interests of the other plaintiffs (smaller claimants) and reduces the recovery to those with "negative value" claims. Yet, on closer analysis, a stronger case can be made for the opposite position: increased opting out benefits all plaintiffs because it may constitute an effective accountability mechanism by which class members can discipline their counsel. Most institutional investors opt out of the class only once a tentative settlement has been reached. Thus, the decision to opt out is effectively a referendum on the adequacy of the settlement. In effect, the opt-outs are "voting with their feet" to reject the settlement. Because their opting out may reduce the settlement size (and thus the likely fees to the plaintiff's attorneys in the class action), the threat of large-scale opting out may deter some weak or collusive settlements. This is an open question, but the eagerness of larger plaintiffs to exit the class appears unstoppable, and it implies that the securities class action will increasingly return to its original role of protecting "negative value" claimants.

One new and ominous storm cloud does today hang over the future of the securities class action. In 2014, the Delaware Supreme Court surprised many with a decision upholding the validity of a board-adopted bylaw that imposed liability on an unsuccessful plaintiff who sued the corporation (or its officers or directors) and did not obtain complete success.[64] This one-way fee-shifting provision went well beyond the British "loser pays" rule, both because it applied only to the plaintiff (and not the defendants) and because it required fee shifting even if the plaintiff recovered a substantial amount (but still significantly less than it had sought). The provision seemed clearly intended to deter litigation, but the Delaware Supreme Court said that that alone was not sufficient to show an "improper purpose."[65]

The response of public corporations to this decision was immediate. Between the decision in May 2014 and the end of September 2014, some twenty-four companies adopted similar provisions, either by board-adopted bylaws (in the case of already public companies) or charter provisions (in the case of companies conducting an initial public offering [or IPO]).[66] For example, the record-setting Alibaba IPO in 2014 contained such a provision.[67] Although twenty-four companies may seem a relatively small number, this number resembles the first trickle through a leak in a dam. Soon the leak will become a torrent, and the dam will burst.

Fee shifting against the plaintiff remains controversial in Delaware because it is likely to chill litigation, thus injuring the leading local industry (i.e., corporate litigation). No other issue has produced the same collision between the interests of the Delaware bar and those of its corporate clients. In 2013, immediately after the decision, the Corporate Law Section of the Delaware State Bar Association drafted legislation to bar fee shifting by corporate action, but this legislation was blocked by corporate lobbyists. A new effort is being made in 2015.

Yet, even if Delaware acts to restrain such fee shifting, the issue will persist, for three distinct reasons: (1) Delaware may place an insufficient chill on the practice; (2) other jurisdictions may tolerate or even encourage fee shifting; and (3) interstate charter competition could intensify, as public companies could migrate away from Delaware and reincorporate in jurisdictions that allow them to adopt fee-shifting bylaws by board action.

The one body that could broadly limit fee shifting is the SEC, which has in similar cases barred mandatory arbitration clauses in corporate charters and also successfully argued that indemnification of securities law liabilities, even if permissible under state law, is contrary to public policy and so preempted by federal law.[68] To date, however, the SEC has remained on the sidelines, taking no position, and it even failed to require disclosure in the Alibaba IPO that such a provision was in Alibaba's charter.

This book will return to the issue of fee shifting in considering needed reforms in Chapter 8. Its view will be that some modest fee shifting may be desirable, but that a ceiling must be placed on any "loser pays" rule to prevent any such bylaw or charter provision from precluding all litigation by shareholders. In the meantime, however, barring action by Delaware and/or the SEC, the future of the securities class action remains uncertain. It has, however, long been in that "cliffhanger" position.

5

MERGER AND ACQUISITION CLASS ACTIONS: LITIGATION ON STEROIDS

MERGERS ARE NATURAL TARGETS for litigation. First, the amounts involved are enormous, and even a modest increase in the share price following a lawsuit could justify a multimillion dollar fee award for the plaintiff's attorney. Second, the law on mergers is relatively favorable to plaintiffs. In Delaware, if the merger involves a majority shareholder seeking to squeeze out the minority shareholders, the defendants must bear the burden of proving the "entire fairness" of the transaction, which requires them to show both a fair price and fair dealing.[1] This is far different than the business judgment rule standard that governs most corporate transactions.

Even when this heightened standard is not applicable (as it would not be in the case of an arm's-length merger), plaintiffs still have substantial leverage because of their potential ability to disrupt the timing of the transaction. For example, if the plaintiffs can make a colorable case that some material disclosure was omitted or some flaw existed in the sale process, they might seek a preliminary injunction. For defendants, who may need the transaction to proceed with clockwork precision (for any of a number of reasons), even a remote threat of delay is sufficient to justify a cheap settlement. A $1 million fee award represents to defendants no more than a modest rounding error in a large multibillion dollar transaction. As a result, plaintiff's attorneys and defense counsel have become adept in settling merger and acquisition (M&A) class actions in nonpecuniary settlements in which additional disclosures are made and used to justify a fee award (typically under $1 million) to plaintiff's counsel. Defendants regard such settlements as extortionate, but would generally rather settle than fight—and, as we will see, they pay next to nothing.

Settlements of M&A litigation were long handled routinely in the Delaware Chancery Court (at least in the case of Delaware incorporated companies). Delaware courts had a long-standing policy of allowing defendants to settle weak (or even frivolous) actions if they wanted to, but they would keep the fees modest in order not to overreward the plaintiffs for a meaningless settlement. Although the process was somewhat tawdry, no one much cared, and transactions went off on schedule.

Then, sometime around 2005, everything began to change, and chaos has followed.[2] The precipitating cause was that many plaintiff's attorneys began to sue outside of Delaware. Why? Opinions vary. Some argue that plaintiff's attorneys decided that other jurisdictions would be more receptive or favorable to their case. For example, they may have wanted a jury trial (which is not available in the Delaware Chancery Court, which is a court of equity). But this explanation cannot account for the suddenness of the transition. A more likely reason is that plaintiff's attorneys found that they could get much higher fees outside of Delaware (whose courts were parsimonious in cases that struck them as meritless). Still others see the underlying cause as the fragmentation of the plaintiff's bar.[3] In the heyday of Milberg, Weiss, it has been argued, that firm could use its oligopolistic power to manage litigation and discourage multiforum battles between dueling class counsel in Delaware and elsewhere. Such battles could embarrass the plaintiff's bar because they predictably produced mudslinging between the rival counsel. A related possibility is that the Private Securities Litigation Reform Act of 1995 (PSLRA) (and its mandated use of institutional investors as lead plaintiffs) forced the smaller plaintiff's firms that had once primarily litigated securities class actions out of that field and into M&A cases in state court (where they did not need an institutional client and could compete by settling more cheaply than their rivals).

All these reasons are plausible. Although it is doubtful that plaintiff's attorneys really cared much about jury trials (as most M&A cases settle within a few weeks and never proceed to trial), many may have wanted to avoid Delaware. In Delaware, absent evidence of a "smoking gun" nature, plaintiffs were unlikely to convince an experienced Delaware vice chancellor to enjoin an arm's-length merger between two unaffiliated companies. Outside of Delaware, however, the case might well have been heard by a state court judge who had never previously been involved in merger litigation. Given the non-Delaware judge's relative inexperience, the outcome would have been less certain. Uncertainty in turn increases the leverage of the plaintiff's attorney. For example, if there was a 20 percent chance that the non-Delaware judge might delay the merger with a preliminary injunction, but only a 5 percent chance that a Delaware judge would do so, the nuisance value possessed by plaintiffs in the non-Delaware forum is substantially greater and may justify a higher settlement value (or, more importantly, a higher fee award).

Still other explanations may better explain the rapidity of the "flight from Delaware" and a more recent partial return. Until fairly recently, if multiple class actions were filed in Delaware, control of the Delaware action would likely go to the first plaintiff's attorney to file an action in Delaware.[4] Thus, if one lost the race to the Delaware courthouse, it made little sense to file in Delaware when one would not get control. If the plaintiff's attorney filed instead in the jurisdiction where the corporation's principal place of business was located, the plaintiff's attorney might expect to be able to control that action (because rival actions were unlikely in that other jurisdiction—at least originally). More recently, Delaware has moved away from its former "first to file" priority rule[5] and today may look to factors such as the client's stake in the litigation (i.e., a parallel to the federal "lead plaintiff" rule), the skill of the counsel, or the relative quality of the pleadings filed by the various contending counsel. This may have had a double-edged effect. It could have encouraged some attorneys to file in Delaware even though they were not first, but it probably told others that, even if they were first, they would not be given control in Delaware (and so they should file elsewhere). M&A class actions were long known to attract some counsel thought to be "bottom fishers" by their fellow attorneys, meaning that these attorneys did not litigate actively, did not conduct discovery, file motions, or take depositions. Rather, they just waited for defendants to make a settlement offer. "Bottom fishers" follow a strategy of investing little money or time in the action in order to be able to settle more cheaply than their more active rivals (who need a higher fee to cover their greater efforts).[6] Defendants anticipate that they can settle cheaper with inferior counsel (or, phrased more politely, with counsel who are not in a position to go to trial). Once Delaware moved away from its "first to file" procedure and began to emphasize the relative quality of the counsel, the so-called bottom fishers had less reason to file in Delaware because the highly experienced Delaware judges knew them by their reputation and would not select them.

Thus, for multiple reasons—pursuit of higher fee awards, the desire to maximize legal uncertainty, cost economies that favored filing in their own jurisdiction, the inability to control the action in Delaware—plaintiff's counsel began to migrate out of Delaware and file in a variety of other state courts (but rarely in federal court). This leakage moved from a trickle to a dam break after 2005.[7]

At the same time, the overall rate of litigation in M&A cases began to soar. As of the 1990s, the litigation rate was moderate. For example, one study found that, over the period of 1994 to 2010, 48 percent of large M&A transactions generated litigation.[8] This study may overstate the historical rate, because it includes years after 2005 when the litigation rate had already begun to rise dramatically. Another study finds that only 12 percent of M&A transactions involving public companies attracted a lawsuit in 1999 and 2000.[9] Whatever the precise number, prior to 2000, the M&A litigation rate was clearly under 50 percent.

Then, sometime around 2005, the pattern changed. Table 5.1 shows the increase in the litigation rates from 2009 to 2012 on M&A deals valued over $100 million.[10] In short, in both 2011 and 2012, a medium-sized or larger merger stood a 93 percent chance of attracting multiple lawsuits (between 4.8 and 5.3). Moreover, larger mergers had an even higher probability of attracting litigation. If the merger was valued at over $500 million, the percentages increased to over 95 percent, as shown in Table 5.2.[11]

Table 5.1   Litigation rates in M&A transactions, 2009–2012

	Acquisition announcement year			
	2009	2010	2011	2012
Number of lawsuits filed	349	792	742	602
Percentage of deals litigated	86%	90%	93%	93%
Average number of lawsuits per deal	4.3	4.9	5.3	4.8
Average number of days between deal announcement and lawsuit filing	14	16	17	14

Table 5.2   Litigation rates in deals over $500 million, 2007–2012

2007	2008	2009	2010	2011	2012
63%	72%	92%	95%	96%	96%

To sum up, in 2011 and 2012, no matter what the terms of the deal or the size of the merger premium, the merging parties in a transaction that was of more than minimal size (i.e., $500 million and up) had only a 4 percent chance of avoiding litigation. The speed of this transition (from under 50 percent to 96 percent in a few years) poses a mystery. Legal change usually occurs at a slower pace, and even the highly lucrative securities class action examined in Chapter 4 took decades to develop. Nothing new had happened in the transactional structure of mergers to attract more litigation, and indeed the rate of merger activity has declined substantially since the 2008 financial crisis. Yet, mergers now attract not one private attorney general, but on average between 4.8 and 5.3. However much one likes the concept of the private attorney general, four to five teams of private attorney generals per transaction seem too many. Somehow, the incentives to sue have become excessive, and litigation is growing out of control, like algae in a petri dish.

The migration out of Delaware has recently slowed. It appears to have peaked around 2009, and more recent data for the years 2011 and 2012 show that Delaware has begun to recover some of its lost market share, as shown in Table 5.3.[12]

The recent return of some cases to Delaware likely reflects recent higher fee awards in Delaware. But, if that is the motivation for this return, it

Table 5.3 Jurisdiction of filing for M&A lawsuits, 2009–2012

	2009	2010	2011	2012
State court (other than Delaware)	225 (64%)	500 (63%)	431 (58%)	320 (53%)
Delaware	96 (28%)	198 (25%)	237 (32%)	239 (39%)
Federal court	28 (8%)	94 (12%)	74 (10%)	49 (8%)

will do nothing to curb the excessive rate of litigation and may eventually lead to an even higher number of lawsuits per transaction.

Once these suits are filed (in Delaware or elsewhere), what happens in this litigation? The short answer is: very little. Typically, M&A litigation is filed quickly after the deal's announcement, usually within a few days and often before the proxy statement is even filed with the SEC.[13] This race to the courthouse resembles the same pattern earlier seen in Chapter 4 in securities litigation before the passage of the PSLRA when cases were filed at a breakneck pace on the premise that the first filed action was more likely to win control. But less chaos arose in the federal securities class action context because the Judicial Panel on Multidistrict Litigation would consolidate these rival actions before one federal judge for the purposes of all pretrial motions (and typically for settlement). In contrast, multiforum litigation at the state level has no similar coordinating body with the result that the level of uncertainty and chaos is greater.

Partly as a result of this uncertainty, little actual adversarial activity follows after an action's filing. Indeed, one Delaware vice chancellor has accurately characterized the distinctive feature of M&A litigation as being that "No One Litigates Anything."[14] Motions are not made; discovery is not pursued; and depositions are not conducted. Instead, silence reigns, and the case's docket at the courthouse has few entries until a settlement is announced in one of the multiple jurisdictions. Very much unlike securities class actions, M&A litigation is feigned litigation.

Nonetheless, weak as these cases appear to be, they overwhelmingly settle, as Table 5.4 shows.[15] The 61 to 64 percent settlement rates shown in Table 5.4 between 2009 and 2012 very likely understate. The category of "voluntarily dismissed" probably includes many cases in which the

Table 5.4   M&A litigation outcomes, 2009–2012

	2009	2010	2011	2012
Settlement	91 (61%)	225 (62%)	184 (58%)	119 (64%)
Voluntarily dismissed	32 (22%)	116 (32%)	110 (34%)	59 (33%)
Dismissed by court	25 (17%)	18 (5%)	26 (8%)	8 (3%)
Judgment recovered	__ (0%)	5 (1%)	__ (0%)	__ (0%)

defendants settled with other plaintiffs in a different jurisdiction. More revealing is the fact that, from 2010 to 2012, less than 10 percent of M&A cases were dismissed by the court. This implies a nearly 90 percent success rate, which would compare favorably with plaintiffs' success rates in any other field of litigation (remember, for example, that around 40 percent of securities class actions are dismissed at the motion to dismiss stage).[16] But this high settlement rate does not imply that M&A litigation is generally meritorious. Rather, it suggests that courts are largely bystanders, either powerless to act or, more likely, unwilling to interfere with defendants' decisions to pay ransom to plaintiffs because of the nuisance value that they pose.

The most striking fact about M&A litigation is how little the class members gain from it. One 2013 study finds that only 4.8 percent of the settlements in M&A litigation over recent years provided for any compensation to the class members, while the vast majority provided only for additional disclosures.[17] The plaintiff's attorneys, however, receive substantial fees for providing such limited benefit to the class. In 2012, the average agreed upon plaintiff's fee award was $725,000.[18] This is a relatively modest amount in comparison to securities class actions where fee awards can exceed $100 million in a single, large case, but it is adequate to attract those attorneys who cannot win control of securities class actions. If a settlement is highly likely (and it is), then little is risked, and a modest return can attract those plaintiff's attorneys with a low opportunity cost. Plaintiff's fee awards are even smaller in "disclosure-only" settlements. In those weaker settlements, plaintiffs' fee awards have declined for the last four years from $730,000 in 2009, to $710,000 in 2010, to $570,000 in 2011, to $540,000 in 2012.[19] Such a decline suggests that courts perceive these actions to be largely meritless and do not want to award windfalls to attorneys who have done little. All in all, the plaintiff's attorneys bringing these cases are usually not the pride of the plaintiff's bar, but marginal (or worse) performers, who see M&A cases as a low-risk payday that will pay their rent.

Ultimately, the policy question is, how should we define the harm from this hyperactive rate of litigation? That definition of the harm in turn shapes the design of the remedy. Here, there are two distinct perspectives: First, a high litigation rate (even well short of the current 96 percent figure) can be viewed as a "litigation tax" on all mergers and acquisitions, because virtually all mergers attract suit. To secure a small nuisance-based settlement with plaintiff's attorneys, shareholders must absorb the unwanted costs of disposing of generally weak litigation (which includes the costs of counsel on both sides of the litigation). This is the business community's primary complaint, and it seems valid.

But a second problem may be more serious: such litigation is likely to result in collusive outcomes and a phenomenon known as the "reverse auction."[20] That latter term refers to a process by which defendants seek out the plaintiff's firm willing to settle at the lowest price (which is often the firm that has done the least work on the case) in order to buy protection from more meritorious suits. Suppose, in a hypothetical case, the board of a merging company has "sold out" the interests of its shareholders to that of the majority stockholder, who is seeking to squeeze out the minority. Although this is not a frivolous action, the same pattern will follow, with litigation being brought in multiple forums. Predictably, the defendants will seek to settle cheaply with a plaintiff's attorney with a weaker case and avoid those plaintiff's attorneys who have worked actively on their case. Such a weak settlement, if approved by an inexperienced (and probably non-Delaware) judge, will carry preclusive effect under the Constitution's Full Faith and Credit Clause and bar all other related litigation.[21] In short, multiforum litigation invites collusion. Vivid examples of "reverse auctions" are rare,[22] but quick and quiet settlements without pecuniary relief are now standard. Both sides have learned to follow a safe protocol to reach settlement. So viewed, the real harm here is a Gresham's Law Effect: weak cases drive out stronger cases.

Many reforms have been proposed to address the M&A litigation crisis. They include federal legislation, Delaware legislation, and private ordering remedies (such as charter and bylaw amendments). Several might work, but all have their problems. This topic of reform will be postponed because the immediate question is what we learn from this context about entrepreneurial litigation. Here, one lesson seems obvious: while access to justice is desirable, it appears that there can be too much of a good thing. Ironically, a multiplicity of private attorney generals appears to hurt, rather than help, the clients that they represent. In reality, the underlying problem is less that there are too many plaintiff's attorneys and more that "common pool" problems deny any attorney the ability to invest in the action with a view to actually litigating it. Instead, "feigned" litigation and "reverse auctions" result because there are no clear rules for allocating control over the case in an efficient manner. Unless multiforum litigation can be better designed, chaos will continue.

6

THE MASS TORT CLASS ACTION:
QUICK RISE, FASTER FALL

IN THE PRECEDING CHAPTERS, we have chiefly examined various forms of business litigation. In most of these cases, the class action served to aggregate small claimants holding "negative value" claims into an entity that had sufficient leverage to negotiate a settlement superior to what individual litigants could obtain on their own. Although the business community may view such aggregation as encouraging extortion, the goal of providing a remedy for "negative value" claims seems at a minimum legitimate.

This chapter will examine the mirror image of such aggregation. Mass tort class actions quickly blossomed at the end of the 1980s and flourished until they were curtailed by the Supreme Court in the late 1990s. But they shared little in common with "negative value" classes. Here, it is useful to recall that the class action was imported into the United States from England on the original rationale that it would serve the interests of judicial economy by minimizing duplicative litigation.[1] That rationale was largely ignored by the two Advisory Committees that wrote and rewrote the Federal Rules of Civil Procedure in 1937 and 1966. Nor was this original rationale relevant to the rise of civil rights class actions or securities class litigation in the 1960s and 1970s. During this period, academics instead championed the class action for its ability to activate the private attorney general. But mass tort class actions seldom, if ever, enabled "negative value" claims to be brought. Rather, mass tort class actions uniquely show the influence and impact of the judicial economy rationale—and the costs of that rationale.

Mass tort class actions are unlike the types of representative litigation earlier examined in two fundamental respects: First, they typically aggregated claims of substantial value, not "negative value" claims. To be sure, many marginal, or even frivolous, claims were regularly swept into these classes, but mass tort classes were unprecedented in being "large claimant" classes. Their claims—for example, for mesothelioma in asbestos cases—could have been resolved in most cases in the traditional tort system where plaintiff's attorneys would have represented them on a contingent fee basis.[2]

Second, the driving force behind these class actions was not the usual instigators (i.e., ambitious and entrepreneurial plaintiff's attorneys— although they were certainly present), but rather a coalition of odd bedfellows: (1) defendants who were often facing a choice between a bankruptcy reorganization or a "settlement class" action that would resolve all the mass tort claims against them and (2) a judiciary that was increasingly fearful of inundation by an approaching tidal wave of mass tort claims. The fact that it was the defendants who actively sought class-wide resolution of mass torts distinguishes this litigation context from all others.

Mass tort class actions were controversial within the plaintiff's bar, where they pitted the traditional plaintiff's trial lawyers, who believed in individual litigant autonomy (and insisted on each client's "right to his day in court") against the class action bar, who saw the need for a collective solution to a massive social problem and who dismissed litigant autonomy as an out-of-date, illusory ideal. In their recurrent battles, both sides of the plaintiff's camp were motivated by both greed and idealism, and both accused the other of acting solely out of greed. That is, both the plaintiff's trial lawyer handling individual asbestos cases (often on a 40 percent contingency) and the class action plaintiff's attorneys seeking to structure a multibillion dollar settlement class anticipated very lucrative fees if they could resolve a mass tort in the way that they preferred.

As a result, mass tort class action settlements typically involved three cornered fights among (1) defendants, who were also actively considering a bankruptcy reorganization; (2) class action plaintiff's attorneys, eager to reach a settlement for billions of dollars; and (3) plaintiff's trial lawyers, often with large inventories of clients, who were convinced (probably accurately) that they could obtain higher value settlements for their clients in individual cases. Overseeing this process were courts that were, themselves, conflicted by their strong desire to protect their dockets from a seemingly unending flood of mass tort cases.

In retrospect, it now seems clear that mass tort class actions fundamentally prejudiced one unique class of claimants that we have not previously encountered: "future claimants." "Future claimants" are persons exposed to a toxic product (e.g., asbestos, tobacco, a prescription drug, or silicone gel breast implants) who have not yet manifested any symptom, but who are destined to develop serious to fatal injuries.[3] Statistically, "future claimants" are a small proportion of the universe of persons exposed to the product or substance (because exposure generally does not produce illness in most of the exposed population). Thus, either because the odds on experiencing illness are in their favor or because they repress the frightening truth, most future claimants tend to remain "rationally apathetic." This exposes them to legal danger because defendants, in contrast, recognize that their greatest risk of tort liability comes from future claimants, not those with existing or "present" injuries. A mass tort settlement will not protect defendants from prospective insolvency, unless it releases them from "future" claims. Hence, securing a release from future claimants is a necessity for defendants.

The resulting negotiations are typically a mismatch. Neither the trial bar, which is focused on their present clients, nor the class action bar has a strong interest in protecting future claimants. As a result, mass tort settlements typically underfunded future claims. This underfunding could occur as a result of (1) underestimating the number of likely future claims against the settlement fund (which was easily done given the long latency periods—up to forty years or more—associated with asbestos and some other products); (2) ignoring the impact of inflation, which trivialized any fixed recovery to be paid a decade or more later; or (3) allowing early claimants to "raid" the settlement fund by filing extravagant claims, thereby depleting the funds available for future claimants. For any of these reasons and others, future claimants were systematically underrepresented and undercompensated in mass tort proceedings (both class actions and bankruptcy reorganizations), and settlement funds in some prominent asbestos reorganizations were quickly exhausted.[4]

The vulnerability of future claimants was long swept under the rug. Academics contributed to this process by confidently offering a "public law" vision of litigation that stressed communitarian values and alternative modes of representation in place of the traditional norm of individual litigant autonomy.[5] But courts were at least as responsible because of their determination to find a solution (indeed, any solution) to the impending caseload crisis that they perceived mass torts to pose for them. This story needs to be sketched in some detail.

A. THE LEGAL AND INSTITUTIONAL BACKDROP

Historically, mass torts had not been subject to class certification. The Advisory Committee that drafted Rule 23 of the Federal Rules of Civil Procedure in 1966 added a note to their new rule stating that a " 'mass accident' is ordinarily not appropriate for a class action."[6] Their reasoning was that individual issues as to causation and defenses would overwhelm the common issues. Even airplane crashes (where the causation was common to all the decedents) were almost never certified as class actions.

But in the 1980s, social behavior changed, and "claiming" increased. As scholars have noted, during the 1980s, "hundreds of thousands of people sued scores of corporations for losses due to injuries or diseases that were attributed to catastrophic events, pharmaceutical products, medical devices or toxic substances."[7] This was a social and cultural phenomenon as much as a legal development, as ordinary citizens began to assert legal claims at a much higher rate. The most prominent mass tort episodes in the 1980s involved medical products (the Dalkon Shield),[8] herbicides (Agent Orange),[9] asbestos, and a few mass accidents (such as the much-litigated collapse of a skywalk at a Hyatt Regency Hotel in Kansas City, Missouri).[10] At the beginning of this decade (and well into it), appellate courts generally rebuffed and reversed those district courts that granted class certification.[11] Again and again, they stressed that problems with proximate causation, differing state laws, and possible defenses made a class action infeasible.

A breakthrough in the resistance of appellate courts to class certification in the mass tort area came in 1986 in a major asbestos case. In *Jenkins v. Raymark Industries,*[12] the Fifth Circuit was candid about the motivation for its sharp departure from prior law and its grant of class certification: "The courts are now being forced to rethink the alternatives and priorities by the current volume of litigation and more frequent mass disasters."[13] Other courts quickly concurred. Later that year, the Third Circuit partially upheld class certification in another large asbestos class action,[14] and a year later the Second Circuit sustained Judge Jack Weinstein's landmark certification of the Agent Orange class action.[15] By the end of the decade in 1989, the Fourth Circuit upheld class certification in the Dalkon Shield case.[16]

Curiously, these cases were "mass exposure" cases, rather than mass accident cases. In principle, certification should logically have been far more difficult in a mass exposure case than in a mass accident case (such as a skyway collapse in a hotel). This is because the facts and the applicable law are likely to vary far more from case to case in a mass exposure case. Unlike a single accident (such as a plane crash), mass exposure may give rise to claims on a nationwide basis and trigger the law of all fifty states. Issues of causation are inevitable where the victims may have been exposed to other toxic substances or had a medical history that offered alternative explanations for their symptoms.

Only one plausible explanation can account for courts certifying mass exposure cases, after having long refused to certify numerous mass accident cases: courts were themselves interested parties and feared inundation if they could not find a way to resolve mass exposure cases. Put more bluntly, in a plane crash or other mass accident, the failure to certify a class might mean that a hundred or more individual cases would have to be heard by the courts (probably in one consolidated proceeding).

But in mass exposure cases, if class certification were denied, the number of individual claims that would likely be filed in court often numbered in the hundreds of thousands. This was precisely because these class members held claims with significant value and could find individual representation from a highly specialized, contingent fee plaintiff's bar. For example, when the Fifth Circuit broke new ground and certified the first asbestos mass tort case in *Jenkins,* the action arose in East Texas, an area that has been aptly described as "the fertile crescent of asbestos litigation."[17] In short, despite the greater doctrinal problems with class certification in a mass exposure case, the courts faced a predicted flood of cases that could potentially paralyze them—unless they could be resolved on a class basis.

B. THE JUDICIARY'S PERCEPTION OF THE CRISIS

During the 1980s, the perception grew that mass torts, unless checked, would eventually clog the federal docket and paralyze the civil litigation system. In some courts, mass torts had already grown to account for 25 percent of the civil caseload,[18] and by 1990, asbestos litigation represented over 75 percent of all new federal product liability filings.[19] And the filing rate was still rising. By 1990, two new asbestos cases were filed each year for every one case resolved.[20]

A sense of crisis began to overtake the federal judiciary. Chief Judge Robert Parker in the Eastern District of Texas observed in one decision that if his district court tried asbestos cases at the rate of thirty cases per month (i.e., better than one a day), it would still take six and one-half years to try all asbestos cases on the existing docket, and at that point the court could anticipate that 5,000 new cases would have been filed in the interim.[21] Multiple commissions and study groups warned of dire consequences and advocated new approaches.

In reality, the impact of asbestos litigation was highly uneven and localized. Forty percent of all federal asbestos filings in the late 1970s and early 1980s occurred in the district courts of Massachusetts, Eastern Texas, and Southern Mississippi, and over 50 percent of all asbestos filings were in the First and Fifth Circuits.[22] These were jurisdictions in which major World War II shipyards had been located and from which the accelerating flow of asbestos cases began.[23] But even if the caseload crisis was more localized than national, it was precisely those district courts most impacted by the asbestos crisis that were called upon to decide whether to legitimize the mass tort class action. Put simply, the new law on class actions was made by the courts most under stress.

Asbestos was not unique in its heavy localized impact. Either as the result of bankruptcy proceedings or, more typically, because of a transfer order by the Judicial Panel on Multidistrict Litigation (JPML), enormous numbers of related mass tort claims came under the control of individual judges. For example, Judge Robert Merhige of the Eastern District of Virginia oversaw the resolution of some 195,000 Dalkon Shield claims,[24] and Judge Jack Weinstein of the Eastern District of New York handled proceedings that resolved 240,000 Agent Orange claims.[25] This pattern was very dissimilar to the prior experience with JPML transfers in securities or antitrust cases. In those fields, the JPML only transferred securities or antitrust cases against one or more connected defendants; here, they transferred all cases involving the same mass tort—i.e., all asbestos, Dalkon Shield, or Agent Orange claims—even if they involved dozens of different defendants. In short, individual judges, some under acute caseload pressure, now had both the motive and the opportunity to attempt a global resolution—by any means necessary.

C. THE DISTINCTIVE DYNAMICS OF MASS TORT LITIGATION

Not only was the number of asbestos and other mass tort cases growing throughout the 1980s, but there were legitimate grounds to expect that their pace would accelerate and that the increased caseload would fall especially intensely on some regions. This shaped the expectations of all the players in this drama. But how events actually played out was determined by the distinctive style of mass torts litigation, which involved three critical and interrelated factors:

1. THE MASS TORT EVOLUTIONARY CYCLE. Mass torts (other than those related to a single crash or accident) tend to evolve according to a predictable cycle.[26] At the outset, plaintiffs allege that a product, drug, or

substance causes certain injuries, but they seldom win at first, both because they lack adequate scientific evidence and because plaintiff's attorneys at this stage do not yet possess the necessary specialized knowledge to effectively try these cases. But over time, the tort begins to "mature," as plaintiff's attorneys invest in acquiring specialized human capital in the field. They acquire relevant scientific knowledge, find experts, and develop effective trial techniques. Once they have made such investments, they exploit their new expertise by searching broadly for individual claimants to represent. As their learning curve turns upward, settlement values rise, and defendants can expect that settlements will become even more costly in the future (thus making an early settlement at today's "bargain" prices more attractive). Correspondingly, as the price of settlement rises, plaintiff's attorneys are incentivized to search for more cases by screening larger populations (and sometimes including weaker cases within their inventories). Hence, the rate of increase in filings can become hyperbolic.

2. INTERDEPENDENT RECOVERIES.   The recoveries in mass tort litigation tend to be highly interdependent—far more so than in ordinary litigation (say, automobile accidents) or in securities class litigation.[27] This is both because there is a high commonality of issues in mass tort cases (particularly as to the scientific and causation issues) and because the plaintiff's bar in specialized mass torts is highly concentrated. As a result, if plaintiffs win a victory in one case by developing admissible scientific evidence to show that asbestos causes mesothelioma (a rare cancer of the lung tissues), that victory in one case will affect the settlement value of all remaining similar cases.

For defendants, the likely increase in settlement values as a mass tort "matures" implies that settlements early in this mass tort cycle are desirable—at least if today's price applies also to tomorrow's future claimants. A further factor here is the typically long latency periods for many mass torts, with thirty or more years often separating the victim's exposure from the onset of illness in asbestos or tobacco cases. Long latency periods incentivize the plaintiff's bar, because they imply that, even after a drug or product is withdrawn from the market, there will still be a lengthy period in which tort claims will continue to arise that they can successfully assert against the defendants. Thus, plaintiff's attorneys can invest rationally in acquiring specialized knowledge and searching for cases through mass screenings, knowing that once they have developed a successful trial strategy, they can realistically expect to reap the benefits of their expertise for many years.

3. MARKET CONCENTRATION.   Many types of high volume litigation do not lead to concentration within the plaintiff's bar (for example, automobile litigation). But mass tort litigation is at the opposite end of this spectrum, and high concentration followed from both the need for specialization and the attractiveness of inventory settlements. Less than fifty firms specialized in asbestos litigation, and a handful dominated the field.[28] Some thirty firms also represented the majority of the Dalkon Shield claimants.[29]

Earlier, this same pattern of high concentration was found to exist in the case of securities litigation, but there is an important difference. Attorneys specializing in mass tort litigation tend to accumulate large inventories of clients with similar claims; this is the efficient way to exploit their investment in specialized expertise. They obtain these clients both through direct advertising and through referrals (often paying referral fees). More importantly, they settle their cases on an inventory basis. No securities plaintiff's firm has 1,000 individual cases in its portfolio; nor could it settle all its different cases at once. But in the mass tort field, many plaintiff's attorneys had inventories numbering in the thousands, and their preferred approach was to seek wholesale settlement of their inventory of cases.

Concentration on the plaintiff's side in mass tort litigation was more than matched on the defendant's side. A defective product or toxic substance is usually produced by a single manufacturer. Even in the asbestos field, there were no more than thirty asbestos producers, and these producers organized into a common defense consortium to mount a common defense, typically through a limited number of defense counsel.[30] As a result, on both sides, repeat players regularly confronted each other.

Even more unusual, this concentration and ongoing interaction between the adversaries was paralleled by a corresponding consolidation at the judicial level. Mass tort cases tend to arise in specific areas (such as the Gulf Coast or other sites of naval shipyards), and they tend to be concentrated in one specific district by the transfer orders of the JPML. Whether as a result of a bankruptcy reorganization or a JPML transfer, one judge, typically chosen because the judge was already experienced in the field, obtains control over most of the pending federal cases involving that specific tort.

This pattern of universal transfer to a single judge implied that a global resolution of all cases was feasible. Repeat players were meeting repeat players in a single forum, and the court was afforded an opportunity to seek a global settlement. The only obstacle to such a global resolution was the difficult problem of estimating the number of future claimants who would experience serious to fatal injuries over an extended latency period. Given the eagerness for a settlement on all sides and the predictable passivity of the future claimants, that obstacle proved to be surmountable.

4. THE RUSH TO A GLOBAL ASBESTOS SETTLEMENT.   In early 1991, the Judicial Conference's Ad Hoc Committee on Asbestos Litigation, which had been established a year earlier by Chief Justice Rehnquist, reported that "what has been a frustrating problem is becoming a disaster of major proportions to both the victims and the producers of asbestos products, which the courts are ill-equipped to meet effectively."[31] It recommended a "national asbestos dispute scheme that permits consolidation of all asbestos claims in a single forum."[32]

Shortly thereafter, eight federal district judges with heavy asbestos caseloads petitioned the JPML to consolidate all asbestos personal injury cases in the federal system in a single forum.[33] Despite having refused earlier similar requests on several occasions, the JPML decided in 1991 to go with the flow and order such a transfer, emphasizing, in particular, the risk of future corporate bankruptcies if it did not. On July 29, 1991, the JPML transferred all pending asbestos personal injury cases in the federal system to Judge Charles R. Weiner of the Eastern District of Pennsylvania (i.e., Philadelphia)—a jurisdiction with a particularly heavy asbestos caseload.[34]

Two days later, on August 1, 1991, Judge Robert Parker, chair of the Judicial Conference's subcommittee responsible for overseeing asbestos litigation and a former member of the Ad Hoc Committee appointed by Chief Justice Rehnquist, wrote to Judge Weiner, urging him to deal aggressively with the challenge that lay before him:

> We now have an opportunity to prove that the federal courts are not impotent. It is incumbent upon us to establish that we are viable as an institution and that we can provide modern solutions for modern problems. If we fail to rise to the task, I fear far reaching consequences.
>
> I deeply believe we are not irrelevant—that we do have a role in our society that is greater than refereeing one-on-one litigation in an expensive and cumbersome manner . . .
>
> I view your role as one of the commanding generals. You are the Eisenhower of this D-Day operation. The rest of us are colonels prepared to take orders in this joint effort . . . The magnitude of this assignment is unprecedented in federal court history.
>
> I would encourage you to at all times maintain a focus on the problem as a whole and not let the lawyers mire you into individual or small group considerations. If you let them, they can dominate your time to the point of rendering the transferee judge ineffective as far as the overall solution is concerned. Case management as applied to individual cases or consolidated groups simply will not work on this problem.
>
> I would encourage you to be reluctant to grant exemptions to transfer. The fact that some judge may have X number of cases scheduled to go to trial two months or six months from now and on that basis (contrary to the MDL Order) gains an exemption from this process, in my judgment, is counterproductive. I think we have to continually focus on the larger problem. This focus will produce dynamics that should work toward the larger solution.[35]

Clearly this letter dropped any pretense of judicial restraint or impartiality. Instead, it asked Judge Weiner to stay all pending asbestos litigation, grant very few "special hardship" transfers back to the court from which individual cases were transferred, and generally maintain the pressure on the plaintiff's side to induce them to accept a global settlement. So admonished, Judge Weiner did indeed slow the pace of asbestos litigation in the federal courts—to the point that fewer than one dozen asbestos cases in federal court appear to have been tried to a verdict or fully settled between the July 29, 1991, transfer date and July 1992.[36]

More importantly, the foregoing Parker/Weiner correspondence indicates that asbestos litigation had transcended the usual bilateral context of private litigation and had become a public policy concern in which the judiciary was determined to play a proactive role. In overview, the consolidation of asbestos litigation was the culmination of a coordinated campaign by federal district judges to pressure plaintiffs (and their attorneys) to enter into global settlement discussions with defendants. Pursuant to that goal, nationwide defendants' and plaintiffs' asbestos steering committees were formed, and, throughout the remainder of 1991, exploratory talks continued between the two sides.

Contemporaneously with these developments, defendants' behavior toward pending asbestos cases changed sharply. Because, without Judge Weiner's consent, plaintiffs could no longer proceed to trial in federal court, their only recourse was to settle in private negotiations. But defendants now began to stonewall, resisting any individual settlements. Despite repeated requests from plaintiffs' attorneys to allow a transfer of cases back to their original jurisdictions, Judge Weiner remained as adamant as Judge Parker had hoped that he would be. Gradually, Judge Weiner's message became clear: no individual settlements would occur outside a global resolution of all asbestos claims.

Despite this pressure, the plaintiffs' steering committee held out, and in November 1991, it rejected the defendants' steering committee's offer of a global asbestos resolution.[37] The traditional trial lawyers and the class action specialists on the plaintiffs' steering committee simply could not agree. Seeing this split on the plaintiff's side, the asbestos industry then implemented a novel strategy. They approached the two co-chairmen of the plaintiffs' steering committee and invited them to negotiate with them on an individual basis a separate settlement covering all future personal injury claimants in the United States. In effect, if the plaintiffs' steering committee would not agree, the defendants would attempt to strike a deal with its two co-chairs. Their proposed deal came in two steps. Both these co-chairs—Gene Locks and Ron Motley—controlled large inventories of "present" asbestos cases and thus were uniquely advantaged by the prospect of an inventory settlement, at a time when all cases in federal court were stayed and all other settlement discussions suspended. They alone were being invited to settle their considerable inventories. Ultimately, the asbestos industry entered into inventory settlements covering 14,000 clients of these two firms for a total payment of $215 million.[38] Although the contingent fees these two firms received is not known (because discovery was not permitted by Judge Weiner), it seems highly likely that they did not receive less than the standard contingency fee of one-third (which here would amount to more than $71 million).

The next step was even more surprising, but logically predictable. On January 15, 1993, the same plaintiff's attorneys and the asbestos industry filed a complaint, an answer, a joint motion for class certification, and a 106-page stipulation of settlement in the Eastern District of Pennsylvania.[39] These documents set forth a comprehensive settlement of all "future" personal injury asbestos claims in the United States. In short, this was a "settlement only class," achieved without motions, discovery, or preliminary litigation in which the plaintiff class was represented by the same two attorneys who had just received the $215 million settlement for their "present" clients. To the plaintiff's trial bar (which was largely opposed to such a class action settlement), the suspicion was irresistible that the two deals were linked so that the $215 million payment in the inventory settlement was conditioned on the two attorneys' agreement to represent the proposed class in a global class action settlement. Still, in the absence of discovery, this could never be shown. Adding to the suspicion, however, was the unusual fact that the asbestos industry agreed to pay any attorney fees awarded to the class by the court approving the class action settlement.[40]

Next, and equally quickly, on February 1, 1993, two weeks after this filing, Judge Weiner conditionally certified the proposed class—without holding a hearing.[41] Judge Weiner did, however, appoint another federal district judge to conduct the fairness hearing on the proposed settlement.[42] After extensive and contested hearings, the settlement was eventually approved in 1994, and the court then enjoined all class members from "initiating or maintaining any asbestos-related personal injury or death claims" against the asbestos industry defendants.[43] In principle, objecting class members could opt out for a brief period, but opting out is unlikely in the case of future claimants who do not yet know or anticipate that they have been seriously injured.

The terms of settlement in this global class action—now known as *Georgine v. Amchem Products, Inc.*[44]—were surprising in several respects. First, the settlement was framed to catch only future claimants and not existing litigants. This was a strategic move to lessen resistance from the plaintiff's trial bar, which would as a result be able to settle their "present" claims, but not bring future cases. This strategy worked, at least to the extent that only a few of the firms in the plaintiff's trial bar formally objected to the settlement.[45]

Second, the substantive terms of the settlement were far inferior to the contemporaneous inventory settlements that the defendants had reached with the same plaintiff's attorneys or that had been reached in recent bankruptcy reorganizations.[46] Future claimants would be compensated only if they satisfied strict standards as to the duration of their occupational exposure (for example, in the case of lung cancer, occupational exposure of between eight and fifteen years was required, depending on the victim's job classification).[47] No similar limits were recognized by tort law. One Harvard Medical School expert testified at the fairness hearing that *Georgine*'s minimum eligibility criteria would eliminate 50 percent of the victims that the doctor had diagnosed with asbestos-related lung cancer.[48]

Third, the *Georgine* settlement also imposed strict limitations on the number of qualifying claims that may be paid in any year for various disease categories. Thus, no more than 700 lung cancer cases, 700 mesothelioma, and 200 "other cancer" cases would have to be paid in any year, with the remainder being placed in a queue to wait indefinitely (and possibly never be paid).[49] Unlike other settlements and most asbestos bankruptcy reorganizations, *Georgine* made no effort to estimate the number of future claimants likely to file claims. Actually, that number made little difference to the defendants because they had already shifted the risk that the fund would be inadequate to the future claimants by agreeing to compensate only a limited number of cases each year. Still, from a public relations standpoint, ignorance was bliss, and *Georgine* was approved without any estimate of how many future claims were likely to arise (and be deferred by the settlement).

All in all, the *Georgine* settlement (1) screened out many (and possibly most) of those who would receive compensation in the tort system, (2) paid future claimants less than had been paid contemporaneously in other settlements, and (3) subjected those who were to be paid to a potentially extended and indefinite delay. In addition, lengthy as the delay might be, there was no adjustment for inflation. Further, if a future claimant filed a claim decades later (after a long latency period), that claimant also had no right to any inflation adjustment.[50]

Nothing in this description suggests that the class action was functioning as the individual claimant's weapon of choice or that the private attorney general was performing its intended role. Perhaps, if *Georgine* had stood alone, it might be dismissed as an aberration that did not prove the inadequacy of the class action to the mass torts challenge. But *Georgine* was swiftly followed by other class actions largely modeled after it.

The next such case, filed months after *Georgine* but negotiated contemporaneously, was *Ahearn v. Fibreboard*,[51] which was an attempt by an asbestos producer that was bordering on insolvency to negotiate a global resolution of all future mass tort claims, based almost exclusively on its insurance policies. Immediately before its settlement, Fibreboard Corporation had unpaid obligations in excess of $1 billion and over 50,000 asbestos-related actions pending against it.[52] These claims exceeded its net worth, and Fibreboard was too cash constrained to be able to enter into the same settlement as the other asbestos producers had done in *Georgine*. Still, it followed the same game plan on its own. In December 1992, Fibreboard first reached an inventory settlement covering approximately 20,000 existing asbestos claims with the same law firm (Ness, Motley) that had principally negotiated the $215 million inventory settlement that preceded *Georgine*.[53] Later, this settlement was extended to cover another 45,000 pending asbestos-related personal injury claims against Fibreboard. Even more significantly, this inventory settlement required Ness, Motley to recommend the same terms to any future claimants that it later represented.[54]

That set the stage for the critical next step. In August 1993, Judge Robert Parker, the same judge who had earlier written to Judge Weiner to encourage toughness on the latter judge's part, appointed Ness, Motley (along with two other law firms) "to act as negotiating counsel on behalf of . . . a class of future claimants."[55] Less than three weeks after this appointment, Fibreboard and the newly appointed counsel informed the court that they had reached an agreement in principle, covering all future claims. On September 9, 1993 (a month after he had appointed plaintiff's counsel to explore a settlement), Judge Parker certified, for settlement purposes only, a class defined to cover all persons with asbestos-related personal injury claims against Fibreboard that they had not yet asserted (i.e., all its future claimants).[56]

In short, as in *Georgine*, the same plaintiff's law firm almost simultaneously represented both present claimants in an inventory settlement and future claimants in a "settlement purposes only" class action. The official class action notice estimated that the present claimants represented by Ness, Motley in the inventory settlement "may exceed 50,000" and, on that assumption, they would receive approximately $500 million (of which roughly one-third, or almost $167 million, would be paid to plaintiff's counsel as its contingency fee).[57] Going one aggressive step beyond *Georgine*, the *Fibreboard* negotiations also expressly conditioned the inventory settlements on the approval of the class action settlement of the future claims.[58] Thus, class counsel had a strong interest (i.e., $167 million) in the approval of the class action settlement, even apart from the fees it would receive for representing the class.

Fibreboard's own contribution to this settlement was extraordinarily small. Although its two principal insurers were to contribute $1.525 billion into a trust fund for future claimants, Fibreboard was to add only a minimal $10 million to this fund.[59] Expert testimony advised the court that, once its asbestos liabilities were resolved, Fibreboard would have a going concern value of probably between $230 to $300 million.[60] Thus, it was escaping billions of potential liabilities by paying a trivial $10 million that amounted to around 3 to 4 percent of its resulting estimated value. As the settlement was negotiated, Fibreboard's stock price rose from a low of $2.13 in 1992 to a high of $22.88 during the month that the settlement was announced. By the end of 1993, after the settlement was approved, that price rose further to a high of $35.63.[61]

The lesson for corporate defendants from this settlement was that a class action was far superior to a bankruptcy reorganization as a means of scaling down tort liabilities. In bankruptcy, the tort creditors often received the lion's share of the assets (sometimes receiving 80 to 90 percent of the stock in the reorganized entity). But, to the extent that the Fibreboard settlement became the template for future settlements, the equity shareholders in a class action settlement could retain most of their firm's value, while the tort victims got only what the company's insurers were prepared to settle for. Making the settlement even more oppressive, Judge Parker certified it as a mandatory class, under Rule 23(b)(1)(B) of the Federal Rules of Civil Procedure, so that no class member had the right to opt out.[62] Effectively, the class members were locked in.

For the community of corporations facing mass tort problems, this was too good to be true. Prior to *Fibreboard*, they had understood that, if they became insolvent, their assets would be pooled and distributed to the creditors. But now, they were finding that, on the doorsteps of a mass tort-driven insolvency, they could use their insurance assets, putting them into what the court declared to be a "limited fund," adding only a small contribution of their own assets, and thereby force their tort victims to accept only that limited fund (and with no right to reject the settlement by opting out). This ideal outcome required only that defendants be able to find cooperative counsel in the plaintiff's bar that would agree to such a settlement (and the price of such agreement in both *Georgine* and *Fibreboard* appeared to be a settlement of that counsel's much smaller inventory of existing claims).

Ultimately, both *Georgine* and *Fibreboard* did in fact prove to be too good to be true. In a careful, scholarly opinion by Judge Edward Becker, the Third Circuit rejected the *Georgine* settlement on a variety of grounds primarily relating to Rule 23 of the Federal Rules of Civil Procedure.[63] Judge Becker in particular objected to the district court's assumption that the standards for class certification were easier in a "settlement class" action than in a class certified for purposes of litigation. He insisted that the standards were the same for both contexts. This displeased the asbestos producers in *Georgine*, who believed that a "settlement class" should presumptively be certified on the grounds that the fact of settlement alone deserved considerable weight in the judicial balancing process. Judge Becker once told this author that he wanted to affirm *Georgine*, but "the decision just wouldn't write." Much as he also wanted to see an end to the asbestos crisis, he could not find *Georgine* compatible with either Rule 23 or due process.

When the Supreme Court granted certiorari in *Georgine* (now renamed *Amchem Products, Inc. v. Windsor*), most assumed that the issue they would focus on would be whether "settlement classes" had to meet the same standards as litigation classes. The defendants hoped that the Court would approve a more relaxed standard for settlement classes (while maintaining a rigorous standard for litigation classes). Although that view received some support at the Supreme Court, the liberal and conservative wings of the Court formed an unexpected coalition against the middle to reject the *Amchem Products* settlement by a 6-to-2 vote. The conservatives (most notably, Justices Rehnquist, Scalia, and Thomas) did not like class actions at all, while the liberal Justice Ruth Ginsburg (who wrote the decision) concluded that the class members had been overreached in a way that implicated due process concerns. Only the "moderates" (Justices Breyer and Stevens) dissented, believing that the district courts should have great discretion to approve settlement classes.

Justice Ginsburg's decision found that the *Amchem* settlement flunked both the "adequacy of representation" requirement of Rule 23(a)(4) and the "predominance" requirement of Rule 23(b)(3). She emphasized that those failures could not be cured by any finding as to the settlement's fairness. Her opinion opened with the following two sentences that framed the issues:

> This case concerns the legitimacy under Rule 23 of the Federal Rules of Civil Procedure of a class action certification brought to achieve global settlement of current and future asbestos-related claims. The class proposed for certification potentially encompasses hundreds of thousands, perhaps millions, of individuals tied together by this commonality: each was, or some day may be, adversely affected by past exposure to asbestos products manufactured by one or more of 20 companies.[64]

From here, it was downhill sledding to her central conclusion that the *Amchem* class was just too sprawling with too little "unity" (in her phrase) because it included too many diverse subgroups that were not given separate representation through subclasses. She stressed the diversity within the class: "[C]lass members in this case were exposed to different asbestos-containing products, in different ways, over different periods, and for different amounts of time; some suffered no physical injury, others suffered disabling or deadly diseases."[65] This gave rise, she concluded, to serious conflicts: "Most saliently, for the currently injured, the critical goal is generous immediate payments. That goal tugs against the interest of exposure-only plaintiffs in ensuring an ample, inflation-protected fund for the future."[66] To this point, the Court's critique of the *Amchem Products* settlement required only moderate reforms, such as the use of subclasses (and more lawyers to represent each subclass). So read, *Amchem Products* was not necessarily fatal to the ability of class actions to resolve mass torts.

But then, in discussing the "adequacy of representation" standard of Rule 23(a)(4), Justice Ginsburg went further. In emphasizing that the fairness of the settlement did not resolve whether the class was certifiable, she wrote,

> [I]f a fairness inquiry under Rule 23(e) controlled certification, eclipsing Rule 23(a) and (b), and permitting class designation despite the impossibility of litigation, both class counsel and the court would be disarmed. Class counsel confined to settlement negotiations could not use the threat of litigation to press for a better offer, see *Coffee, Class Wars: The Dilemma of the Mass Tort Class Action*, 95 Colum. L. Rev. 1343, 1379–1380 (1995), and the Court would face a bargain proffered for its approval without benefit of adversarial investigation.[67]

This idea (borrowed from this author) that a "disarmed" class counsel could not provide adequate representation was a more serious threat to "settlement classes." It seemingly implied that if the class could not be certified for purposes of litigation, it could not be settled as a settlement class, because the plaintiff's attorney would have too little leverage to provide adequate representation.

Although that was precisely what Judge Becker had held at the Third Circuit stage, Justice Ginsburg drew back from the full implication of this position and announced a compromise. The fact that the case had settled was relevant, she wrote, because the Court "need not consider whether the case, if tried, would present intractable management problems . . . for the proposal is that there be no trial."[68] As a practical matter, this compromise freed the settling parties from the requirements of Rule 23(b)(3)(D), which required that, in deciding the propriety of certification, the Court should consider "(D) the difficulties likely to be encountered in the management of a class action."

On this basis, a "settlement class" had to meet all the requirements of a "litigation class," except that it need not show that the class was "manageable." Many suspect that this concession may have been necessary to win the votes of some "swing" justices, as Justices Breyer and Stevens in dissent were holding out for the position that the fact of settlement alone constituted a strong factor in favor of approval of the settlement. On balance, the result of Justice Ginsburg's concession was to preserve a measure of ambiguity and allow settling parties to tell a district court that it could consider the standards for class certification to be somewhat lower for their settlement. But, if the class failed the "predominance" test of Rule 23(b)(3) or if counsel were conflicted, a settlement class could not be certified.

In overview, *Amchem Products'* basic message was that "sprawling" classes could not be certified, at least not without some "structural assurance of fair and adequate representation for the diverse groups and individuals affected."[69] That probably necessitated the use of subclasses, with each subclass represented by its own counsel. The feasibility of the intraclass bargaining that would follow is uncertain and has seldom been tested.

A major reason that practitioners have not sought to push the envelope in this area is that Justice Ginsburg's opinion ended with an emphatic warning. Her opinion ducked the issues of whether appropriate notice had been given, or even could be given, to the future claimants, but it recognized that it was "highly problematic" whether notice could be given to "persons with no perceptible asbestos-related disease at the time of the settlement."[70] Because class certification had been rejected on other grounds, she did not need to rule on this issue of the sufficiency of the notice to the future claimants (which the Third Circuit had found inadequate), but she warned, "[W]e recognize the gravity of the question whether class action notice sufficient under the Constitution and Rule 23 could ever be given to legions so unselfconscious and amorphous."[71] Thus, even if all the conflicting subclasses could bargain out a settlement under *Amchem Products'* new standards, it was still not clear that future claimants could be bound by that settlement. If they could not, corporate defendants had little interest in structuring elaborate class action settlements just to pay off present claimants. They could be handled through inventory settlements with individual attorneys. So long as this uncertainty remained, mass tort class action settlements lost their attractiveness for defendants.

A year after it heard *Amchem Products,* the Supreme Court took up *Ahearn v. Fibreboard* (now renamed *Ortiz v. Fibreboard Corp.*).[72] *Ortiz* was far more vulnerable than *Amchem Products* because it involved a mandatory class action based on a "limited fund" theory where the fund was "limited" only by the parties' agreement. That is, the settling parties had agreed to contribute only Fibreboard's insurance proceeds (obtained in a parallel settlement with its insurers) to the settlement (plus a trivial contribution by Fibreboard). Again, the Court divided along the same lines as in *Amchem Products,* with seven justices finding no basis in Rule 23 for such a "limited fund," and Justices Breyer and Stevens again dissenting on their same theory that the fact of settlement should be a major consideration in determining the propriety of class certification.

Essentially, the Court found that the proponents of the settlement had to show that (1) Fibreboard's total liabilities exceeded its total assets, fairly valued; (2) the whole of the limited fund was to be devoted to the overwhelming claims; and (3) the claimants were treated equitably among themselves.[73] Understandably, the Court encountered problems with each of these three required elements and held that the "limited fund" could not be limited to simply those assets that the settling parties had agreed to contribute. Even more clearly than in *Amchem Products,* the Court found that the plaintiff's attorneys could not provide adequate representation because of the conflicts created by their inventory settlements (and their preexisting agreement to bind future clients to the proposed settlement's terms). Finally, the Court warned counsel in future cases to avoid "adventurous application" of

Rule 23.[74] *Fibreboard*'s message was clear: do not attempt to develop novel settlement techniques that can only be justified by unprecedented extension of Rule 23's already broad reach.

Read together, *Amchem Products* and *Ortiz* spelled the end for tort reform through settlement class actions. The case for asbestos reform may have been compelling, but the Court was saying that the proponents of asbestos reform had to make their case before Congress and not ask it to devise the solution by rewriting Rule 23. Predictably, asbestos litigation (and other mass torts) soon returned to their prior mode of resolution through individual settlements, with transaction costs as a result consuming the majority of the total expenditures made.[75]

Because this approach was costly and inefficient, practices evolved. Plaintiff's attorneys and defense counsel turned increasingly to aggregate global resolutions of mass tort claims. For example, in 2007, Merck, the pharmaceutical company, entered into a $4.85 billion settlement with plaintiff's law firms representing over 33,000 claimants with respect to Vioxx (a drug marketed by it).[76] No attempt was made to certify a class action, but the settlement was an aggregate one with the same terms offered to all claimants. More controversially, the participating plaintiff's attorneys were required to recommend the settlement to all their clients and to withdraw from representing those clients who refused to accept the settlement.[77] As others have argued, aggregate settlements may be as abusive to clients as the settlement classes in *Amchem Products* and *Ortiz*.[78] After all, where there is no class action, there is also no court to approve the fairness of the settlement or the reasonableness of the attorney's fees.

In short, group litigation that is the functional equivalent to a class action has come to supplant the class action in the mass tort field. Thousands of cases involving the same drug or product are transferred by the JPML to a transferee court, and that court may seek to maintain oversight over the settlement process. The term "quasi–class action" has developed to describe this new form of group litigation,[79] and a few courts have sought to exercise close scrutiny over the process, including by limiting the fees of the plaintiff's attorneys handling these cases.[80] This controversy can be postponed for the moment, but it should remind us that limiting the reach of the class action does not necessarily solve the problems of group litigation (and may even give rise to a wholly unregulated Wild West).

At this point, it is time to ask what the experience with mass tort class actions teaches us about the concept of the private attorney general and entrepreneurial litigation? Above all, it shows us that the private attorney general can be corrupted. Under enormous pressure from mounting asbestos liabilities, the asbestos producers needed a global solution and were able to find experienced plaintiff's attorneys willing to join in their efforts, even though it deprived most future claimants of meaningful compensation. Perhaps, this should not be surprising. If one maxim applies here, it is Lord Acton's aphorism that "Power corrupts, and absolute power corrupts absolutely." Particularly in the case of passive future claimants, plaintiff's counsel had the near equivalent of absolute power.

Beyond the sheer discretionary power possessed by counsel, structural problems are also revealed by the mass tort experience. Private attorney generals do not occupy the higher-profile positions of public officials; nor are they subject to the same rules or level of transparency. Eager for settlements, courts that were under pressure acquiesced, tolerated dubious conflicts of interests, and did not exercise objective oversight. In retrospect, it was probably foreseeable that, when offered extraordinary financial inducements, plaintiff's attorneys would fail their clients. In this light, the accountability problems associated with the private attorney general (and entrepreneurial litigation generally) grow with the case's scale: The greater the size of the class and the liabilities at stake, the greater the prospect of fiduciary failure. The incentives for collusion become "too big to decline."

Judicial performance during the asbestos crisis is harder to evaluate. Ultimately, judges at the highest level—Judge Becker in the Third Circuit and the Supreme Court—came to realize that settlement class actions were being misused and curbed their use (at least marginally). Judges in the lower federal courts, however, were not merely passive participants, but active instigators, motivated by an urgent desire to end the caseload crisis that they perceived to be engulfing them. On balance, this episode suggests that according great discretion to the private attorney general carries considerable dangers, because judicial oversight may be weak or compromised. Equally important, because the private attorney general operates in the relative shadows, it will remain subject to less public or political accountability.

If the private attorney general failed its clients in the case of mass torts, it must also be remembered that mass torts was the unique context in which the services of the private attorney general were not truly required. Asbestos (and similarly tobacco) class actions were characteristically "large claimant" class actions in which those more seriously injured could have generally obtained counsel on an individual and contingent fee basis. Because future claimants are ordinarily passive, they were foreseeably exposed to opportunistic behavior by plaintiff's counsel.

This assessment suggests a pragmatic compromise. "Negative value" claimants need the class action (and the private attorney general) because they have few alternatives. Claimants with larger claims that can be handled in the traditional tort system, however, do not depend on the class action. Thus, institutional investors regularly opt out of securities class actions, and claimants with high-value claims similarly seek exclusion from mass tort classes. The attempt to extend the class action to reach all claimants may go a bridge too far. As applied to both larger claims and future claims, the class action may be less the plaintiff's sword and more the defendant's shield. The asbestos class actions provide a sad illustration of how the immense wealth at stake ultimately seduces even the most aggressive of plaintiff's attorneys. Prudence therefore dictates that society be cautious in how far it extends both the class action and the private attorney general concept.

PART THREE

THE SEARCH FOR REFORM

ACROSS A VARIETY OF CONTEXTS—derivative actions, state class actions challenging mergers and acquisitions, mass torts litigation—we have seen evidence of dysfunction. Sometimes, plaintiff's attorneys and defendants achieve an equilibrium that benefits them, but not the plaintiff's attorney's clients. In these cases, a low monetary recovery to the class is exchanged for an above-market award of plaintiff's attorney's fees.[1] Both sides, after much experience, seem to have recognized that it is better to settle than to fight—particularly if the settlement can be structured (as it often is) to meet their special needs.

In other cases (such as the mergers and acquisitions [M&A] context), a transaction that may justify litigation triggers instead a stampede of lawsuits in multiple jurisdictions, which are ultimately resolved in low visibility ways that again seem to benefit only the lawyers. Once more, there is much sound and fury, but it signifies little. Collectively, these examples suggest a hypothesis: American law and legal institutions generate an excessive incentive to litigate.

But this is only half the story. We have also surveyed the world of securities class actions, where each of the ten highest class action settlements exceeds $1 billion. In this context, the plaintiff's law firm has proven itself a formidable adversary with little interest in collusion.

Much as one may question the ethics of the various partners at Milberg, Weiss who served jail time, little basis exists for doubting that they aggressively pursued their adversaries and sought to maximize the financial recovery for their clients. Collusion was not their business model. Nor is this pattern of hard-fought litigation unique to securities litigation. Multibillion dollar recoveries have been won by plaintiff's attorneys under the antitrust laws, and large settlements have been obtained in employment discrimination, environmental, and consumer protection cases.

A key issue is thus posed: why does the private attorney general (or, more specifically, the entrepreneurial plaintiff's law firm) work well in some contexts and not in others? Compounding this mystery is the curious fact that some law firms are active in both contexts, earning large fees in securities class actions and modest fees in derivative actions that are settled for nonpecuniary (and seemingly cosmetic) relief.

The explanation for these very mixed results begins from a very basic starting point: sometimes, it pays the entrepreneur/lawyer to focus on the legal merits of the action, and sometimes it does not. Take, for example, a large securities class action where the sudden decline in the corporation's stock price may amount to a total loss in the billions of dollars and the expected recovery can approach $1 billion. In such a case, plaintiff's attorneys rationally have less interest in collusion. They can expect to be paid a fee largely determined as a percentage of the recovery to the class (with fees sometimes exceeding $100 million). This percentage-of-the-recovery formula largely aligns their interests with those of the class. That they settle for, typically, only 1 to 5 percent of the total loss (in terms of the decline in the stock market capitalization of the defendant company) largely reflects a variety of factors (the litigation odds, the defendant's limited capacity to pay, and the delay in the recovery if there is likely to be an appeal), but not collusion.

In contrast, now take a derivative action challenging a corporate business decision that proved (in hindsight) to be an egregious and costly blunder. Here, the plaintiff's attorney must face both the demand rule, which will give virtual immunity to a public company with an independent board, and the likelihood that the company has a charter provision that exculpates directors from liability for breach of the duty of care.[2]

These are both formidable obstacles that collectively dwarf the lesser obstacles facing the plaintiff in a securities class action (which chiefly consists of the need to plead scienter with particularity), and they make the chance of a litigated victory remote. But the plaintiff's attorney in the derivative action does have one remaining source of leverage that is not related to the merits of the action: a litigation cost differential that favors the plaintiff's side, making it more economical for the defendant to settle (cheaply, if possible) than to seek a complete victory in litigation. In reality, the defendant corporation may or may not elect to settle (much will depend on whether it is a repeat player that will face future nonmeritorious actions), but overall defendants settle often enough in derivative actions that some plaintiff's attorneys can earn a "normal" profit on their investment of time and money (even if the majority of their cases are dismissed).

Similarly, in the M&A class action context, the plaintiff's leverage may come from timing considerations: delay will be costly to the defendant. In addition, even if the plaintiff's firm believes that its action is meritorious, it also knows that in multiforum litigation, it may lose out to others who can more quickly settle a parallel case in another forum, thereby preempting its action. In this imperfect world, neither side can focus on the merits alone, and the economically rational course of action may be to settle—and early.

To be sure, some plaintiff's law firms will not seek to litigate cases based on their nuisance value and will limit themselves to cases where they see a probability of victory. That is the difference between the aristocrats of the plaintiff's bar and the "bottom fishers." In recent years, the plaintiff's bar has become increasingly stratified, with some firms reaching an institutional size comparable to mid-sized corporate law firms, while the majority of plaintiff's firms are still composed of no more than a handful of lawyers.[3] With differences in organizational size come differences in behavior. Smaller plaintiff's firms generally cannot attract large institutional clients who can win control of the litigation; nor can they afford to fund the costs of a large case for years until a distant and uncertain recovery. Thus, they pursue lower-cost strategies, such as filing "copy cat" actions or "tagalong" derivative actions, which offer only a modest return but do pay the rent.

To sum up: In a hypercompetitive legal marketplace, some plaintiff's law firms, typically those struggling to survive, will seek to exploit the nuisance value in cases. This nuisance value may sometimes be based on a favorable litigation cost differential, sometimes on the fact that delay is more costly to defendants than plaintiffs (as in a merger case), and sometimes on the fact that risk-averse individual defendants would prefer to settle if they can arrange to do so based on someone else's money (e.g., the insurer, the indemnifying corporation, or the party bearing the costs of a nonpecuniary settlement).

The litigation odds also figure into this settlement calculus. Although a larger plaintiff's law firm can rationally bring an action that it knows it is unlikely to win, this requires that the plaintiff's law firm maintains a sizable portfolio of cases (of which a significant percentage must settle) in order that its fees on those cases that it settles can cover the costs on its cases that are lost (and still also generate a "normal" profit for our rational attorney entrepreneur). Much depends here on (1) how generously the law firm can bill on its victories and (2) how much it can economize on its investment in cases while still convincing its adversary to settle. Obviously, different styles and strategies are possible.

This analysis is not intended to justify attorneys exploiting the nuisance value in their cases, but it is meant to explain why there can be an excessive incentive to litigate. Such behavior is rational and predictable—particularly as the legal marketplace becomes more stressed and competitive.

Against this backdrop, it becomes possible to put the search for reform in perspective. At the heart of this problem of abusive litigation is not the availability of the class action, which can be used to assert both meritorious and frivolous claims, but the lack of any downside for the attorney/entrepreneur who is deciding whether to assert a nonmeritorious claim based on its nuisance value. Reform requires that the merits need to matter more. How do we get there? Under a legal system that either incorporated a "loser pays" rule or some seriously enforced system of sanctions for the assertion of weak claims, there would be such a downside. But, go too far in this direction, and entrepreneurial litigation ends.

Why then is there not more discussion of a "loser pays" rule and less of a focus on the class action, itself? The short answer is that few defendants want the optimal reform; they want instead the reform that most protects them and their interests. Because defendants are threatened both by meritorious actions and frivolous actions, they prefer overbroad reforms that will chill both types of actions to a remedy that will only deter frivolous actions. It is naïve therefore to expect defendants (or the defense bar) to favor a narrow remedy that only penalizes frivolous actions. This means both that we cannot accept defendants' proposed reforms at face value and that there is only a limited constituency interested in optimal reforms that do not "throw the baby out with the bath water."

This part will focus on how the class action, and entrepreneurial litigation generally, might be reformed in order both to maintain the viability of the "negative value" class action and to limit the prospect for litigation abuse. Chapter 7 will initially focus on recent developments in class action practice, where several important Supreme Court decisions have clouded its future. Although we earlier examined the securities class action, it has been uniquely exempt from the changes otherwise sweeping through this field. Chapter 7 will then turn to and assess the standard critiques of the class action. For example, the claim that class actions result in extortion is frequently heard but seldom carefully examined.

Chapter 8 will return to the topic of reform. It will focus less on the technical issues of Rule 23 or other procedural rules and more on the broader issue of what is necessary to make the private attorney general work in the interests of its clients.

Chapter 9 will then examine public enforcement. Can it (and should it) be restructured to utilize the entrepreneurial efforts of plaintiff's attorneys? As we will see, this is already occurring in low visibility ways.

7

A PRELUDE TO CLASS ACTION REFORM

A. WHERE ARE WE TODAY? MAPPING THE LEGAL TERRAIN

The pendulum has been swinging toward the curtailment of the class action for at least two decades. The last major decision to truly liberalize class certification was *Basic Inc. v. Levinson* in 1988, which adopted the "Fraud-on-the-Market Doctrine."[1] Soon afterward, the climate turned more hostile toward class certification in the federal appellate courts, particularly when attempts were made to certify nationwide classes in mass torts cases for purposes of litigation.[2] Correspondingly, over this same period, defendants gained even greater protection in the legislative arena. Briefly, the following three statutes stand out:

1. 1995: THE PRIVATE SECURITIES LITIGATION REFORM ACT OF 1995 (PSLRA).   This was Congress's first attempt to adjust the balance of advantage in class action litigation. Essentially, it immunized "forward-looking statements," gave presumptive control of the class action to a "lead plaintiff" who had suffered the largest loss (which effectively meant that control went to the largest institutional investor to volunteer for the role), and imposed stricter pleading rules.[3] Despite predictions that the

PSLRA would be the death knell for securities class actions, not that much has actually changed. Today, the majority of securities class actions continue to survive motions to dismiss. Although the number of securities class actions has declined in recent years, their settlement size has increased, as earlier noted.[4] The "megasettlement" has substantially (but not wholly) replaced the nuisance suit.

2. 1998: THE SECURITIES LITIGATION UNIFORM STANDARDS ACT (SLUSA). Plaintiffs responded to the PSLRA by migrating to state court to sue under state "Blue Sky" statutes or even the common law of fraud. To prevent this flanking maneuver, Congress responded in 1998 with SLUSA, which preempted state class actions (and also certain consolidated proceedings that arguably resembled a class action).[5] This preemption applies to class actions (whether filed in state or federal court) that were based on either state statutory law or common law where the complaint alleged in substance (1) a misrepresentation or omission of a material fact or (2) the use of manipulation, a deceptive device, or a contrivance in connection with the purchase or sale of a security. This language paralleled the wording of Rule 10b-5 but also applied to state laws based on negligence. Individuals and small groups could still sue (and several exemptions allow certain specific types of litigation, such as Delaware merger and acquisition class actions, to continue). On balance, plaintiffs lost not only a state court forum, but also the ability to sue on strict liability or negligence-based state law causes of action in federal court.

3. 2005: THE CLASS ACTION FAIRNESS ACT OF 2005 (CAFA). Sometime after 2000, in light of *Amchem, Ortiz,* and a series of similar lower court defeats, plaintiff's attorneys began to abandon federal forums to sue in state courts, opting in particular to sue in several especially friendly forums (known as "rotten boroughs" or "hellholes" to the defense bar).[6] The most infamous of these was Madison County, Illinois. Possibly, these state courts were more hospitable to plaintiff's attorneys either because elected state judges (in contrast to appointed federal judges) needed to raise political contributions or because elected state judges were more aligned with the Populist and anticorporate sensibilities of their constituents in some areas of the country. Whatever the reason, state courts clearly applied lower and laxer standards toward class certification, regularly permitting what defendants termed "drive-by certification."[7]

CAFA abruptly ended these practices by generalizing SLUSA's approach to state securities litigation. Specifically, it created a new removal provision, specially tailored for class actions, so that defendants could remove multistate class actions to federal court (and away from elected state judges). Once in federal court, the removed class action would have to satisfy the significantly higher class certification standards established by *Amchem* and subsequent cases.

There things stood until 2011 when the Supreme Court handed down two major decisions, both highly adverse to class action plaintiffs.

First, in *Wal-Mart Stores, Inc. v. Dukes,*[8] a 5-to-4 majority rejected class certification in a much publicized case that constituted the largest female employment discrimination case ever brought. To do so, it employed an entirely new theory to reach this result. Essentially, the majority found that the *Wal-Mart* class did not satisfy the "commonality" requirement of Rule 23(a)(2). Prior to *Wal-Mart,* commonality had been an easily satisfied requirement of Rule 23 that was automatically satisfied if there was even one common legal or factual issue. Shifting the focus of the "commonality" inquiry, the majority ruled that the appropriate test looked to whether there were dissimilarities, not similarities, within the proposed class.

Because *Wal-Mart* is a controversial case, it seems best to start with an objective statement about it: No circuit, other than the Ninth Circuit, would have then certified a class this broad and sprawling, covering both alleged discrimination in the hiring of new employees and in the promotion of existing employees. Wal-Mart was the nation's largest private employer, and the class consisted of "about one and a half million plaintiffs."[9] The critical and distinctive fact about the case was that Wal-Mart broadly delegated discretion to its store managers over all pay and promotion decisions. That discretion was exercised in a largely subjective fashion by individual store managers at some 3,400 Wal-Mart stores.

Thus, unlike most employment discrimination cases in which there is a specific practice (for example, an employment exam) or a specific biased manager, the issue in *Wal-Mart* was whether this policy of delegated discretion could be, itself, deemed an unlawful employment practice, given apparent statistical evidence that female employees were disadvantaged. Normally, this would be viewed as an issue of "predominance" under Rule 23(b)(3), but because plaintiffs had styled their case as a Rule 23(b)(2) class seeking both injunctive and monetary damages, the predominance requirement was not applicable in such a Rule 23(b)(2) case.

Unable to rely on the predominance standard, the majority had only the "commonality" requirement of Rule 23(a)(2) on which to rest its decision, and they rewrote that standard fundamentally. Under prior law, the common issue could have been: did an employment system of delegated discretion disadvantage female employees? But, the majority insisted that the proper focus had to be not on the existence of common questions but whether the plaintiff's theory of the case proposed common "answers to common questions."[10] Clearly, delegated discretion did not injure all Wal-Mart's female employees, in part because many store managers were female. Thus, Justice Scalia framed the new governing standard, as follows: "Without some glue holding the alleged reasons for all those decisions together, it will be impossible to say that examination of all the class members' claims for relief will produce a common answer to the crucial question *why was I disfavored*."[11] In short, to satisfy *Wal-Mart*'s standard, the class members have to suffer the "same injury" attributable to the same cause.[12]

On this basis, a class action might be certified with regard to employees at an individual store (on the theory that the store manager was biased), but nationwide disparities in hiring or salary practices do not demonstrate that all 3,400 store managers have discriminated (some presumably did, and some presumably did not). The necessary "glue" holding together the class would exist only if plaintiffs could frame a common answer that explained the alleged discrimination. Plaintiffs did attempt to show that Wal-Mart, as an organization, was shaped by a traditional, male-dominated corporate culture, but that was too weak a "glue" for the majority, who mocked plaintiffs' expert witnesses for their overreliance on sociological jargon.

Although many issues remain under the *Wal-Mart* decision, its broader impact seems clear: *Wal-Mart* implies a radical downsizing of the size and scope of class actions, particularly those in the employment discrimination field. A class action may remain feasible on a plant by plant, store by store, or locality by locality basis, but a nationwide (or even regional) class seems infeasible when all class members must share the same theory of what caused their adverse treatment.

The Court's second major class action decision in 2011—*AT&T Mobility LLC v. Concepcion*[13]—also was a 5-to-4 decision written by Justice Scalia, which upheld a class action waiver. Although California law had deemed class action waivers in arbitration agreements to be "unconscionable" (and thus unenforceable), the majority held that California law was preempted by the Federal Arbitration Act. *Concepcion*'s clear implication for the future is that any time that defendants can induce an employee, consumer, borrower, shareholder, investor, or other person to sign a boilerplate arbitration agreement, that agreement will be presumptively enforceable according to its terms, regardless of what state law says. Such mandatory arbitration and class action waiver agreements are now standard in the documentation used by most financial institutions, and their use is rapidly spreading to all forms of consumer and employment agreements in light of *Concepcion*.

Speculative as it is to predict just how broadly mandatory arbitration clauses can be imposed on consumers, one straw in this wind is revealing and troubling. In 2014, General Mills, the maker of Cheerios, inserted mandatory arbitration clauses on coupons it distributed to its Cheerios customers and announced on its website that persons receiving any "benefit" from it would be bound by mandatory arbitration and thus compelled to abandon the right to sue it. In response to questions from the *New York Times,* General Mills acknowledged that its intent was to compel all users of its products or services to be bound by arbitration clauses.[14] Ultimately, General Mills backed down under consumer pressure and adverse publicity and dropped this arbitration provision (at least for the time). But its legal position, while certainly open to challenge, was not untenable. This is but one of numerous examples in which "forced" arbitration clauses are being imposed on largely unaware consumers (and often in the face of state laws that would consider such contracts "unconscionable" and unenforceable).[15] Over time, the use of arbitration clauses will only spread, predictably covering most persons in contractual relationships with a company and also applying to at least some tort claimants, disabling both groups from suing in court.

Arbitration is not the only dark cloud on the class action's future. In 2013 and 2014, the Court maintained its momentum in curbing class actions with two decisions that will constrain future antitrust and securities class actions. First, in 2013, the Court decided *Comcast v. Behrend*,[16] a case in which the antitrust violation seemed relatively clear, but in which class certification was denied, again on the same 5-to-4 division of the justices. The majority found that antitrust claims cannot be certified under Rule 23(b)(3) unless the plaintiffs present a damages model demonstrating that antitrust injury and the damages attributable to the antitrust violation can be proven on a class-wide basis through evidence common to the class. This is a tall order. Proving that the defendant's conduct caused injury to each class member on a class-wide basis and without resort to individualized assessments of each class member's position may often be infeasible, even when the misconduct is egregious. For example, in *Comcast,* it was clear that acquisitions of overlapping cable systems had lessened competition, but the injury was different for different customers, depending on their geographic location and their access to other competitors. Although *Comcast* has received less public attention than *Wal-Mart,* it may prove an equally restrictive decision. Only in securities class actions are class-wide damages easily proven by common evidence. Even in a clear-cut environmental case, involving, say, an oil spill, the damages to each class member may be highly variable.

In 2014, the Court faced a major opportunity to end the securities class action in the *Halliburton* case by reversing the Fraud-on-the-Market Doctrine, but in a divided decision, it declined to do so.[17] Instead, it tilted the playing field marginally in the defendant's favor by giving it the ability to demonstrate at class certification that the alleged misstatement had no "price impact." Balanced and fair as the decision was in the eyes of most observers, it still implied that defendants won increased rights to challenge class certification.

What message should we draw from these cases? The class action may be dying the death of the one thousand cuts. No one judicial decision is fatal to it, but the cumulative impact of many decisions may prove to be. To understand this claim, consider now five hypothetical cases in which a class action was historically possible:

1. A company sells a defective product nationwide (say, a toaster), which regularly bursts into flames when it is used, causing fires and rendering the product unusable and worthless;

2. A drug is found to have an undisclosed side effect, which causes strokes in older patients (and research to this effect was suppressed by the manufacturer);

3. An employment discrimination class action is brought against a corporation, employing workers in seven states, that hires employees based on interviews and a subjective personality assessment test;

4. A lender charges a usurious rate of interest to its retail customers but has a mandatory arbitration clause in the loan documents; and

5. A catalog mailed nationwide by a drug wholesaler makes materially false claims about an herbal product, promising that it will restore youth and sexual potency to its users.

Today, it is unlikely that a class action can be successfully maintained in any of these cases.[18] In cases (1) and (2), the barrier will be the "predominance" test of Rule 23(b)(3). The toaster in (1) was sold nationwide, meaning that laws of different states will apply. In the parlance of class action lawyers, this gives rise to a "choice of law" problem, because the applicability of different laws means that there are "individual" issues of law that could outweigh the common legal issues and thus easily cause the class to flunk the "predominance" standard of Rule 23(b)(3). Plaintiff's attorneys can respond to this problem by dividing the class into subclasses for each state (or at least for each group of states having similar legal rules), but whether this answer will work is highly problematic. If there are more than a few such subclasses, the class action will likely not be viewed as "manageable" under Rule 23(b)(3).[19] Further, if an attempt is made to recover for the fire damages caused by these toasters, the individual variations among these claims in terms of the causation of each fire would likely also cause the class to fail the predominance standard.

Next, the stroke-causing drug in (2) will give rise to individual issues of proximate causation and damages, and issues as to notice will arise with respect to future claimants (i.e., those who have not yet manifested symptoms). In (3) above, *Wal-Mart* will be the barrier, unless plaintiffs can demonstrate that a common official or common procedure produced a disparate impact. In (4), the barrier is *Concepcion,* and both a class action and class-wide arbitration appear unavailable in light of it. In (5), it would be necessary to establish that each class member individually relied on the false statements to prove a fraud-based cause of action, and reliance is an individual question that will cause this class to fail the predominance standard.[20] The depressing bottom line here is that the predominance requirement now bars most fraud classes (not involving securities) because of the need to show individual reliance, most multistate contract or consumer law classes because of the applicability of multiple state laws, and most personal injury cases because of the "individual" issue of proximate causation.

So when does the class action still survive? Federal claims under the securities and antitrust laws today remain certifiable as class actions—but increasingly the camel must pass through a steadily narrowing eye of a needle. The fate of the antitrust class action is in greater doubt, as the problems after *Comcast v. Behrend* of proving damages on a class-wide basis are only now being faced by the lower federal courts. Even in a simple price-fixing case, it may be difficult to prove that the injured consumers would have all sustained the same damages (as different prices might have been charged in a free and open market to different consumers in different areas). This leaves only the federal securities laws as generally amenable to class action treatment—and even here the Court has reinterpreted the Fraud-on-the-Market Doctrine to impose additional burdens on the plaintiff.[21] In addition, if in the future the Securities and Exchange Commission (SEC) were ever to permit arbitration clauses to be inserted into corporate charters or bylaws (or if a court were to order the SEC to do so), both securities class actions and derivative actions might then be effectively precluded.

Still, even if there are threatening storm clouds on the horizon, the death knell of the class action has not yet been sounded, and several recent Supreme Court decisions have declined the opportunity to cut back drastically on the class action.[22] Nonetheless, after a long, steady retreat for nearly two decades, the domain of the class action has substantially shrunk—much like a grape in the sun, drying slowly into a raisin.

B. CLASS ACTION CRITIQUES

The class action has probably been more criticized than any other procedural innovation—and for very different and often inconsistent reasons. Before proposing reforms, it is necessary to evaluate these critiques.

1. THE EXTORTION CRITIQUE.   At least a minority of the Supreme Court believes that the certification of a class action coerces the defendants into settlement and renders defenses and other legal rules largely irrelevant. This critique was first sounded by Columbia Law Professor Milton Handler, who had earlier helped to pioneer plaintiff's antitrust litigation in the electrical equipment cases. In 1971, he published a famous law review article that argued that the class action amounted to "legalized blackmail."[23] Very quickly, this assessment was repeated by others, including distinguished federal judges such as Henry Friendly[24] and Richard Posner.[25] Empirical researchers have, however, generally found this charge "overstated."[26] The authors of a respected Federal Judicial Center study were skeptical that "the certification decision itself, as opposed to the merits of the underlying claims, coerces settlements with any frequency."[27] This distinction is critical because most settlements are driven by a fear of losing at trial.

Aggregation of claims, of course, increases the pressure to settle, but this does not alone make that increased pressure illegitimate. If the merits of the action are strong, it would normally seem desirable that defendants settle. Moreover, if the legitimate role of the class action is to aggregate "negative value" claims, it would be hopelessly inconsistent to consider the aggregated impact of these claims alone to be extortionate. More is needed to make the extortion thesis coherent.

In fairness, some proponents of this extortion thesis have offered more. Professor Handler's original thesis was that class actions were too complex and costly to ever go to trial.[28] In his view, defendants would become enmeshed in costly, unending litigation and would settle to escape. The threat here is not the risk of a ruinous judgment, but the inability to get to a trial or other resolution. In effect, this is the plot of Dickens's *Bleak House* applied to class action defendants.

The problem with this version of the extortion thesis is that class actions regularly are resolved—either through a variety of pretrial motions or occasionally at trial. Professor Handler wrote at the very outset of the modern class action, and his prediction that they would be unresolvable has proven false. Moreover, the Federal Rules of Civil Procedure were expressly amended to protect defendants from this threat by permitting interlocutory appeals of class certification.[29] This was done explicitly on the premise that defendants facing a proposed class action needed protection from extortionate pressure.

A very different variant on the extortion thesis was articulated by Judge Henry Friendly, who argued that small claims should not be aggregated in class actions because the compensation was meaningless to the class members—or at least too trivial to justify the burden on courts.[30] In his view, federal courts should not handle small claims, and the focus should be instead on injunctions and other remedies to stop the wrongdoing. This is a far broader claim than Handler's, and it arguably "throws the baby out with the bath water" by largely rejecting the "negative value" justification for class actions. Today, forty years later, this seems politically unrealistic. Imagine that a defendant misappropriates $1 dollar from 1 million citizens. This is the paradigmatic "negative value" case, but the recovery of the lost money is not important to any individual. Nonetheless, all may demand restitution because they are outraged: "You cannot do that to me!" is a strong, visceral, and recurrent emotion.

More nuanced theories of extortion, however, have been advanced that deserve greater attention. Judge Richard Posner refused to certify an "immature" mass tort in one well-known decision on the premise that defendants might be compelled to settle an enormous class action based on still novel and untested claims, whereas the defendants could resist, and had in fact successfully resisted, settlement in similar individual cases that had been brought against them.[31] His view appears to have been that the threat of a ruinous billion dollar judgment, even if remote, could induce settlement because of risk aversion on the defendant's part. In other words, the defendant would take to trial 1,000 individual cases for $1 million each but would not risk the firm on a single billion dollar trial. This view that the risk of an all-or-nothing single judgment triggers a risk averse settlement is a conceivable thesis (although corporate defendants are probably less risk averse than individual plaintiffs). But, at most, it justifies the denial of class certification in the fairly unusual case of "immature" torts (which is all that Judge Posner required).

A context where the extortion thesis may make greater sense involves the combination of class actions and treble damages or other penalties. The purpose of punitive damages (including trebled damages) is to punish, not to compensate. But how much punishment is too much? When Congress authorized treble damages in the Sherman Anti-Trust Act in 1890, the modern class action did not then exist. Arguably, Congress would not want to punish at the astronomic level that the class action makes possible. Still, this critique implies only a limited reform, namely, that treble damages or other penalties should not be available in class actions.[32]

The most plausible theory of extortion is that the inevitable aggregation of strong individual cases with weak individual cases in a class action may give enhanced (and unjustified) settlement value to the weak claims. In effect, the weak cases hide behind the strong. From this perspective, the class action camouflages the weak cases and so arguably extracts overpayments. Although never expressly emphasized by the Supreme Court, this is precisely the problem that the *Wal-Mart* decision addresses. That case posed the corporate defendant's worst nightmare: a class consisting of 1.5 million employees. In such a setting, it is highly likely that halfway diligent plaintiff's attorneys can find a dozen or more instances of egregious discrimination. If these few cases (amounting to only a microscopic percentage of the class) can be presented at trial to convince the jury that discrimination was pervasive, then weaker cases may receive an undeserved recovery, because neither a judge nor a jury can review all 1.5 million cases.

Necessarily, class actions lead to a trial by anecdote, in which a single biased store manager could infect the entire case. The jury might attribute that individual's biased attitudes to the thousands of other store managers who they did not encounter at the trial. Plausible as this scenario for extortion may be, *Wal-Mart* has already imposed the remedy that this problem calls for: the class must show that it suffered the same injury through the same mechanism to be certifiable.[33] Under *Wal-Mart*, one store manager's bias may not be attributed to others. Whether or not *Wal-Mart*'s reinterpretation of the "commonality" requirement was justified can be debated at length,[34] but it has greatly reduced the potential for extortionate class action settlements.

To sum up, the extortion thesis is overbroad, but a problem does exist to the extent that plaintiff's attorneys can gain great leverage by presenting a few vivid examples at trial.[35] By downsizing the scope of the class action, *Wal-Mart* addresses this problem but does not eliminate it. Additional reforms may be desirable that also address plaintiff's problems as well, as will be discussed later.

2. THE RIP-OFF CRITIQUE.   The polar opposite critique to the "legalized blackmail" thesis is the thesis that class actions systematically exploit the class, generating huge fees for the plaintiff's attorneys and no tangible benefits for the class.[36] Indeed, CAFA opens with legislative findings to precisely this effect.[37] CAFA's special whipping boy and symbol of class action abuse was the "coupon" settlements (in which a class that had bought a defective product receives as its only compensation the opportunity via coupons to buy a revised version of the same product at a modest discount, while class counsel typically receives a generous fee in cash, not coupons).[38]

Objectionable as coupon settlements generally are, they are only illustrative of a broader pattern. Other kinds of nonpecuniary settlements involving only corporate therapeutics pose the same issues. At bottom, all these cases involve collusion, which necessarily takes "two to tango." Corporate defendants (and their counsel) are buying off plaintiff's attorneys to settle their cases on a basis below their true value—in effect, a polite bribe is being paid, which an overworked or inattentive court does not detect (or decides to ignore). Real and recurrent as this problem is, it does not justify ending the class action. The holders of "negative value" claims are not better off if the class action were abolished, because an imperfect remedy is better than none at all. What this critique really shows is that class members need protection from collusion. We will shortly return to that topic.

3. THE "NO ONE BENEFITS" CRITIQUE.   Here, the claim is that, even if there is a large settlement, it does not truly benefit the class. Given the

extensive judicial time and effort necessary to monitor class actions, this is essentially an assertion that the class action's costs exceed its benefits. To understand why the costs may exceed the benefits, we need to consider two different contexts: (1) ordinary class actions and (2) securities class actions.

a. The Ordinary Class Action. Suppose a large settlement—say, $100 million—is negotiated, out of which fees and expenses totaling $25 million are to be paid to plaintiff's counsel. What happens next? The remaining $75 million will be paid to eligible class members who submit claims documenting their loss. Generally, a claims administrator is appointed (again at a substantial fee) to handle this process. If the class involves fairly small claims—say, $100 or less on average—it is unlikely that the majority of the class will even file claims, and the percentage could be as low as 10 percent or less. Much will depend on how complex and demanding are the claim forms that the claimant must file to prove his or her loss.

Why would these claim forms be especially demanding? Here, the answer could be that the defendant may have negotiated a reversionary (or "claim made") settlement, under which the amount in the settlement fund not validly claimed by class members is returned to the defendant. But why would the plaintiff's attorneys permit the defendants to employ complicated claim forms that discourage the filing of claims? By now, this should seem a naïve question, and the obvious answer is that they may be indifferent because their fee is based on the total settlement fund, not the amount actually paid out to class members. An early Supreme Court case appeared to bless this result of looking only to the size of the initial fund (and ignoring whether it was paid out),[39] and its impact was to encourage illusory settlements in which money goes into a fund and later is returned to the defendants, never reaching the class. Such "evaporating" settlements benefit both plaintiff's counsel and defendants and are thus easy to negotiate, even if they do little for the class.

Today, sophisticated judges will generally not approve reversionary settlements, and, as later discussed, the federal securities laws discourage them in other ways. But, the problem of a low filing rate among class members persists, in part because the plaintiff's attorneys in nonsecurities cases have little incentive to encourage claim filing by class members. Thus, if the claims filing rate remains low and reversionary settlements have been discouraged, the new beneficiary of a low claiming rate is the more substantial and sophisticated class member, who necessarily receives a larger share of the pie. In some cases, the excess funds in the settlement that are not claimed will be distributed in a *cy pres* settlement to a related charity or for a benevolent purpose, but recent judicial decisions have tended to discourage (or at least downsize) this approach.[40] Increasingly, the excess funds that are unclaimed will today be redistributed among those class members that did file claims. This can also create a perverse incentive—now on the part of sophisticated class members—to favor, or at least tolerate, complex claim forms in order to obtain such a "second helping" of the settlement fund.[41]

Overall, the settlement context in class actions demonstrates the uncanny ability of lawyers to reenact Charles Dickens's *Bleak House* and complicate everything to the point of self-parody. The best example at this stage is a new entrepreneurial player: the "professional" objector. Once a settlement is announced, its terms must be communicated to class members, who may object to the court (either as to the fairness of the settlement's terms or, more typically, as to the proposed attorney's fee award). No one doubts that class members should have such a right to object, but the process can get carried to an extreme. The contemporary pattern is that, in a large class action, "professional" or "serial" objectors will appear to challenge the settlement's terms or the fee award.[42] Usually, these are attorneys motivated by the hope that either (1) they can convince the court to award them a portion of the amount by which the court cuts the proposed plaintiff's attorneys' fee award or (2) they will be paid off by class counsel not to appear at the hearing. "Professional" objectors are unloved figures, particularly within the plaintiff's bar, but there is an unconscious irony in plaintiff's attorneys' characterization of them as "extortionists." In reality, an idea is being pushed to the limits of its logic: entrepreneurial attorneys monitor defendants, and now entrepreneurial objectors monitor entrepreneurial plaintiff's attorneys. Conceivably, in the future, the objector may get its own monitor.

From the outset of the modern class action, it has been recognized that the settling parties have a strong desire to blind the court to the imperfections in their settlement, and so lock arms and compliment each other. Judge Henry Friendly made this point in several justly famous decisions.[43]

Still, to demonstrate the persistence of this problem, it is useful to examine the facts of a recent case. In *Eubank v. Pella Corp.*,[44] the redoubtable Judge Richard Posner described this case's facts as "scandalous,"[45] but the key point is that the settlement was approved by the district court. On appeal, it was quickly rejected by the Seventh Circuit, once subjected to the rigorous scrutiny of Judge Posner. Yet, other appellate courts might well have approved the district court's decision without comment, and similar settlements were once regularly approved (before CAFA) in state court consumer class actions. In *Eubank,* the case was a standard commercial class action in which the product (windows) allegedly had a design defect. But the red flags were numerous, virtually self-evident, and included:

1. The original class representative, a dentist, was the father-in-law of the class counsel (whose wife, his daughter, was also a co-counsel in the case). The result was a "palpable" conflict, Judge Posner found, because the family unit stood to gain more from attorney's fees than from the relief to the class.

2. Although the case was originally certified based on two subclasses to reflect the differing merits of cases in which the windows had been replaced versus those in which they had been repaired, the settlement agreement created a simple, nationwide class consisting of all owners of the windows produced by the defendant, Pella Corp. This was exactly the kind of nationwide class that would normally be uncertifiable because of "choice of law" problems inherent in the application of the differing law of all fifty states to one defendant's product.

3. Early in the case, four other class representatives were added to minimize the conflict created by class counsel representing his own father-in-law. But when the settlement was presented for preliminary approval, these additional four all opposed the settlement. At this point, class counsel removed these four as class representatives (even though he had handpicked them) and substituted four replacement representatives.

4. The settlement provided for $11 million in attorney's fees (based on the plaintiff attorney's claim that the benefit to the class from the settlement came to $90 million). But the settlement did not actually require any payment to the class at all, but only established an elaborate claim

resolution process. Although the settlement agreement stated that it had a value of $90 million, the defendant itself publically estimated its value at $22.5 million.

5. Class counsel had an urgent need to reach an immediate settlement. He was facing disciplinary proceedings that could result in a sanction that suspended his ability to practice law (or share in a fee award). Also, his former partners were suing him for embezzlement of the firm's assets. Given class counsel's need for the funds, it was symptomatic that the settlement agreement provided for an immediate $2 million advance of attorney's fees to him, even before notice of the settlement was sent to class members.

6. Under the settlement agreement, some class members were entitled only to coupons (with which they could purchase a product with an allegedly defective design), while others received only an extension of their warranty. Some were eligible to seek arbitration, but were subject to low ceilings on individual recoveries and the defendant preserved a variety of defenses (including a comparative fault defense and a defense relating to a failure to mitigate damages). The claim form was thirteen pages long and required the claimant "to submit a slew of arcane data" with respect to each affected window (including the code numbers for each window).[46]

7. Some 225,000 notices were sent to class members, but only 1,276 claims were filed (of which only 97 sought arbitration—or roughly 0.04 percent). These total claims amounted to only $1.5 million, and Judge Posner estimated that the defendant would be able to knock 75 percent off the damages sought by class members who filed for arbitration. He estimated the likely total recovery at closer to $1 million.[47]

8. Worse yet, if the proposed attorney's fee award of $11 million was reduced, the amount of the reduction would go not to class members, but would revert to the defendant.

In short, the case was a study in class action pathology, as a weak settlement was apparently being exchanged for a high fee award. But it was approved! One must suspect that equally suspect settlements have escaped reversal in other circuits.

So where does this leave us? Examples like these show that outside and independent expertise is needed at the settlement approval stage because (1) the trial court is too easily motivated by the desire to get a complicated case off its docket and (2) it knows much less than the parties about the case (and they reveal information only selectively). Although there are some respected "public interest" objectors who do provide valuable assistance to the court, they are typically able to appear in only the most egregious cases (and even then the court may prefer to ignore them). The only feasible answer here appears to be encouraging (or insisting that) public enforcement agencies appear at the settlement hearing and provide their own evaluation of the settlement. Courts would find it more difficult to ignore a prominent federal agency (which might even appeal). Chapter 11 will flesh out this idea further.

b. The Securities Class Action.   Uniquely, securities class actions regularly produce large settlements, and their litigation defines a special legal industry. Indeed, between 1997 and 2012, over 3,050 securities fraud class actions were filed, which resulted in settlements exceeding $73.1 billion.[48] Between 1997 and 2007 (a shorter period), plaintiff's attorneys earned nearly $17 billion in fees from securities class actions (and probably defense counsel earned fees that approached this level).[49] These are staggering numbers and reflect an extraordinary concentration of resources focused on litigating basically "stock drop" cases (cases in which a public corporation's stock suddenly declines and the plaintiff seeks to prove that this loss was caused by a fraudulent misstatement or omission).

But does anyone truly benefit from all this activity? This is a much harder question than it initially seems, because the flow of funds is normally circular. That is, investors are paying investors, with the individual defendants largely escaping personal liability. To understand this point, one needs to first recognize that in the typical securities class action, the plaintiff shareholders are essentially suing the other shareholders. Their claim is that they bought the issuer's stock in the open market at a time when material adverse information had been allegedly misstated or withheld. When the omitted material information is eventually disclosed, the issuer's stock price drops, and these investors sue to recover their losses. Such a class action essentially pits the plaintiff shareholders, who bought within the class period (i.e., the period during which the omitted information was not disclosed), against all other shareholders (because the latter will bear the net cost of any settlement that the corporation makes).

At first glance, the class action may seem a zero-sum game between these two shareholder groups (neither of whom committed or condoned fraud). But the problem goes deeper. One must next recognize that most shareholders (and particularly institutional shareholders) are diversified. They own many stocks, and they probably also own shares in the issuer that were purchased both inside and outside the class period (so that these shareholders have interests on both sides of this suit). Assume hypothetically (but realistically) that an institutional investor that we will call "CalPension" owns stock in 1,000 companies and, over a given period, 200 of them are sued in securities class actions. In these 200 suits, CalPension owns stock purchased within the plaintiff class period in one hundred, owns stock purchased outside the plaintiff class period in one hundred, and has purchased stock both inside and outside the class period in fifty. If we assume (as a simplifying assumption) that all these cases settle, CalPension then wins in one hundred (those in which it purchased in the class period) and loses in one hundred (those in which it did not purchase in the class period), and in fifty it is both winning and losing. At best, it is breaking even as a diversified shareholder. On this basis, securities litigation results in an involuntary wealth transfer under which money largely moves from one pocket of CalPension to another, as it wins in some cases and loses in others.

But in reality its winnings will not equal its losses. Why? Litigation costs must be deducted. Specifically, in the cases in which CalPension is within the "winning" class, plaintiff's counsel will charge roughly 25 percent of the settlement as its fee, and another 5 to 10 percent will be deducted as expenses of the litigation. Also, CalPension and the other shareholders bear indirectly the hidden costs of defense counsel (which may be as great as those of plaintiff's counsel) plus other incidental costs (for example, the company's directors and officers [D&O] insurance premiums may go up and much managerial time is diverted). Thus, on our assumed facts, CalPension loses in half the cases and settles, receiving a partial recovery, in the other half, so that on balance it is systematically losing.

From this compensatory perspective, only the lawyers seem to benefit from securities litigation. Immediately, however, the response will be heard that this analysis uses too narrow a perspective and ignores the deterrent justification for securities litigation. Certainly, securities litigation should produce a deterrent benefit, but the reality is more complex. Ideally, for deterrence to work, the penalties need to fall on the culpable—namely, the corporate executives responsible for the fraud or misconduct. That, however, rarely happens because the settlement is generally funded exclusively by the corporation.[50] Even when corporate executives or directors do contribute to the settlement, their payment is almost always funded by D&O insurance or corporate indemnification payments.[51] Thus, the cost is still passed back to the company's shareholders, and deterrence is undercut.

Defenders of the current system will respond that, even when the liability is fully insured, a deterrent benefit can still be generated if the cost of the insurance goes up in line with the corporation's relative riskiness. Although this increased cost would still fall on the shareholders, there would at least be a signal that the company carried high legal risk. But the reality is again that this does not happen. Careful observers have investigated and reported that D&O insurers do not price their policies to reflect relative risk.[52] As a result, because all public companies carry D&O insurance, low-risk companies (and their shareholders) subsidize high-risk ones. When insurance is too cheap, a moral hazard problem surfaces—and misconduct is encouraged.

Another plausible argument for a deterrent benefit is that securities litigation may generate reputational penalties that will chill the incentive to commit securities fraud. In fact, SEC enforcement does appear to generate substantial reputational penalties and in amounts that are a multiple of the financial penalties levied by the SEC.[53] But the evidence that private securities litigation does anything similar is weak to nonexistent. A recent study by Lynn Bai, James Cox, and Randall Thomas focused on 480 companies that settled securities class actions that were brought after 1996 (the point at which the PSLRA became effective).[54] They found that defendant firms experienced no significant decline in sales opportunities as a result of either the lawsuit or the settlement, but may have experienced some reduced level of operating efficiency while the lawsuit was pending (but not after it was settled). This is consistent with securities litigation being a nuisance but not a long-term threat.[55] Some firms also experienced liquidity problems and even entered bankruptcy, but it is difficult to ascribe this primarily to the litigation and settlement (as opposed to the underlying fraud). Private litigation may add to a financially strained company's problems, but it does not seem to generate any lasting stigma.

The equivocal nature of this evidence concerning reputational penalties should not surprise us. Although the SEC is respected as the "policeman of Wall Street" (and probably concentrates its limited resources on the worst offenders), no similar level of respect surrounds private enforcers, and private litigation that is perceived as abusive or nonmeritorious elicits no reputational penalty. Nor is there any reason to believe that plaintiff's attorneys focus on the most culpable defendants; rather, they rationally take aim at the cases where the damages seem greatest. All in all, settlement of a private class action carries little, if any, stigma. Even a substantial settlement can be rationalized as the product of defendant's fear of a jury trial before an unpredictable decision maker.

No claim is here made that private litigation can never generate a reputational penalty, but the bottom line remains that private enforcement rarely punishes the wrongdoer but instead levies its sanctions on the corporate issuer (and thus its shareholders). It does so because plaintiff's attorneys have no economic incentive to punish and much incentive to settle quietly. Once again, defendants and plaintiff's attorneys have found a resolution that works for them but not for investors or the public interest.

From the standpoint of stockholders, private securities litigation produces a double penalty. Not only do the costs fall on them, while the managers escape financial sanction, but the filing of a securities class action usually leads to a significant stock price drop, which is independent of, and in addition to, the initial price decline on the corrective disclosure.[56] Although this could be because the market learns something new from the filing of the action, the more likely explanation is that the market anticipates waste, settlement costs, and disruption as a result of the litigation. In effect, shareholders are punished twice: first, when the market declines on the filing of the action and, second, when the action settles at their expense.

From a cold-blooded economic perspective, this stock price drop on the filing of a securities class action could have a potential deterrent impact. Shareholders could react to this punishment and discipline or oust the responsible managers. But the costs of shareholder collective action are high, and if the episode looks like a one-time event, rational shareholders will see little point in demanding retribution. In any event, follow-up litigation rarely, if ever, imposes the cost of the corporate settlement on corporate managers. This failure reveals the high agency costs associated with the private attorney general and underscores the central problem of circularity: the federal securities laws perversely protect shareholders by punishing shareholders.[57] This approach can only work if angry shareholders take action, and they usually do not.

Clear as this failure should be, academics who are committed to private enforcement have still found ways to rationalize this problem of circularity. Some even claim that shareholders should be punished in this fashion, because they are not, in their view, "innocent" but should have been more diligent.[58] In effect, shareholders are guilty of allowing managers to lie to them. This is a strange view and an impossible standard. It is much as if Congress passed a law making it a crime negligently to suffer a burglary. Such a law might make homeowners more diligent in protecting their homes, but it would be morally incoherent because Congress would be punishing the real victim.

Another standard rationalization of the circularity problem is to point out that not all shareholders are diversified and argue that undiversified shareholders may benefit (to a modest extent anyway) from securities litigation.[59] But this argument gets things exactly backward. In reality, the retail investor is the party most disadvantaged by the current structure of the law. Retail investors are usually "buy and hold," long-term investors. They make relatively few changes in their portfolios because they must pay much higher brokerage commissions than do hedge funds and other institutions. Because they trade less frequently than activist investors, retail investors are much less likely to have purchased within the relatively narrow class period.[60] Thus, they will typically be among the shareholders who are not in the class and who therefore bear the cost of the settlement. As a result, securities litigation today typically results in a wealth transfer from retail investors to hedge funds and other frequent traders. It is hard to imagine a set of rules that would be less politically acceptable (if they were understood) than a system that involuntarily transfers money from ordinary citizens to hedge funds.

A last possible justification for private enforcement through the securities class action is that private enforcers may discover a fraud that was missed by public enforcers, who respond to this discovery by bringing a public action that would not otherwise have been brought. This argument has validity in the case, for example, of private antitrust litigation (where plaintiff's attorneys have indeed discovered antitrust conspiracies missed by public enforcers) but applies poorly to securities litigation. Typically, securities litigation does not begin with an investigator discovering fraud; rather, it usually follows a sharp price drop in the issuer's stock, implying that the market, itself, first discovered that some number was overstated or understated. Then, the plaintiff's attorney basically pursues the market's discovery, seeking to fill in the gaps by demonstrating that the earlier omission or misstatement was not innocent, but rather fraudulent. The irony then is that securities litigation persists (and at a high volume level), while other types of class actions are disappearing, even though securities litigation may generate a lesser benefit in terms of its social value.

This sober assessment that private securities litigation today largely results in pocket-shifting wealth transfers among institutions and even greater real wealth losses for retail investors does not mean that there is no deterrent benefit from securities litigation. Managements, of course, do not want to be sued, and adverse publicity is feared. But these benefits are modest, and there is really only one major exception to this generalization, namely, private securities litigation does produce a significant deterrent benefit when it is directed at secondary participants, including, most notably, accountants and investment bankers. For example, the private class actions in the *Enron* and *WorldCom* cases were directly solely against officers, investment bankers, and accountants (because those two corporations were bankrupt and could not be sued), and the two actions settled for amounts in excess of $7 billion and $6 billion, respectively. Similarly, actions brought by bondholders against corporate issuers are also exempt from the circularity problem, and the real victims receive compensation.

In any event, the Supreme Court has significantly restricted Rule 10b-5 litigation against secondary participants, and bondholders may not be able, at present, to use the class action (because bonds do not trade in an efficient market and so do not qualify for the Fraud-on-the-Market Doctrine). Thus, where securities litigation works best, it is most discouraged. Nonetheless, it would "throw the baby out with the bath water" to seek to eliminate all private securities litigation. The goal should be instead to reconfigure private securities litigation around a deterrence rationale by focusing it on two groups: (1) individual corporate officers and (2) corporate gatekeepers (accountants, consultants, investment bankers, and experts). These are the actors who need to be deterred but are not today. We will examine specific reforms to this end in Chapter 8.

One last irony about private securities litigation must be considered: even when there is a payoff, it often tends to be ignored. Settlements in securities class actions have been more closely studied than the settlements in other class actions, and the evidence shows a surprisingly low filing rate by eligible class members. One well-known study found that less than 30 percent of institutional investors with provable claims perfect those claims in the settlement process, thereby leaving billions "on the table."[61] This is counterintuitive because institutional investors are presumably more sophisticated and organized than retail investors, and characteristically they have much larger claims. In all likelihood then, retail investors file at an even lower rate. This finding has two implications: (1) most investors (i.e., those who do not file) are not compensated; and (2) those who do file may be overcompensated, because they receive the payments that should have gone to other class members. This "overpayment" results in part from the fact that reversionary settlements (under which unclaimed settlement proceeds are returned to the defendant) have been discouraged by the PSLRA in the case of securities class actions—with the result that the "excess" recovery today goes instead to those class members (largely institutional investors) who do file.[62] This may help explain why some institutional investors are happy with the current system.[63] They should be happy (and may even receive a windfall in some cases), but they are not the "negative value" claimants that the class action was intended to serve. With the "institutionalization" of share ownership so that 70 percent or more of the stock in large public companies is today held by institutions, securities class actions have simply outgrown the "negative value" justification that motivated courts to facilitate them.

In short, small claimants are not the likely beneficiaries of securities litigation (both because they own a low percentage of the stock traded during the class period and because they tend not to file claims even when there is a recovery for which they are eligible). This fact compels us to face a troubling question: Who does the securities class action principally benefit today? Who would have lost if the Supreme Court had closed down the securities class action by rejecting the Fraud-on-the-Market Doctrine? In reality, the inescapable truth is that the securities class action primarily benefits institutional investors by increasing the recovery they can obtain. Without the class action, they could still sue in individual suits, but the class action magnifies the damages obtainable by including the losses of smaller and foreign shareholders (who typically do not participate or share in the recovery). Yet, even institutional shareholders seem—increasingly—to believe that they will do better by opting out and suing individually.

This blunt evaluation does not mean that the securities class action should be closed down as a policy failure, but it does underscore that the securities class action makes sense only if it can be refashioned to generate real deterrence. To be sure, this is primarily a problem of substantive law, not procedural law. The real issues here should not be the availability of the class action, but whether corporate indemnification and D&O insurance can be restricted and whether corporate officers can be otherwise required to contribute more to the settlement. Unfortunately, changes in the state laws relating to insurance and indemnification are unlikely. But one path to reform still remains. Federal public enforcers (including the SEC) can prevent indemnification of the penalties owed to them.[64] In part for this reason, Chapter 11 will call for greater integration of public and private enforcement in order, in certain cases, to preclude indemnification. Otherwise, the best practical response is to collect more of the settlement from someone other than the corporate issuer.

A sad irony now comes fully into view. Current law comes close to making the nontrading corporate issuer an insurer of the accuracy of its stock price, but it simultaneously immunizes from private liability those actors who cause its violation.[65] From a policy perspective, this may be exactly backward, if we wish to generate deterrence. Reversing these two rules (i.e., reducing the corporation's liability but increasing that of the corporate officer and the aider and abettor) would make better sense if our goal is to generate deterrence. Still, curbing the class action is not a logical means to this end.

4. THE POLITICAL CRITIQUE. ARE CLASS ACTIONS UNDEMO-CRATIC? This is a critique still debated largely within the faculty lounge and unlikely to influence courts (but it could shape future legislative and administrative action). The critique is advanced on two levels, one simplistic and the other subtle. On the simplistic level, some aggressive and free-swinging critics, most notably Professor Martin Redish,[66] have attracted considerable attention by arguing that the class action is "undemocratic" because

1. Judicial rulemaking is inherently a legislative process, which the Supreme Court, an unelected body, has improperly arrogated to itself; thus Rule 23 (the class action rule) is invalid;
2. The class action transforms substantive law in a way that violates individual rights, including an asserted right to "freedom from association"; and
3. Settlement classes are unconstitutional because they are not true "cases or controversies" within the scope of Article III of the U.S. Constitution.

In contrast, the subtler critics argue that private enforcement is poorly coordinated with public enforcement and should be subject to greater control by administrative agencies (including through a possible veto power). This latter claim will be discussed in Chapter 11, while this chapter will focus primarily on Professor Redish's and similar critiques.

Redish's first claim is essentially a "separation of powers" argument that is beyond the scope of this volume,[67] but his second and third arguments are relevant to any discussion of class action reform or to any discussion of global efforts to achieve a system for group representation. Both compel us to focus on the value of litigant autonomy. How much should we respect it and at what cost?

The key assertion behind Professor Redish's claim that the class action sacrifices litigant autonomy is that the American system of opt-out class actions improperly treats inaction as consent. Other countries have developed opt-in class actions (which bind only those who elect to participate), but only a few nations tolerate the opt-out class. (Of course, this could be based either on principle or political expediency, because defendants have every reason to oppose the much more threatening opt-out class action and to justify their opposition based on a resort to the rhetoric of high principles). Litigant autonomy is abused, according to Professor Redish, because class members are forced into unwanted association.[68] A short answer to this claim is that objecting class members can opt out (at least from a Rule 23(b)(3) class action for money damages).[69] Class members generally do not do so because they are (in the language of law and economics) "rationally apathetic." Either the amount in question is too small to justify any action on their part, or they are willing to see the action proceed so long as it costs them nothing.

Implying consent from inaction, in the way that American class action law does, relies on a dubious inference, and it will clearly not satisfy those who want citizens to participate in an idealized New England town meeting. Still, in evaluating Redish's claim that the class action sacrifices litigant autonomy, we have to ask the obvious question: Compared to what? How much autonomy does the individual possess under any alternative approach for resolving the same dispute? Viewed this way, the goal of litigant autonomy appears more illusory than real.

Take, for example, the special context of mass torts. Mass torts were for a brief time resolved through class actions but today are resolved typically through either inventory settlements or bankruptcy reorganizations. In neither of these latter two modes of resolution does the individual litigant have much autonomy. Although the individual client can, in theory, reject an inventory settlement, individual claimants can be (and are) asked by their attorneys to agree in advance to be bound by a settlement that receives the approval of a majority (or supermajority) of their fellow claimants.[70] Even in the absence of such a provision, the individual client may be required to find a different attorney if he rejects the settlement.[71] And none may be available, as the specialists in this field wish to settle on a group basis. Economies of scale make group settlement the norm and individual litigation the exception.

Correspondingly, the bankruptcy reorganization can only be stopped if the class votes to reject the reorganization plan (and, even then, the plan of reorganization can still be "crammed down" on the class).[72] In short, litigant autonomy quickly gives way to majority rule under these approaches, and the key decision makers become the attorneys.

Litigant autonomy is viable as a norm only in the context of large claimant litigation, and there it does flourish. Opting out has become the preferred course for large claimants in securities class actions. For the "negative value" claimant, however, litigant autonomy is rhetoric—and little more. To tell the "negative value" claimant that he or she cannot benefit from the "opt-out" class action because it robs that claimant of his or her autonomy is to place a high value on a very formal and limited right. To paraphrase Anatole France, the law in its majestic equality tells the rich and the poor alike that they may not steal bread, and Professor Redish would similarly tell the large claimants and the small claimants alike that they may not sue as a group unless formal consent was individually given in advance. Litigant autonomy comes then at a high price.

Professor Redish also claims that the settlement class is illegitimate,[73] and this claim may rest on a stronger empirical foundation. Settlement classes (by which he means a class that is filed and typically settled on the same day) do not resemble, in his judgment, true "cases and controversy" that fall within the legitimate sphere of courts. Here, he makes a somewhat more substantial case. Settlement classes often lead to claims resolution processes that were never mandated by the legislature or any administrative body. (In truth, however, inventory settlements in non-class mass tort disputes often produce about the same outcome.) Still, the heyday of the settlement class is probably over, as the settlement class can no longer dispose easily of "future claims" because of the parties' inability to give adequate notice.[74] To be sure, despite *Ortiz,* settlement classes persist to a degree, but the better answer to the settlement class may be to introduce a greater element of adversarial procedure into the settlement hearing.[75]

Curiously, the most surprising feature in Professor Redish's critique of the political legitimacy of the class action is what he does not challenge. The keystone in the U.S. system is not the class action but the private attorney general. The private attorney general is a private enforcer performing a public role in order to solve collective action problems but without authorization by the legislature.[76] Even if the concept has its flaws (with self-interest regularly triumphing over idealism, as we have repeatedly seen), the private attorney general arguably still performs a critical failsafe role by protecting the public against nonenforcement by public enforcers. Here, we reach the true issue for democratic theory: should a law be enforced when it has not been repealed but those politically accountable officials controlling public enforcement choose not to enforce it? Put differently, should the executive branch be able to make a decision not to enforce the law? Liberals would argue that, although the majority can repeal the law, the executive branch alone cannot abandon a valid law through systemic nonenforcement. In such a debate over the ethics of public enforcement, both sides may seek to prove too much, but clearly the private attorney general offers the most feasible answer to public underenforcement of law.

For its proponents then, the great virtue in the private attorney general concept is that it tends to ensure continuity of enforcement. They fear that a new and more conservative administration will cease to enforce the policies that they disfavor. Thus, they rely on the likelihood that, even if a new administration abandons enforcement in a particular area, the private attorney general will remain the enforcer of last resort. As a result, if a legislative majority wants to ensure consistent, long-term enforcement of a particular policy, it logically should authorize private enforcement, because it knows that change in the executive branch is much more likely than change in the legislative branch (and only the latter can end private enforcement).[77] Those who want environmental, civil rights, or consumer protections laws to be enforced consistently should regard the private attorney general as their guarantor of enforcement stability.

Although the debate will continue, the contemporary American consensus seems likely to remain that the private attorney general is socially desirable.[78]

To sum up, Professor Redish boldly asserts what everyone already knew: that procedural law affects substantive law, and can distort it. But styling the issue as protecting litigant autonomy adds little. The focus needs to be on protecting the "negative value" claimant (including from wholesale subversion of the individual claimant's rights through settlement classes), while also penalizing nuisance value suits. That balance is not easy to strike, as discussed in Chapter 8.

8

THE NEEDED REFORMS

WE HAVE JUST SURVEYED the limited reach of the class action today. As courts have lost confidence in the class action, they have curbed its reach, primarily by an increasingly strict interpretation of the "predominance" requirement of Rule 23(b)(3). But limiting the class action's reach does not truly resolve the underlying problems. They persist in only modestly altered form. For example, in the case of mass torts, the same problems of collusion and opportunism that characterized mass torts class actions have resurfaced in the "quasi-class action," as plaintiff's attorneys with inventories of several thousand individual clients each behave much like the class action plaintiff's attorney. The key implication then is that procedural, substantive, and structural reforms are all needed. Accordingly, this chapter will assess possible legal reforms, holding off for Chapter 11 a discussion of whether the relationship of public and private enforcement needs to be more fundamentally restructured.

Probably the clearest candidate for reform is merger and acquisition (M&A) class litigation. Here, the problem is not limitations on the availability of the class action, but the inability of courts to control dueling class actions in multiple jurisdictions. The contrast could not be sharper between the efficient centralization of competing class actions in the federal system (where the Judicial Panel on Multidistrict Litigation [JPML] quickly consolidates overlapping cases before one district court judge) and the absolute chaos at the state level, where copycat class actions challenge virtually every merger and produce dueling class actions in different jurisdictions. This recurrent and destructive competition presents structural problems that cannot be successfully resolved simply by "tweaking" the procedural language of Federal Rule of Civil Procedure 23. Redesign is needed.

Similarly, we have also seen that, even if the "extortion" critique of the class action is usually overstated, it does have some legitimacy. Aggregation of cases within the class allows plaintiff's attorneys to hide weak cases behind strong cases. In the M&A context, frivolous actions are filed because there is no penalty and the corporation is under time pressure. From these premises, the following reforms logically flow:

1. THE MULTI-FORUM PROBLEM AND THE NEED FOR EFFICIENT CONSOLIDATION ACROSS JURISDICTIONS. Looking back, one can now understand that the most successful step taken in the administration of aggregate litigation in the United States was the creation of the JPML in 1968 as a consequence of the electrical equipment antitrust cases. This achievement may have been the product of dumb luck, because the JPML was created even before the modern class action arose. In the absence of a JPML, the same chaos that now prevails in state M&A litigation (and in some derivative action and mass tort battles) would also likely persist at the federal level. Instead, a workable system functions relatively smoothly, which largely prevents interjurisdictional warfare among cases in different federal courts. Both sides gain from it: defendants avoid duplicative discovery and motions in overlapping cases, and plaintiffs gain a mechanism that allocates control of the case (and thereby enables the winner in this competition to invest in its action and litigate it effectively).

Multi-forum litigation produces not only chaos, but also collusion. When there are multiple overlapping cases pending in state court, the first case to settle wins and preempts the others because courts must accept that settlement (once approved by the state court) as dispositive under the Full Faith and Credit Clause of the U.S. Constitution. Both defendants and plaintiffs understand how to exploit this provision. To the inexperienced observer, it may seem strange that in response to a merger, class actions are filed in multiple state courts—but are not actively litigated. Yet, the attorneys behind these "sleeping beauties" have a rational plan. They are hoping and waiting for Prince Charming (the defendant) to choose one of them to settle with. That settlement will block those who have litigated the case intensively—at least as long as it precedes any resolution in the actively litigated case. Thus, the less work the passive plaintiffs do, the more cheaply they can afford to settle. Sadly, passivity pays.

On the federal level, this problem is largely mitigated by the JPML. But even here, there are serious problems—largely caused by a modern Supreme Court decision. In *Matsushita Electric Industrial Co. v. Epstein,*[1] the Supreme Court was faced with dueling class actions, one in federal court and one in state court. Both challenged Matsushita's acquisition of MCA Corporation (the parent of Universal Studios) in a friendly tender offer (which acquisition was on terms that were arguably unduly favorable to MCA's controlling executives). One team of plaintiff's attorneys sued on state law grounds in Delaware (where MCA was incorporated), and the other team sued in federal court in Los Angeles, asserting that the defendants had violated the federal takeover rules under the Williams Act. This was a novel claim, but federal courts had exclusive jurisdiction over the federal securities law and thus it could not be asserted in Delaware.

Nonetheless, defendants and the Delaware counsel proposed a global settlement in Delaware that released all claims, both state and federal. Initially, the Delaware chancellor (to his credit) refused to approve the settlement, ruling that the federal claims were too speculative to value at this stage. Later, the Ninth Circuit did uphold the federal claims, but, before it did, the Delaware Chancery Court had approved a revised global settlement that released all claims. The Ninth Circuit refused to defer to this settlement because it concluded that Delaware plaintiff's counsel could not settle claims that it could not litigate (given the exclusive federal jurisdiction over these claims).[2]

The case then went to the Supreme Court, which, in a closely divided decision, reversed the Ninth Circuit. The dissent, written by Justice Ginsburg, doubted that the Delaware counsel could give "fair and adequate" representation to the plaintiffs in the federal actions when they could only settle, but not litigate, their claims. The majority, however, found that the Delaware counsel had made an honest and reasonable attempt to value these claims.

Ignored by the majority was the strong incentive here for collusion. Delaware plaintiff's counsel knew that, if they did not settle the federal claims that they were unable to litigate, the rival plaintiff's team in Los Angeles would eventually do so (and earn much or most of the resulting total fee awards). Ironically, the Supreme Court ruled one year later in 1997 that plaintiff's attorneys could not settle claims that they were unable to litigate in a mass tort class action (because they were "disarmed" and thus could not give "adequate representation" to the class),[3] but in 1996 the Court found that plaintiff's attorneys could settle equally un-litigatable claims in a state court class action. The two decisions are in unresolved tension and may show that the majority of the Court is willing to accept almost any technique to resolve securities class actions.

In any event, *Matsushita* lays out a practical roadmap for plaintiff's counsel in state court litigation: settle all claims (even those they cannot litigate) before counsel in the federal action litigates and/or settles them. Defendants are more than happy to oblige the state court counsel, because such a handicapped counsel will typically settle cheaper than the rival counsel in federal court (who can actually litigate these claims). The result, however, is to partially undermine the ability of the JPML to prevent (or at least discourage) collusion.

This problem is susceptible to an obvious reform: expand the authority of the JPML so that it could consolidate cases in different states, or in state and federal court, before a single judge for the same purposes of pretrial coordination. If only state cases were involved, a panel of state judges (possibly selected by the Chief Justice) could perform this same function, assigning the case to an experienced state judge to hear all pretrial motions and discovery disputes (and quietly serving as a mediator to encourage settlement). Politically difficult as such a reform would be to adopt, it faces no serious constitutional problem. Duplicative, multi-forum litigation burdens corporations, taxes shareholders, and creates uncertainty. Thus, the Commerce Clause can justify such a statute, because the burden on interstate commerce is clear. Still, federal legislation is not the only means to this end. States could themselves agree to an interstate compact establishing the same rules.[4] Probably no more than eight or so key states in which such litigation is common would need to agree to make such a reform effective. The problem lies in inducing these states to see their common self-interest.

This proposal to expand the JPML's scope can be framed either ambitiously or modestly. A minimalist version would authorize consolidation by the JPML only when class actions in different courts overlapped (and therefore could preclude each other). This would cover both the *Matsushita* fact pattern and the M&A context, but little else, because the Securities Litigation Uniform Standards Act (SLUSA) and Class Action Fairness Act (CAFA) largely preclude multistate class actions. To preserve the primacy of state corporation law, however, these statutes were written so as to expressly exempt class actions involving state corporate governance issues (the so-called Delaware carve out).[5] Thus, it is uniquely in the M&A context (and only a few other corporate governance areas) where actions challenging the same conduct under the same governing law and involving the same class of plaintiffs can be brought in different courts. These are the cases that most justify consolidation.

A more ambitious version of this proposed reform could authorize the JPML (or a similar body created by the state courts) to consolidate actions any time they (1) involved the same general factual allegations against the same defendant, or (2) involved the same product (or type of product). This is the governing standard today at the federal level, and its generalization would eliminate much duplicative discovery and parallel pretrial motions. Indeed, this was the original rationale in the electrical equipment antitrust cases in the 1960s for creating the body that eventually evolved into the JPML. Admittedly, there are plausible counterarguments against this more ambitious proposal: for example, it would involve the transferee court resolving issues under the different procedural rules of another jurisdiction (for example, the discovery rules of a different state). This problem does not arise today at the federal level, because all federal cases handled by the JPML are subject to the same federal procedural and evidentiary rules.

Probably the best argument against even the more modest version discussed above is that it may be unnecessary because a simpler reform is gaining ground that could also work, namely, forum selection clauses.

These clauses, adopted in a corporation's bylaws by its shareholders or its board of directors, typically require that any class or derivative action, or any other suit based on fiduciary duties, must be brought exclusively in the corporation's jurisdiction of incorporation (which effectively would mean the Delaware Chancery Court for the majority of public corporations). An important recent Delaware decision has upheld such a clause, and it may curtail duplicative litigation.[6] Indeed, this is the preferred solution of the corporate bar, and many companies are today adopting this self-help remedy.

But the problem with relying on the forum selection clause as the optimal remedy is that it solves only half the problem; that is, it protects against extortion, but not against collusion. Most companies adopting a forum selection clause draft the provision so as to give the corporation a choice whether or not to waive its application in any actual case. Today, the boilerplate clause will typically say "Unless the Corporation consents in writing to the selection of an alternative forum, the sole and exclusive forum . . . [will be]."[7] Thus, there can be another forum if the corporation consents. Why would it do so? Giving the corporation the option to waive this provision preserves the possibility of the reverse auction. In effect, the corporation sends an implicit message to anyone filing an action outside of its jurisdiction of incorporation that: "We can have this case dismissed quickly—unless you are willing to settle cheaply." Predictably, some will file and settle on that basis.

In reality, the problem of multi-forum litigation is two sided: (1) weak litigation taxes the corporation and its shareholders unduly and (2) multiple forums invite collusion in those cases that may be meritorious. The current version of forum selection clauses deliberately addresses only the first of these problems, whereas the proposal for an expanded JPML addresses both. Precisely for this reason and also because of the predictable reluctance of the states to cede power to the federal government, this proposal for an expanded JPML probably stands the least chance of adoption of the proposals made in this chapter.

2. THE COMMON POOL PROBLEM: HOW SHOULD CONTROL OF A CLASS ACTION BE ALLOCATED? The first battle in most class actions is the struggle for control among rival plaintiff's law firms. Thus,

even if an effective system of consolidation were developed to prevent cross-jurisdictional warfare and "reverse auctions," the problem of how to allocate control remains; it is there even when the multiple parties seeking to bring the same action are all in the same jurisdiction.

In overview, control is a valuable asset because class actions usually settle, and the attorney or attorneys named class counsel will, on average, receive a lucrative fee award—but only if the attorney can first win the competition for control of the action. The policy goal here should extend beyond simply preventing excessive profits to the plaintiff's attorney and should seek to incentivize the plaintiff's attorney to invest time and money in the action in order to resolve it for its full economic value.

This latter goal is not easy to realize. The key difficulty here is what the economist calls a common pool problem: if no one has a property right in an asset, no one will invest optimally in its development.[8] Similarly, if every plaintiff's attorney willing to participate in a class action can do so, the result will be an inefficiently large team of plaintiff's lawyers that inflates the costs and dilutes the return to all. Basically, common pool problems result in underinvestment in the action, with consequent smaller recoveries. Empirically, much plaintiff's litigation (particularly in the M&A context) appears to be underfunded and passively litigated. This seems at least partially the result of common pool problems. Forced to share the expected return with loafers, free riders, and others who do not contribute materially, the better attorneys will logically limit their own investments (in time and money) to the case. Efficiency then requires an early assignment of the action to one team of plaintiff's attorneys.

The traditional rules for assigning control of an action compounded this problem. A "first to file" rule that gives control to the first attorney on the scene rewards premature filing and slapdash complaints. Alternatively, conferring complete discretion on the court (particularly at the state level where most judges are elected and need to raise campaign funds) encourages a patronage system. Finally, elections of the class counsel by the participating plaintiff's attorneys invite logrolling and overstaffing, as the attorney with the most allies (rather than the best attorney) may win the election. Democracy alas gives too many a share in the action, with the consequence that the most capable attorneys have reduced incentive to invest time or money in the action.

For this reason, some have proposed an auction system that would assign the role of class counsel to the law firm willing to bid the lowest in terms of the fee award that it would receive if successful. Although once a popular idea, the bloom on this rose has faded, as it has become obvious that there are many flaws in proposals for auctions of either the counsel position or the lawsuit itself (most obviously, the cheapest attorney is generally not the best attorney).[9] A more practical answer is the "lead plaintiff" approach of the Private Securities Litigation Reform Act of 1995 (PSLRA), which assigns control to the party with the largest stake in the action, but this approach cannot be broadly generalized as the preferred solution for all class actions. This is because most class actions (at least those outside the securities law context) do not normally have large claimants. Also even where there are large claimants, they increasingly tend to opt out and settle quietly on their own.[10]

What system would work best? Here, it is easier to identify the worst answer and work backward from it. The worst system would give control to a large amalgam of firms that agreed to litigate the action together as a team. This outcome is often the consequence if the plaintiff's attorneys are permitted to elect their own lead counsel or lobby the court for a joint appointment. Such a team actually resembles a cartel—that is, an attempt by the leading firms to organize the case by agreeing to share the fee rather than compete for the role of lead counsel. Inevitably, this approach will produce free riders and overstaffing necessitated by the need to give everyone a lucrative role in the case in return for their vote.

The better approach should rely on judicial selection and asks the court to assign control to the single firm that has the best attorneys who are willing to commit their time and money to the action. This smaller team could later invite in other attorneys (possibly for their expertise or possibly to diversify the risk with them), but this would be a voluntary decision, not one that was the product of a strategy to win control of the case. Thus, the court could attempt to identify the best, most competent counsel by evaluating the initial pleadings that they filed (as Delaware courts today often do). Or, the court could establish ground rules and select the best candidate that came forward (but not necessarily the lowest bidder). Here, it is important that counsel agree to commit time and money to the case in order to avoid the kind of feigned litigation that today characterizes many M&A cases. Finally, the court must be prepared to revisit its choice and remove class counsel if the case is inactively litigated.

Ultimately, once we discard the theoretical, but impractical, possibility of an auction, the "real world" choice is between (1) a "political model" that invites all the interested plaintiff's counsel to participate and share in control and (2) an "entrepreneurial model" that seeks the most competent counsel most willing to make a substantial investment (in time and money) to litigate the case and confers the property right to do so on that counsel. Efficiency points toward the latter as the better model.

3. CLASS CERTIFICATION.   As we have seen, the "predominance" requirement of Rule 23(b)(3) is the great obstacle to, and grim reaper of, class actions for money damages. Its impact is far reaching. For example, it will typically bar (1) a fraud-based class action (because of the need to show individual reliance); (2) a mass tort class action (because of the need to prove proximate causation of the individual class member's injury); and (3) consumer protection or other multistate class actions (because of the likely application of the laws of multiple states, thus creating "individual" legal issues). In the future, the Supreme Court's decision in *Comcast v. Behrend* implies that the predominance requirement may also bar any class action for money damages, unless a class-wide theory of damages can be shown (and only securities class actions seem effectively exempt from this problem).[11]

Formidable as the predominance requirement is, there is one means by which it can be outflanked (and without legislation). The answer is known as "partial" or "issue" certification, and it is expressly permitted by Rule 23(c)(4) of the Federal Rules of Civil Procedure.[12]

Although appellate courts today are divided over when partial certification may be used, an example will show its potential utility: imagine a billion dollar, common law fraud case in which the plaintiff's attorneys can easily prove both the materiality of defendant's misstatements and defendant's intent to defraud, but cannot show individual reliance (because it is an individual issue that needs to be shown in this nonsecurities case by each of the estimated 20,000 class members). The federal court could certify a class on the issues of materiality and scienter (and all other requisite elements of the cause of action, except for individual reliance). This would be a "partial certification" under Rule 23(c)(4). If this action were successfully resolved, each class member could then sue in state or federal court and be required to prove only the one missing element of individual reliance. In effect each claimant could make use of these class-wide findings to estop the defendant from denying them.[13] Being required to prove only reliance on the omitted information is not a difficult burden for an individual litigant (who can easily testify as to his own thought processes), and traditional contingent fee plaintiff's lawyers could easily prosecute such cases.

Correspondingly, in a mass tort case involving a drug with dangerous side effects, the class action trial could resolve the major issues of liability (causation is usually the key issue on which scientific experts may disagree), and class members would be left to prove proximate causation (i.e., that the drug caused their personal injury) in individual cases. This would also allow the defendant to raise any special affirmative defense applicable to this claimant in the individual trial (whereas such special defenses usually tend to get ignored in the class setting, especially if there is a settlement).

The logic to this proposal is that it avoids duplicative relitigation of the same issue (i.e., general causation in a tobacco case). This goal of judicial economy was the original rationale for the class action in England and Colonial America. It also reflects and responds to the fact that smaller claimants cannot usually afford to prove complex scientific issues (which require expensive scientific experts) on their own. The more complex and expensive issues are generally "common" issues that can be resolved in the class action (which larger plaintiff's law firms would handle). The individual and more fact-specific issues would be handled in individual trials (by the same or different lawyers, as the individual client elects). This would be an efficient allocation of issues between the group and individual proceedings.

One hidden advantage of this approach favors defendants: it would deny class attorneys the ability to hide weak cases behind strong cases. Suppose in an asbestos class covering persons with current injuries, the class action attorneys have a number of "strong" (i.e., truly injured) claimants, but also many class members with feigned or dubious injuries (a slight cough which they attribute to asbestos exposure decades before). These weak cases could be screened out at the individual stage. Thus, partial certification is the most logical answer to the one valid theory of extortion encountered earlier (namely, that class actions can involve a masquerade in which weak cases hide behind the strong ones). Nor would there be any risk that the defendant would effectively be denied its right to assert individual affirmative defenses, as they could be raised at this stage.

So why do not both sides favor partial certification? On the defendant's side, it is better to block class actions in their entirety than to reform them, and the current law on class certification does largely eclipse the class action in many contexts. Defendants have no desire to change that. On the plaintiff's side, there is also a difficult problem: attorney's fees. How are fees to be shared between the attorneys representing the class and the attorneys representing the individual class members in the follow-on proceeding?

Class action attorneys are not interested in bestowing valuable findings on the attorneys in the individual actions (where the actual recovery will come) unless they are fairly compensated for so doing. In their view, they have pulled the lead oar, and the individual attorneys should not receive a windfall for filling in the one remaining blank in plaintiff's theory of liability. In principle, this problem can be solved if the court handling the class action mandates that fees be paid out of any individual recovery to the class attorneys, but this is not easy to implement. A state court awarding a recovery in an individual action may find it easier simply to ignore (or may never learn of) the order of a federal court a thousand miles away that some of the recovery should go to the class attorneys. Ultimately, this problem can be largely solved (including through self-help remedies),[14] but this reform pits the traditional trial bar against class action attorneys. Still, class action attorneys have few alternatives to it.

At present, the likelihood is that the current Supreme Court will not expand partial certification under Rule 23(c)(4) and may simply ignore this issue. Conversely, there are even colorable constitutional issues that could lead them to reject partial certification.[15] Because many of the Court's recent decisions on class actions (most notably, *Wal-Mart, Concepcion,* and *Comcast*) have involved 5-to-4 splits on key issues, it is speculative to predict the Court's future behavior. Suffice it to say that a future Supreme Court could save the "negative value" class action through a liberal ruling on this issue of partial certification. But, if it does not, the combination of the new strictness with which the predominance requirement is being read and the spread of mandatory arbitration across the legal landscape implies the slow extinction of most class actions.

4. "LOSER PAYS." Repeatedly, this volume has suggested that an excessive incentive to litigate can arise under American law. Sometimes, this is the result of a cost differential that favors the plaintiff; other times, it results from the key fact that directors and officers insurance will cover a settlement, but not necessarily an adverse judgment, which implies in turn that defendants will often prefer settlement to litigation, even when facing weak cases. Finally, the American rule incentivizes the plaintiff's attorney to impose costs on the adversary, while economizing on its own costs, knowing that it is immune from fee shifting. The net result is to encourage weak litigation that taxes the economy and is not necessary to preserve the "negative value" class action. But any remedy has to be a balanced one—or otherwise plaintiff's attorneys could be constantly threatened with punitive fee shifting that will deter them from bringing meritorious cases.

Often, when a plaintiff's attorney sues a large defendant, the litigation costs are radically asymmetric, with the plaintiff's side expending far less than the defendant's. Thus, by shifting these costs, a pure "loser pays" rule would amount to a "one horse/one rabbit" trade. For example, the defendant in securities litigation might reasonably incur costs of $10 million, while the plaintiff's side correspondingly incurred costs (in terms of its lodestar time) of only $1 million. If we wish to avoid a Draconian response that could render the private attorney general extinct, then the fee shifting against the plaintiff's attorney should be limited to a reasonable amount in relation to the plaintiff's own costs and expected payoff. This need for balance could be addressed either by an ex ante legislative rule that permitted fee shifting against the loser (but placed a low ceiling on the amount that could be so shifted) or by ex post monitoring by the Securities and Exchange Commission (SEC), which could intervene in cases where the proposed fee shifting seemed so disproportionate as to chill future meritorious litigation from being brought.[16]

This suggested approach for limited fee shifting differs sharply from current law, under which the court can impose sanctions on either side (typically under Rule 11 of the Federal Rules of Civil Procedure) only if the court deems either side to have misbehaved. At least three major problems have made this approach (i.e., the use of court-awarded sanctions) ineffective:

First, sanctions under Rule 11 can only be imposed on very limited grounds, and a plaintiff's attorney can file a "long shot" class action, knowing that it faces only a low risk of sanctions.[17]

Second, courts dislike imposing sanctions and try by all possible means to avoid doing so, in part because they believe it delays settlement. In contrast, the proposed limited fee-shifting approach is automatic and would not depend on the court's discretion.

Third, sanctions typically go to the court (and thus the U.S. Treasury).[18] As a result, although the defendant may want the plaintiff's attorney to be punished, the award of sanctions does not benefit the defendant and thus may not affect its own decision-making calculus. For example, if the defendant believes that it will cost it $4 million to take a case to trial, the fact that the plaintiff's attorney will be penalized $2 million (if the plaintiff loses) will not reduce the costs to the defendant. Thus, the defendant may decide that it is better to settle for $3 million than to expend $4 million to reach trial (and a still uncertain outcome).

All this changes under a fee-shifting approach. For example, under the foregoing example where the settlement costs the defendant $3 million and a trial costs it $4 million, the shifting of as little as $2 million of the defendant's expenses to the plaintiff's attorney changes the calculus for the defendant. Now, on the foregoing facts, the net cost of going to trial may fall to $2 million, and hence the defendant may not settle as easily for $3 million. Much will depend, of course, on its estimate of the outcome at trial. Fee shifting thus encourages the defendant to resist what it sees as "meritless" litigation but has less impact on cases where the merits are stronger. Plaintiff's attorneys would similarly recognize that the prospect of fee shifting reduces the prospect of small settlements based on the differential in litigation costs. As a result, fewer "weak" cases would be filed.

This proposal could be softened even further to avoid Draconian results. The worst abuses occur in cases that never get within a country mile of a trial. These are the true "nuisance" suits, brought by an attorney who largely remains passive. To isolate these cases, a legislatively adopted "loser pays" rule might apply only to those cases that do not survive a motion to dismiss. The premise here is that surviving a motion to dismiss indicates that the case had at least some potential merit. Limiting fee shifting against the plaintiff to cases that do not survive a motion to dismiss would effectively limit the plaintiff's attorney's maximum exposure to fee shifting. So limited, fee shifting would not be likely to bankrupt any firm.

Discussions of the "loser pays" rule, as applied to U.S. courts, have long had a theoretical quality, because there was little chance that the Federal Rules of Civil Procedure would be amended to include any provision imposing anything similar to a "loser pays" rule. But the possibility of a "loser pays" rule has suddenly become ominously plausible. In 2014, in an unexpected decision, the Delaware Supreme Court held that a bylaw, adopted by the board of directors of a Delaware nonstock corporation, could shift attorney's fees and costs to the unsuccessful plaintiffs in intracorporate litigation.[19] The issue arose in federal court litigation, and the federal court certified the question of the enforceability of this bylaw to the Delaware Supreme Court. As a result, the court's decision was abstract and did not consider the factual circumstances, but only the general principle. Nonetheless, the Delaware Supreme Court clearly held that such a bylaw was facially valid, could be adopted by the board of directors (without a shareholder vote), and applied to shareholders who acquired their shares before the time of the bylaw's adoption. Whether the bylaw was enforceable, it said, depended on the manner in which it was adopted and whether it was being used for "an inequitable purpose."

The Delaware Supreme Court's decision opened the door for self-help remedies and experimentation. Some companies have adopted very sweeping bylaws or charter provisions under which the fees and expenses of the defendants (individual and corporate) are shifted to the plaintiff unless the latter is completely successful.[20] This trend is accelerating, and it could become part of the standard package of provisions adopted by a company preparing for an initial public offering.

Because only about half of the publicly held corporations in the United States are incorporated in Delaware, Delaware cannot alone solve this problem (and it may provoke interstate charter competition and a "race to the bottom" if it adopts a strong legislative response totally barring fee-shifting bylaws). The SEC is better positioned to strike a sensible balance, but it to this point has remained passive. It could attempt to define the point at which fee shifting moved from a desirable deterrent to a punitive penalty that blocks meritorious litigation, and it could intervene selectively on a case-by-case basis.

The advent of fee-shifting bylaws and charter provisions can be greeted with both pessimism and optimism. The grounds for pessimism are obvious, but these developments also imply that real change is possible. At least in intracorporate litigation, private ordering may be both feasible and justified, and appropriate disincentives to frivolous litigation can be designed. To be sure, some efforts may go too far (and may or may not invite judicial rejection). But the floor is now open for a robust debate over what the optimal disincentive should be, and this chapter has made its modest (and timely) proposal.

5. REFOCUSING THE SECURITIES CLASS ACTION. The current irony is that class actions are most viable in exactly the context where they are least needed and most problematic, namely, the securities context. As earlier argued, the circularity problem undercuts the compensatory role of most private securities litigation and implies that such actions largely yield only pocket-shifting wealth transfers. Although some deterrence probably is generated by such actions, considerably more deterrence would likely result from holding liable the corporation's officers and gatekeepers (e.g., its accountants, lawyers and investment bankers). This diagnosis leads naturally to a prescription: private securities litigation under Rule 10b-5 should be refocused on corporate officers and agents, including its gatekeepers. Today, these gatekeepers are largely exempt because Supreme Court decisions have largely immunized secondary participants from the reach of Rule 10b-5.[21]

Based on these premises, it is now time to propose a Missouri Compromise that has benefits for both sides. First, aiding and abetting liability should be legislatively restored (with possible safeguards in the form of statutory ceilings on liability). Second, corporate liability in cases where the entity is not itself trading should be limited, either by entirely exempting the corporate entity from liability or, more likely from a political perspective, by placing a ceiling on its maximum liability.[22] The entity's liability would thus be more symbolic than economically threatening. Plaintiffs will like the first proposal and hate the second, and defendants will have the reverse reaction. Only in combination is such a package politically feasible (or even conceivable).

The net effect of such a proposal would likely reduce the total amount of securities litigation (and, depending on where the ceiling is set on corporate liability, the settlement value of many cases) and shift the target of such litigation. Plaintiff's attorneys would understand that large recoveries required them to pursue officers and secondary participants. But, by restoring aiding and abetting liability, deterrence would be enhanced, and the corporation's gatekeepers (its accountants, investment bankers, and attorneys) are probably the parties who can most feasibly prevent corporate misconduct.

Restoring civil liability for aiding and abetting makes obvious sense because aiding and abetting a securities fraud remains a criminal offense.[23] To say the least, it is anomalous that a person can go to prison for fraudulent conduct that does not entitle the victim to sue that person. Moreover, the circularity problem that confounds compensation in most securities class actions does not apply in this context, as the payments do not flow between different classes of shareholders. Significant compensation can also be obtained in such actions. For example, in the *Enron* and *WorldCom* securities class actions, the settling defendants (who were all secondary participants and primarily consisted of investment banks) paid approximately $7.3 billion and $6.5 billion, respectively.[24] The one significant argument against such liability is that it could destroy an accounting or investment banking firm as an entity. Even so, this danger does not justify immunity, but only a ceiling on such firm's liability. The specifics of such a ceiling need not be fine-tuned here.[25]

The idea of placing a ceiling on the nontrading corporation's liability will seem unthinkable to some. But, in fact, Canada recently adopted just such a ceiling on the corporation's liability at the same time as it authorized a class action applicable to open market trading in its securities markets.[26]

6. THE FRAUD-ON-THE-MARKET DOCTRINE.   One last major question remains to be addressed: should Congress seek to revise or restore the Fraud-on-the-Market Doctrine? In *Halliburton Co. v. Erica B. Jong Fund, Inc. (Halliburton II)*,[27] the Supreme Court declined to overrule the doctrine, but did give the defendant an enhanced ability to rebut the doctrine's presumption of reliance at class certification by demonstrating (probably through event studies) that the market did not respond to the corrective disclosure, implying that the market was never deceived in the first place. This was a compromise that moved the law marginally in the direction of defendants but still permitted the relatively easy certification of securities class actions. The decision leaves in place the key rule (first announced in *Basic v. Levinson* in 1988) that individual reliance need not be shown because the plaintiff investors are presumed to have relied on the market to properly price the securities. *Basic*'s elimination of the need to show individual reliance allowed plaintiff's attorneys to overcome the "predominance" hurdle of Rule 23(b)(3), and its presumption of reliance (at least if the market was efficient) enabled the securities class action to flourish.

Now, in *Halliburton II,* the Court has said that defendants can seek to rebut that presumption at the class certification stage. Actually, the defendants always could rebut this presumption at trial or on a motion for summary judgment, but now they can do so before the court at class certification. This may prove a significant difference, because lay jurors typically have little understanding of the complex economic issues (or the event studies and other evidence) that are disputed before them. Defendants are unwilling as a group to rely on the jury to understand and pay attention to these issues. Hence, to delay issues, such as price impact of loss causation, to the trial stage is to submerge them as a practical matter and compel defendants to settle. At class certification, the court will now play a screening role, deciding whether defendants (who will have the burden of proof) have shown that there was in fact no fraud on the market because the corrective disclosure did not trigger any adverse market reaction. That would imply that the market was not surprised or defrauded. From a policy perspective, it seems desirable that, before defendants are compelled to settle the case at potentially $1 billion or more, the court play such a screening role. As earlier noted in Chapter 4, over 60 percent of securities class actions settle, but this statistic does not imply that they are meritorious to that same degree. Rather it tends to show that defendants dare not go to trial. If so, an expanded judicial screening role makes sense and reduces the prospect of extortion.

The Fraud-on-the-Market Doctrine, as it existed after *Basic* but before *Halliburton II*, had other flaws as well.[28] Primarily, it was underinclusive. By emphasizing market efficiency as its justification, the doctrine was largely inapplicable to stocks not traded on an "efficient" market (which in practice meant the New York Stock Exchange or the upper reaches of Nasdaq). But the classic American securities fraud is the "pump and dump" scheme, in which the fraudsters control the supply of a thinly traded stock, limit sales for a period of time to create an artificially limited supply, then pump up the stock's price with false rumors, and finally dump their shares into an inflated market. These cases generally cannot be certified as class actions today because the shares do not trade in an "efficient" market. Yet, little reason exists for using market efficiency as the test of class certification. The real issue should be whether there is evidence that the market price was distorted, and a price decline on the release of the corrective disclosure shows that, both in efficient and inefficient markets.

Interestingly, the Fraud-on-the-Market Doctrine did not always rely on proof of market efficiency. When the doctrine was first formulated by the Ninth Circuit in 1975, it was justified entirely in pragmatic terms: absent the doctrine, the Ninth Circuit said, class certification would not be possible, and there would be no feasible remedy for securities fraud.[29] In *Basic v. Levinson*, the Supreme Court carried on this theme, emphasizing that presumptions exist mainly to do justice.[30] However, more recent federal courts have read the doctrine to require proof that the market was efficient as a precondition for dispensing with proof of individual reliance. That was unfortunate. Ideally, the doctrine should focus not on the level of market efficiency, but on proof that the market was clearly distorted by the alleged misstatement or omission. If proof of price distortion is substituted for proof of market efficiency, both sides benefit in different ways.[31]

Ultimately, the Fraud-on-the Market Doctrine should be read not as an empirical statement that investors do in fact rely on an efficient market (which is debatable), but as a normative statement that investors are entitled to rely on the integrity of the market. Viewed this way, the doctrine asserts not a factual premise, but a normative entitlement: investors are entitled to an undistorted market. This entitlement justification has little connection to the issue of reliance (which is relevant only from a compensatory perspective), but instead places at center stage the social interest in an accurate and undistorted market.[32] To sum up, although *Halliburton II* was a statesman-like compromise by the Supreme Court, its outcome should be legislatively liberalized still further by eliminating the need to prove market efficiency, as a prerequisite to the Fraud-on-the-Market Doctrine's application. Thus, this book proposes a unique, but balanced, compromise for securities litigation: (1) place a ceiling on the corporate entity's liability, (2) restore the aiding and abetting liability of secondary participants, and (3) liberalize the Fraud-on-the-Market Doctrine still further.

7. ATTORNEY'S FEES. This is the lever—the carrot, rather than the stick—by which the law can most easily change the behavior of plaintiff's attorneys. For example, higher fees should be awarded for recoveries obtained from officers and secondary participants in securities class actions (because more deterrence is likely generated in such cases). Similarly, attorney's fees could be reduced when the case merely "piggybacks" on an earlier public enforcement proceeding (because the risk was low). The real question is less the fee award criteria than how such rules could be communicated and enforced (because federal judges are notoriously independent and persuading them is like herding cats). One answer may be manuals, or guidance from the Federal Judicial Center, but the most that can be hoped for here is mild progress.

8. CONCLUSION. This chapter has proposed a number of reforms that are each unlikely to be adopted on an individual basis. But, collectively, they both make sense and are balanced. In the case of the securities class

action, reducing corporate liability and restoring aiding and abetting liability are substantially offsetting, but each is logically justified. The overall goal is to shift the securities class action from being a flawed vehicle for achieving compensation into an effective means of deterrence. In the case of other class actions, plaintiffs would benefit from the availability of partial certification, and the better plaintiff firms would gain from an expansion in the jurisdiction of the JPML. Correspondingly, defendants would be eager to see any movement toward a "loser pays" rule (even on the modest terms here proposed).

In the current polarized political climate, realism compels the concession that legislative reform is a remote possibility at best. But, if at some future moment, both sides could recognize that the current system is dysfunctional (as it is), this chapter has offered a road map for reform.

These largely technical reforms are not the only reforms needed. Law also has expressive goals that entrepreneurial litigation does little (and can do little) to further or affirm. Chapter 11 will consider how private and public enforcement could be better combined and coordinated, in part to better realize the symbolic objectives of civil justice.

9

PUBLIC ENFORCEMENT AND THE
PRIVATE ATTORNEY GENERAL

To this point, we have seen that entrepreneurially motivated plaintiff's attorneys can organize efficiently to litigate complex actions successfully in a variety of fields but that there are high agency costs associated with this activity. Not infrequently, the interests of the clients in class and derivative actions are subordinated to the interests of their attorneys.

But one cannot stop there. If private enforcement has its problems, so too does public enforcement (as discussed later in this chapter). Also, private enforcement has clearly had its successes as well, with numerous settlements exceeding the $1 billion level. Indeed, if we focus just on civil litigation and measure success by the magnitude of the recovery, private enforcement has been much more effective than public enforcement. To see this, Table 9.1 compares the recovery in private securities class action with the parallel recovery by the Securities and Exchange Commission (SEC) in its enforcement actions.[1]

As Table 9.1 shows, the margin between the private and public recovery is often 10:1 (or greater). Possibly even more important, in some notable instances (such as Lehman Brothers), public enforcers have not sued,

Table 9.1   Comparison of class action recovery to SEC recovery against same
defendants

Company	Securities class action recovery	SEC recovery
Enron	$7.242 billion	$450 million
WorldCom	$6.194 billion	$750 million
Tyco International	$3.2 billion	$50 million
AOL Time Warner	$2.5 billion	$308 million
Bank of America	$2.425 billion	$150 million (as revised)
Citigroup	$1.320 billion	$75 million
Nortel Networks	$2.217 billion	$35 million
Merrill Lynch	$940 million	None
American International Group	$937.5 million	$800 million
HealthSouth Corp.	$804.5 million	$100 million
Xerox	$750 million	$44 million
Lucent Technologies	$667 million	$25 million
Wachovia	$627 million	None
Countrywide Financial	$624 million	$48.15 million
Lehman Brothers	$600 million	None
Washington Mutual ("WaMu")	$208 million	None
National City	$168 million	None
New Century	$125 million	$1.5 million
Wells Fargo (MBS)	$125 million	$6.5 million

while private enforcers have, reaping large recoveries. This should remind us of the "failsafe" or "safety valve" function of private enforcement; it remains available even if public enforcers are "captured" or are otherwise unavailable.

This contrast in the relative recoveries in public and private enforcement frames an important question: could the entrepreneurial energy of the plaintiff's bar be harnessed instead to public enforcement? If it could, this might not only add teeth to public enforcement, making it more potent, but public enforcers might be better able to monitor the private attorney general than can private clients. In short, two goals could be advanced at once: (1) greater deterrence might be generated; and (2) better monitoring might be achieved to reduce opportunistic behavior by the private attorney general.

The most direct route to these ends would involve public enforcement agencies retaining plaintiff's law firms to undertake complex litigation for which public enforcers are either ill-equipped or undermotivated to handle. The feasibility and possible consequences of such a union present timely questions because, in the wake of the 2008 financial contagion, just about every commentator has criticized the inability of financial regulators in the United States to hold accountable senior executives at the major financial firms. Most notably, U.S. District Court Judge Jed Rakoff has rejected some Securities and Exchange Commission (SEC) settlements as unfair and inadequate, and very publicly asked why so few senior executives have been sued or prosecuted.[2]

Incisive as Judge Rakoff's questions have been, he still may have framed the issue too narrowly. The broader issue is not just that few senior executives have been prosecuted (in either criminal or civil actions), but that, even when only the corporate entity is sued, the penalty has been modest. Why then has public enforcement in the financial sector been so equivocal? This book will not address the special and sensitive issues in the use of the criminal sanction, but on the civil side, the SEC has been repeatedly singled out for criticism for its lackluster efforts.[3] In particular, its failure to take action against any officer of Lehman Brothers with respect to Lehman's dubious and recurrent "Repo 105 transactions" has puzzled many, particularly when the experienced bankruptcy examiner appointed to investigate that case filed a voluminous report urging the filing of fraud actions against these executives.[4] The possible response that no one committed any fraud conflicts with the Financial Crisis Inquiry Commission's much documented conclusion that fraud was at the heart of the 2008 crisis.[5] A depressing conclusion thus seems hard to avoid: an agency long viewed as a model administrative agency and clearly staffed by intelligent, hard-working, and honest personnel seems to have been pulling its punches, letting culpable officials off without even an attempt to hold them accountable. But why?

A. WHY DOES PUBLIC ENFORCEMENT RECOVER SO LITTLE?

In fairness, benign reasons can explain some of the disparity between the recoveries in private and public enforcement.[6] Still, most critics have focused on one or more of the following less benign explanations:

1. THE SEC IS UNDERFUNDED, RESOURCE-CONSTRAINED, AND CANNOT AFFORD TO LITIGATE THE COMPLEX CASE. No reasonable person can disagree with this assessment. Congress has failed to fund the SEC adequately, for various reasons. Republicans may doubt the need for more enforcement, particularly against their allies in the business community, and members of both parties view the SEC with greater skepticism as a result of some notorious failures (most notably, its long failure to detect Bernie Madoff's Ponzi scheme, despite warnings, for over thirty years). Undermanned and underfunded, the SEC must settle cases cheaply, because it cannot afford costly trials and lacks the experienced manpower to handle them.

2. FINANCIAL SCANDALS PRODUCE SUDDEN FLOODS OF CASES, PERIODICALLY STRETCHING THE SEC'S CAPACITY TO ITS LIMIT AND COMPELLING WEAK SETTLEMENTS. Cases and crises come in waves. Living on a relatively fixed budget that only expands modestly from year to year, the SEC cannot cope well with the greatly increased volume of cases that flowed from the 2008 financial contagion. Predictably, this problem will recur again, as public enforcers inherently face cycles of feast and famine. Market crashes expose frauds (such as Bernie Madoff's) that have long gone undetected. As Warren Buffett has observed: "You only find out who is swimming naked when the tide goes out."[7] Conversely, few frauds are detected when the market is in a "bubbly" phase. Thus, financial regulation will experience a roller coaster ride of peaks and valleys, and it must anticipate such cycles. Here, one virtue of the plaintiff's bar is that it offers a ready reserve, as plaintiff's law firms can quickly expand to seize litigation opportunities,[8] while a government bureaucracy with fixed resources cannot.

3. RISK AVERSION: THE SEC'S ATTORNEYS GENERALLY LACK TRIAL EXPERIENCE, AND IT WOULD PREFER TO SETTLE THAN RISK A LOSS. This is probably the favorite explanation of the defense bar and some judges. A clear difference exists between the experiences of assistant U.S. attorneys in the Department of Justice and SEC enforcement attorneys. The former start trying criminal cases from the outset of their careers and know the special rules of criminal justice as well (or better) than most corporate defense attorneys. SEC enforcement attorneys are knowledgeable in the securities laws but tend to lack much trial experience. This lack of experience has recently been evident, as the SEC has lost a number of cases that it has taken to trial.[9] As a result, an agency with such a mixed record at trial might prefer to settle than take the risks of trial. In addition, because large financial institutions tend to settle (probably to avoid the adverse publicity of a trial) while senior executives go to trial (both because they are indemnified by their firm and because a fraud verdict could be career ending for them), a risk-averse enforcer will tend to avoid suing individuals.

4. THE NATURE OF LITIGATION HAS CHANGED AND THE COMPLEX CASE HAS BECOME SIMPLY TOO LARGE AND COSTLY FOR THE SEC TO HANDLE.   Once, two or three SEC attorneys could effectively handle a case, but, with the advent of "ediscovery" and other developments, complex litigation has come to require squadrons of lawyers on both sides. Today, literally millions of documents (such as e-mails) may have to be reviewed in even a moderately complex case, and defense law firms assemble large teams of associates, special "contract" attorneys, and paralegals to do this. If the public enforcer cannot similarly staff such document discovery with an adequate number of attorneys, it will be flying blind into a trial with an adversary that knows far more than it. Expert witnesses are also increasingly needed and have become increasingly costly. To the extent that the SEC for these reasons would have to assign a dozen or more attorneys to litigate a case effectively, senior SEC staffers may feel compelled to settle, rather than make such a costly commitment.

This problem less seriously affects the Department of Justice where (1) discovery is largely disfavored and constrained in criminal cases and (2) the agency's budgetary problems are less severe.[10]

5. TO SECURE FUNDING, THE SEC NEEDS VICTORIES, EVEN IF THEY ARE "ILLUSORY."   This explanation views public enforcers as agents of bureaucracies that are in constant competition for limited congressional funding. All the financial regulators were embarrassed by the 2008 crisis (and their inability to foresee or prevent it), but the SEC was

particularly hard hit. The Madoff scandal humiliated it (and also cost it dearly with Congress, which became more tight-fisted about its appropriations). As a result, the SEC has particular reason to fear any embarrassing litigation defeat.

More importantly, to obtain more resources, the SEC needs to show improved results. In recent years, the SEC has responded by bringing and settling more cases than in the past. But, without increased funding, bringing more cases is only possible if the agency bringing simpler cases, arguably emphasizing quantity over quality to impress Congress with its improved efficiency.[11] Indeed, the evidence does show that, after 2008, the SEC shifted its priorities toward bringing smaller, more retail-oriented cases against brokers and low-ranking personnel, while de-emphasizing cases against public companies.[12] In addition, there is some evidence that the SEC has padded its numbers by focusing on smaller, even penny-ante cases (such as cases involving late corporate filings but no fraud).[13]

At a minimum, the SEC needs litigation successes to convince a skeptical Congress to increase its budget. The simplest way to do this is to arrange illusory "victories"—that is, settlements in which the defendants cooperate to make the SEC appear to have won a respectable victory (even if the defendant has negotiated what it considers a highly favorable settlement). Cynical as this may sound, this perspective helps explain the SEC's long-standing "neither admit nor deny" policy under which the defendant may not criticize the SEC's prosecution of it (or even continue to maintain its innocence).[14] This enforced silence enables the SEC to proclaim victory, while the defendant remains mute. To be sure, the defendant avoids having to "admit" wrongdoing (while federal criminal prosecutors in contrast usually do secure such admissions), but in return the SEC gets the stage to itself and can proclaim a victory without any protest or retort from the defendant. Necessarily, the SEC must pay a price for such a staged "victory." Defendants may only cooperate if the price of the settlement is cheap. Both sides gain what they most want: the SEC obtains a victory that it can celebrate and show to Congress, and defendants escape at a lower cost.

This need for public "victories" that can be used to seek increased funding from Congress also may contribute to another much observed characteristic of SEC settlements: few senior executives are charged. If the SEC needs a settlement in order to stage a victory parade, it may be willing to strike a deal, trading a large (and headline-generating) settlement by the corporation in return for the SEC quietly dropping charges against senior executives. Such a trade is never made explicit, but both sides may understand that a generous settlement offer by the defendant will be withdrawn if senior officials are charged. This tactic will work only so long as the financial press and other opinion-shapers can be convinced that the SEC has truly won a meaningful victory, and that may now be changing (as public and press skepticism of such victories has grown). Still, it is a bargain that many public companies would be willing to strike because it is essentially a form of self-dealing (as they are essentially using the shareholders' money to buy immunity for senior officers).

This list of explanations is not exhaustive. Others believe that financial regulators were also politically constrained (possibly by the fear that strong enforcement would destabilize the financial markets).[15] No view is here expressed on this issue, and, in fairness, it must be recognized that there are some signs that the SEC is getting tougher. Still, for the immediate future, it seems likely that it and other financial regulators will lack the resources and manpower (and possibly the nerve) to pursue individuals in cases that will be complex and hard fought.

B. WHAT MIGHT BE THE IMPACT OF PUBLIC AGENCIES RETAINING PRIVATE COUNSEL?

Given the foregoing criticisms, what consequences should follow if public enforcers (including the SEC) were to retain private law firms (sometimes on a contingent-fee basis) to pursue the large complex action that today is seldom brought? There are several levels on which this question needs to be addressed.

First, on the economic level, both firms and bureaucracies necessarily face an unavoidable "make or buy" decision about staffing. Do they try to assemble an enforcement staff capable of handling all cases under all circumstances? Or, do they hire a permanent staff to handle the "run of the mill" case load and then go outside the firm to "buy" talent in the legal market to handle major or specialized cases for which they do not have an in-house capacity? One only has to look at the behavior of any large corporation to see the logical answer. Almost invariably, large corporations will have in-house legal departments to handle recurring and simple cases. But they do not internalize the ability to handle every case. If they encounter a major "you-bet-your-company" case, they will turn to outside legal assistance from a major law firm and its "star" litigators. This is cost efficient, as it would be infeasible to keep a high-priced "superstar" litigator on the payroll to handle the infrequent and unpredictable litigation that could imperil the firm. The logic of "make or buy" decisions dictates that a firm should internalize only the capacity to handle recurring and/or perfunctory litigation, while the unusual or life-threatening case should be sent outside (either because very specialized legal talent is needed for a rare problem or because the legal threat justifies paying a premium for the very best talent available).

This same logic applies even more forcefully to public bureaucracies, such as the financial regulators. Such bureaucracies have "civil service" legal staffs that are paid well less than the "going rate" in the private legal marketplace. Dedicated and professional as such in-house attorneys may be, the best of them are usually seduced away over time by the greater profits available in the private bar (this is equally true for the Department of Justice as the SEC). Thus, use of outside counsel might both (1) reduce the imbalance that often arises when agency "in-house" lawyers face the "stars" of the private bar in major litigation and (2) provide a supplementary reserve of manpower if the agency's caseload waxes and wanes with recurrent crises.

From a political, rather than an economic, perspective, another key advantage to the use of outside counsel is that it allows the agency to outflank budgetary constraints. The agency is effectively shifting the upfront cost of the litigation and much of the downside risk of defeat to entrepreneurial plaintiff's law firms, which will willingly bear such risk if they can charge a contingent fee that adequately compensates them. Also, the agency is tapping resources that are otherwise not available to it. Public enforcement annually produces large recoveries, but they do not benefit the public enforcer. Instead, they go to the federal treasury. For example, in 2011, the SEC recovered some $2.8 billion,[16] but none of these funds went to the SEC. Instead, some are returned to investors, but most revert to the Treasury Department.[17] If the public enforcer could retain and pay private counsel out of such recoveries, it would be essentially obtaining free funding.

To be sure, the use of contingent fees may produce some undesired consequences: (1) the public may resent contingent fees that strike it as excessive and wasteful; (2) Congress may resist any attempt to outflank the budgetary limitations it seemingly placed on the agency; and (3) the generous reward offered to the private attorney, acting as bounty hunter on a contingent-fee basis, may arguably compromise the objectivity and neutrality expected of persons acting on behalf of the government. Put differently, retaining outside counsel (particularly on a contingent-fee basis) converts the "private attorney general" into much more of a "public attorney general," and greater obligations should follow.

Finally, some perverse incentives are inherent in the use of a contingent fee. For example, a plaintiff's law firm might have little interest in obtaining an injunction or other equitable relief because that relief would not normally increase the fee that the firm would receive. Typically, the plaintiff's attorneys will contract to receive some percentage of the financial recovery under its fee agreement with the agency retaining it, and an injunction will not increase that recovery. Predictably, the plaintiff's law firm will maximize what it is paid to maximize. Even worse, generous fees might also create an excessive incentive to litigate (and possibly even incentivize the firm to take on a long-shot case).

Still, these problems can be addressed in a well-drafted fee agreement. Thus, if one believes that public enforcers are constrained by resource limitations and risk aversion, the use of private counsel on a contingent-fee basis seems the logical response. The playing field would become more level between the two sides. Moreover, at least in principle, the plaintiff's law firm should view the case with a cold-blooded economic objectivity. In contrast to public enforcers (who may be influenced by political or public relations considerations), a plaintiff's law firm has no reason to invest its resources in a losing case for which it will receive no compensation. Finally, to the extent that public enforcement is constrained by risk aversion, the public enforcer may be less inhibited if the blame (in the event of a loss) will fall not on it, but on the private law firm. Indeed, the public may take satisfaction in the fact that a losing law firm will receive nothing.

The political reaction to the use of private law firms presents different problems. Congress may be displeased that its budgetary constraints have been outflanked. Still, it is equally possible that Congress will care little so long as public funds are not wasted. Taxpayers, after all, do not pay when private counsel is retained on a contingent-fee basis. The cost falls instead on the beneficiaries of the litigation (and only when the litigation is successful). Also, budgetary constraints on an agency are not necessarily the result of a deliberate congressional decision; they may instead be the product of minority vetoes, stalemate, or inertia. If congressional paralysis caused the budgetary constraint, this suggests that Congress may be equally paralyzed and unable to halt the use of such an end run around its budgetary powers.

Obviously, it is highly speculative to predict the political reaction to the use of private counsel by public agencies. Precisely for this reason, it is useful to examine contemporary practices in this regard. In overview, the reality is that several financial regulators today make extensive use of privately retained counsel and do sometimes pay them on a contingent-fee basis. Indeed, the practice seems to be growing on the federal level, and the results (in terms of amounts recovered) have been impressive.

C. EXISTING PRACTICES IN THE PUBLIC USE OF PRIVATE COUNSEL

1. THE EXPERIENCE AT THE STATE LEVEL.   The use of private counsel by public agencies, particularly counsel compensated on a contingency fee basis, has a relatively short history. It first burst into view at the state level in 1998 with the settlement of nationwide tobacco litigation. Under the Master Settlement Agreement of 1998, the fifty states struck a $246 billion settlement with the tobacco industry, and some $14 billion was paid to trial attorneys retained to represent the states on a contingent-fee basis.[18] The state attorneys general justified their use of contingency fee arrangements on the grounds that they simply lacked

the personnel, resources, or expertise to undertake such potentially costly litigation on their own. In contrast, the plaintiff's bar had already developed substantial experience in suing the tobacco industry. Since then, several states, and even some counties, have used contingency fee arrangements in connection with other actions, including cases against lead paint manufactures or challenging water pollution.[19] Generally, these cases were sufficiently high risk that the jurisdictions may have felt reluctant to undertake them using taxpayer funds.

To say the least, this use of contingency fee agreements attracted much criticism but mainly on the fear that political favoritism was involved (i.e., that politicians were hiring firms that had supported them). Whether or not true at the state level, this claim is much less tenable at the federal level, where independent agencies, such as the SEC, the Environmental Protection Agency (EPA), or the Federal Deposit Insurance Corporation (FDIC) have less involvement in politics (and their personnel does not seek political contributions).

2. FEDERAL AGENCIES. Three federal agencies—the FDIC, the Federal Housing Finance Agency (FHFA), and the National Credit Union Administration (NCUA)—have recently made significant use of private counsel to litigate actions against firms in the financial industry.

a. The FDIC. The FDIC was the first to do so, beginning in the early 1980s during the savings and loan crisis. Typically, the FDIC sues as the receiver for a failed bank, and it may bring an action against the officers, directors, auditors, or controlling persons of the bank. In an elaborate self-study, the FDIC has found that its use of outside counsel "skyrocketed" between 1989 and 1993, the peak period during the savings and loan crisis, because of such factors as "(1) the limited number of in-house legal staff in relationship to the growing number of receiverships, (2) the diverse geographic location of the receiverships, and (3) the wide variety of legal issues . . . that required specialized knowledge of state laws and legal practice, as well as federal law."[20] During this period, the FDIC often entered into what it termed alternative fee arrangements that often blended a flat fee with a contingent fee.[21]

The FDIC has now had sufficient experience with private counsel that it has prepared a deskbook, specifying procedures and covering most issues that can arise from such retentions.[22] The FDIC's deskbook makes explicit that all important decisions are to be cleared with an oversight attorney within the FDIC who is "responsible for managing all legal assignments and litigation."[23] The deskbook does not expressly refer to contingency fees, but notes that the FDIC will consider "innovative rate proposals,"[24] which appears to include both flat rates for the entire transaction and contingency fees.

How well has the use of outside counsel worked for the FDIC? In one of its most visible cases growing out of the 2008 crisis, the FDIC sued former officers of IndyMac Bank, which failed in 2008. Using private counsel, the FDIC eventually won a jury verdict in California in 2012 for $169 million in damages.[25] This verdict then led the former CEO of IndyMac to agree to a $1 million settlement with the FDIC.[26] In contrast and contemporaneously, the SEC failed to achieve any success in its own action against the same IndyMac CEO and eventually settled for a trivial $80,000.[27] To be sure, this is only one case (and few comparisons are possible because the SEC brings few actions against senior executives), but the contrast here is striking.

More generally, the level of FDIC enforcement activity has recently soared, as it has turned to private counsel. As of September 2013, Cornerstone Research, an economic consulting firm, reports that the FDIC had already filed some thirty-two lawsuits in 2013 against directors and officers of failed financial institutions—a rate that, it projected, would double the FDIC's number of filings in 2012.[28] An even better indicator may be the fact that at all financial institutions that failed in 2009, the FDIC has sued or settled with 41 percent of the directors and officers at these institutions.[29] It is doubtful that anything like that volume of litigation could have been generated by an in-house staff.

In short, if the public wants accountability imposed on financial institutions, the FDIC seems to be generating that with grim efficiency through the use of private counsel. It is not clear to what extent the FDIC is using contingency fees in these cases (they have been conspicuously silent on this controversial issue), but they clearly used them in the past.

b. The FHFA.   The FHFA is a more recent convert to the use of private counsel, but, acting as the conservator of Fannie Mae and Freddie Mac, the FHFA is now following closely in the FDIC's footsteps. In its role as conservator for Fannie and Freddie, it has sued some eighteen major financial institutions, alleging that they packaged and sold toxic mortgage-backed securities to Fannie Mae and Freddie Mac. Already, it has reached a much publicized $5.1 billion settlement with JPMorgan (this was the largest component in JPMorgan's record $13 billion settlement with the Department of Justice, several states, and other agencies).[30] In addition, other defendants—including GE Capital, Citigroup, Wells Fargo, and UBS—have settled with the FHFA, but the amounts have not generally been disclosed. Nonetheless, financial analysts are projecting, based on the terms of the JPMorgan settlement, that the FHFA may ultimately receive as much as $23 billion from the other banks it is suing.[31]

Representing the FHFA in most of this litigation has been the law firm of Quinn Emanuel Urquhart & Sullivan, LLP.[32] Quinn Emanuel is a well-known, respected (or at least feared) example of a "switch hitter" law firm—one that regularly represents both plaintiffs and defendants. These firms are few in number (Boies, Schiller & Flexner and Susman & Godfrey are other leading examples), but rather than the traditional plaintiff's bar, they are likely to be the type of firm that a government agency would retain. This is because they have established clients, their professional reputation is higher, and they employ "star" litigators with obvious credentials. These firms are also unlikely to work on a purely contingent-fee basis; rather, they may negotiate for a "blended fee" or a "success fee." Under such arrangements, they might receive a relatively low hourly rate (for them) plus a contingency fee if certain settlement benchmarks are exceeded. Such a compromise may dampen some of the criticism that surrounds a pure contingency fee.

c. The NCUA.   One federal agency has publicly defended the use of contingent fees in this context. The NCUA, which also retains private counsel in its role as a conservator for insolvent credit unions, was challenged in 2013 by Representative Darrell Issa (R-Calif.), chairman of the House Committee on Oversight and Government Reform, to justify the contingent-fee–based arrangements it had used in securities-related litigation over mortgage-backed securities its credit unions had acquired. Representative Issa had expressed skepticism about whether contingency-fee agreements were "the best possible alternative given the circumstances." NCUA's Inspector General responded that the time and cost involved in "analyzing hundreds of securities containing thousands of mortgage loans, issuing administrative subpoenas, taking testimony of hundreds of witnesses, reviewing tens of thousands of pages of documents, drafting complaints, and developing and relying on a rather unique theory related to each security" would have been prohibitive, particularly given that the NCUA anticipated "protracted litigation" that might well have yielded no recovery.[33]

In a nutshell, that is the debate: some cases could not be undertaken on an hourly rate basis by government agencies but could be successfully litigated on a contingent-fee basis. Although the NCUA was willing to argue the case for contingent fees, other public agencies have preferred to keep a lower profile and (at least for the present) avoid the public use of fee arrangements that will attract congressional attention and ire.

3. THE QUI TAM ACTION

The oldest historical precedent for private citizens bringing actions to enforce public law or obtain recoveries for public agencies is the qui tam action. Although the action's origins date back for centuries in English law, the United States turned to it only during the Civil War to combat war profiteering. Under the False Claims Act, a person who files a false claim with the federal government is liable for civil penalties "plus 3 times the amount of damages which the Government sustains because of the act of that person."[34] Uniquely, the False Claims Act allows a private citizen (known to the law as a "relator") to bring this action on behalf of the United States, even though the citizen has suffered no individual injury.[35] The Attorney General (or his or her delegate) must investigate the private citizen's allegations and may choose (1) to intervene and take over the prosecution, (2) to decline to intervene and allow the relator to prosecute the action, or (3) to move to dismiss the action. If the government does proceed with the action, the relator who initiated it receives "at least 15 percent, but not more than 25 percent of the proceeds of the action or settlement of the claim, depending on the extent to which the person substantially contributed to the prosecution of the action."[36]

In effect, the qui tam action goes well beyond the whistleblower procedures mandated by the Dodd-Frank Act (under which the SEC must pay a defined portion of the recovery to the whistleblower who gave the SEC the initial tip) and authorizes the private citizen to prosecute the case for the government, unless the Department of Justice formally intervenes.

According to a recent study by a prominent law firm, relators bringing actions on behalf of the government received over $532 million in awards in 2011[37] and $439 million in 2012.[38] But the federal government did even better, as the Department of Justice recovered over $5.6 billion in 2011 and $5 billion in 2012 in civil and criminal fraud–related proceeds.[39] Probably the majority of these recoveries came from citizen-initiated qui tam actions, and the total recoveries to the Department of Justice under the False Claims Act from 2009 to 2012 soared to $13.3 billion.[40]

In these cases, private counsel typically negotiates its own fee agreement with the relator, which is usually on a contingency basis. Rather than resist these actions across the board, the Department of Justice has proclaimed its support for a "public-private partnership to fight fraud."[41] To the surprise of some, the Supreme Court has upheld the qui tam action against claims that it violated the "case and controversy" requirements of Article III of the U.S. Constitution because the "relator" had not itself suffered injury.[42]

What the qui tam example really shows is that public enforcers will welcome the assistance of private counsel if they retain the discretion to employ them. In truth, in the qui tam example, public enforcers have less such discretion than in cases where they retain counsel, because they cannot choose the law firm and must intervene to dismiss an action they consider unpromising, which can elicit unwanted publicity and press attention. In contrast, a decision not to retain private counsel is far less visible or politically dangerous.

D. THE LEGALITY OF CONTINGENT-FEE AGREEMENTS BY PUBLIC AGENCIES

1. THE CASE LAW. In the wake of both the 1998 multistate settlement with the tobacco industry and several follow-on state actions over lead paint and water pollution that used private counsel, industry groups, de-

fendants, and conservative academics have challenged the legality of contingent-fee agreements in this context. Some even argued that it was unconstitutional for the states to use contingent-fee agreements.[43] Nevertheless, to date, courts have found such agreements between state attorneys general and private counsel to be lawful and otherwise permissible—at least if the state maintained control and oversight over the litigation.[44] Thus, if the agency insists (as the FDIC's deskbook clearly insists) that all important litigation decisions be cleared with the agency, then the existing precedents suggest that contingent fees paid by financial regulators would be upheld.

Such oversight can be maintained in a variety of ways. In the case of those financial regulators that have broad antifraud jurisdiction (such as the SEC and the Commodities Futures Trading Corporation [CFTC]), the agency would conduct an initial investigation and would first determine that an enforcement proceeding was justified. Only then would it retain private counsel to prosecute the action. This division between investigation and enforcement ensures greater oversight.

Ideally, the agency should first decide that there was a probability that a violation had occurred before it retained private counsel to bring an action, and then it would enter into a detailed retainer agreement that required all important decisions to be brought back to the agency. This would protect against the danger that potentially astronomical damages could lead the private enforcer to accept and pursue a long-shot cause of damages. In theory, a potential recovery of a billion dollars in damages could lead a risk-neutral private attorney to accept an action that had only a 10 percent chance of success—if the costs to it would be hypothetically $33 million or less.[45]

From this perspective, the decision to hire private counsel could resemble the act of an eighteenth century sovereign in commissioning a privateer to roam the high seas to seek out and plunder the Crown's enemies. In reality, however, this is a grossly overstated fear, as contingent-fee–compensated counsel rarely take such gambles (and usually only pursue cases in which it thinks it sees a probability of success).[46] Still, a formal determination by the agency that there was such a probability of success would eliminate this theoretical danger that contingent fees could encourage the pursuit of long shots.

2. EXECUTIVE ORDER 13,433. Even if the case law poses no insurmountable obstacles to the use of contingent fees, a serious administrative obstacle does exist—at least for the present. In 2007, President George W. Bush issued an executive order prohibiting federal agencies from paying contingent fees.[47] Executive Order 13,433 ("Protecting American Taxpayers from Payment of Contingency Fees") was largely a response to the state tobacco settlement, which annoyed Republicans (possibly because it enriched plaintiff's attorneys, who usually support Democratic candidates). Although the executive order contains some major exceptions,[48] it covers the independent federal agencies, including the SEC and CFTC.[49]

To date, the FDIC, FHFA, and NCUA have escaped Executive Order 13,433 by arguing that, as receivers or conservatives, they stand in the shoes of the failed institution and obtain whatever rights and powers that institution had to sue its own officers, directors, and others.[50] In theory, the FDIC, FHFA, and NCUA are not exercising the powers of a federal agency that is subject to the executive order but are simply utilizing the failed institution's own powers. Whatever the merits of this argument, it would not be available to the SEC or CFTC, which do not act as receivers.

Executive orders can, of course, be modified or repealed, and Executive Order 13,433 also permits the attorney general to grant exemptions. Given the long-standing close relationship between the plaintiff's bar and the Democratic Party, it would not be surprising if appropriate amendments were made under a Democratic president to that executive order— at least if the plaintiff's bar decided it wanted to exploit this opportunity.

E. THE POLICY ISSUES

1. THE IMPACT OF PROSECUTORIAL DISCRETIONS. This author has previously argued the case for use of private counsel by public enforcers[51] and received an angry retort from Robert Khuzami, then the immediately past director of the SEC's Enforcement Division, and George Canellos, then the acting director of the Enforcement Division (and the SEC attorney most responsible for the decision not to sue the Lehman

executives).[52] The Coffee proposal, they argued, "assumes that the SEC's general goal is to sue as many deep-pocketed parties, and collect as much in penalties as possible."[53] Instead, they responded, "[T]he SEC's goal is aggressively to uphold the law and serve the interests of justice. That means evaluating each case fairly, suing only those whom the evidence shows violated the law, assessing relative culpability of different participants, and assessing a penalty that is appropriate for the particular violation."[54] Stripped of its rhetoric, this is essentially a claim that prosecutorial discretion is important and would be sacrificed by using private counsel. Of course, prosecutorial discretion is important. But it is not lost, simply because outside counsel is used or contingent fees employed. Every major U.S. corporation uses outside counsel, but does not delegate decisions affecting the corporation's important interests to outside counsel. Instead, the corporation's general counsel monitors closely, and settlement decisions involve the corporation's highest executives. Similarly, a public agency's general counsel or enforcement chief would play an analogous role. As here proposed, the public enforcer would conduct the investigation, make the decision to sue, and then retain outside counsel. The fee agreement would clearly indicate that only the agency could approve a settlement, that it could insist on injunctive and nonpecuniary relief, and could replace counsel at any time.

This is in contrast to private enforcement, where private counsel in a securities class action is monitored only by a lead plaintiff (usually a public pension fund). Although some institutional investors do monitor class counsel in securities class actions (to varying degrees) and do seek nonpecuniary relief (usually involving corporate governance reforms), they do not have the same incentives as a public agency and generally want to maximize the size of the settlement more than obtain other forms of relief. Nor are they politically accountable (as a public agency is). Thus, closer monitoring should be anticipated in this context.

To be sure, plaintiff's attorneys will want to maximize the monetary recovery. This is not necessarily bad. The low recoveries in SEC enforcement actions could be the consequence of the SEC's sense of justice, or it could be the consequence of the SEC's overwhelming caseload, risk aversion, or even the desire of bureaucrats to live the quiet life. In practice, defense counsel negotiates with the SEC by pointing to the settlements in other cases, arguing for parity with the past. Yet, there can be a social need for increased deterrence that this perspective overlooks. Justice does not require treating all cases alike in terms of the penalty levels of a decade ago. The Justice Department has clearly recognized this in its much increased penalties (such as its $15 billion settlement with JPMorgan), but the SEC continues to look backward.

2. THE IMPACT ON AGENCY MORALE.   The 2008 financial crisis demoralized the SEC (in part, but not exclusively, because of the Madoff scandal). Turning to outside counsel for major cases might aggravate this demoralization by reducing the staff's self-image. In their own minds, they might appear to resemble a junior varsity, which has to stand aside in truly major cases. Very likely, this sense of being downgraded undergirds the SEC's adamant refusal to consider use of private counsel.

Yet, the same resistance has not materialized at the FDIC or FHFA. There, in-house counsel seem comfortable with their role as supervising attorneys, from whom outside counsel must seek approval with respect to all major decisions. That role is by no means ego deflating—just as general counsel at public corporations do not resist outside counsel or insist on suing themselves. In-house counsel would also still handle those cases that required immediate action (such as cases needing an injunction to avert irreparable injury).

Nonetheless, adapting to the use of outside counsel would be a major adjustment for SEC staffers, but not for other agencies, where the ability to use private counsel has been easily accepted because it enables the agency to take on major cases that otherwise would not be brought.

F. A HOPEFUL CONCLUSION

Conflicts of interest can arise everywhere, including in the proposed union of public agencies and private counsel. Some scholars have forcefully argued that *elected* state officials are particularly likely to serve as unfaithful agents of class members' interests.[55] Fair as that criticism may be, it is not what is here proposed. Independent federal agencies (the EPA, the SEC, the FTC, the CFTC) do not confront the same conflict between voters and class members that state and elected officials face; federal public agencies have long been active enforcers but have been hobbled by funding and manpower limitations. If a political consensus can be forged that more enforcement is needed, this proposed union of public and private enforcement has fewer risks than either depending on largely unsupervised private counsel suing through class actions or elected state officials suing as the representatives of class members.[56]

PART FOUR

THE FUTURE

THE FOCUS IN THIS PART now shifts to the future. What elements of the American system of entrepreneurial litigation should Europe (and other jurisdictions) adopt to create an effective system for aggregate representation? What substitutes are possible? This part will suggest a hybrid of the model common in U.S. public interest litigation with the entrepreneurial litigation model in order to downsize (but not eliminate) the entrepreneurial component.

Similarly, if the private attorney general often lacks adequate accountability, who can we find to guard the guardian? Courts by themselves seem unable or unwilling to monitor the settlement process rigorously. They need allies. Thus, this part will propose movement toward a "semiprivate attorney general" in which private and public enforcement are better integrated (but without sacrificing the independence of the private attorney general).

10

THE GLOBALIZATION OF THE CLASS ACTION: CAN THE PRIVATE ATTORNEY GENERAL BE EXPORTED?

AMERICAN IDEAS ARE OFTEN COPIED ABROAD. In particular, American legal ideas have proven highly influential. A "rights revolution"—whose centerpiece was the Civil Rights Act of 1964—swept the United States in the last decades of the twentieth century, establishing new protections, not only for civil rights, but also with regard to employment discrimination and environmental protection. In the United States, these new substantive rights soon came to be enforced by the class action, which had been deliberately redesigned in 1966 to encourage the private enforcement of civil rights.[1] Yet, while much of the world has followed the United States in its recognition of these rights, few nations adopted anything that closely resembles the U.S. class action.

As late as 2000, one could only point to three nations—Canada, Australia, and Israel—in which "opt out" class actions were authorized.[2] Since then, a few European countries—most notably, Denmark and Portugal—have adopted litigation procedures that resemble an "opt out" class action for money damages,[3] but, elsewhere in Europe, the preference has been to authorize only relatively pale substitutes that require class members to opt in.[4] More importantly, whatever the "law on the books," the "law in action" reveals even greater disparities in the actual use of class actions. One survey (as of 2010) found that Australia had seen 245 class actions between 1992 and 2009; Canada had experienced 411 class actions between 2007 and 2011; and Israel had seen 750 class action complaints filed between 2007 and 2011.[5] After these three, the next largest number was only 20–30 class actions in Indonesia—obviously implying a dramatic falling off in actual class action activity.

Outside of the United States and a few other "common law" countries, actual class actions remain as rare as unicorn sightings. Even in Australia and Canada, class action practice differs significantly from that in the United States. Although both Australia and Canada permit "opt out" class actions (in which one plaintiff can seek to represent thousands of others without their consent), Australia does not allow contingent fees based on the size of the class recovery, and both Australia and Canada follow the traditional British "loser pays" rule on fee shifting. Although a sizable number of class actions have been filed in Australia, this seems largely attributable to the development in that country of third-party litigation funding, under which financial institutions, not the class counsel, finance the action.

Although the number of class actions actually litigated continues to be small, legal changes are under way, and the number of jurisdictions authorizing them has recently increased. Following the Asian Financial Crisis of 1997, both South Korea and Taiwan authorized class actions but with special constraints. In South Korea (which does not authorize contingency fees and follows the "loser pays" rule), legislation recognized the availability of class actions as of 2005, but the first action was not brought until 2009.[6] To prevent the development of professional plaintiff's firms, the South Korean law precludes any attorney from serving as either lead counsel or lead plaintiff more than three times in the three previous years.[7] Not surprisingly, very few class actions have been brought in South Korea. Taiwan went even further to preclude professional plaintiffs by creating a government-sanctioned nonprofit organization, known as the Securities and Futures Investors Protection Center (or IPC), which alone is authorized to bring securities class actions. As of 2013, it had brought some seventy-one class actions, almost always as a parallel action to a criminal case.[8] This may well represent active enforcement, but it seems doubtful that this should be viewed as private enforcement.

Overall, a 2011 survey found that some twenty-one countries now authorized class actions (most fairly recently),[9] but few permit "opt out" class actions. Generally, the class member is required to opt into the class. Given the rational passivity of the small claimant, an opt-in rule greatly limits the likely size of the class and the potential damages (and thus the economic leverage possessed by the plaintiff's attorney). Most countries also prohibit private attorneys from charging fees based on the amount of the damages obtained, thereby barring "entrepreneurial litigation" (at least to the extent that the attorney serves as the entrepreneur). Finally, many of the countries recognizing the class action in principle have limited standing to represent the class to public officials or nonprofit organizations approved by the government.[10] This standing limitation may be an attempt to preclude "greedy" plaintiff's attorneys from using nominal clients to file broad class actions, or it may reflect a broader skepticism about private enforcement and a European preference for public regulation.

Not surprisingly, American commentators surveying these developments have suggested that legislation authorizing class actions will have little impact unless economic incentives exist to implement these new remedies.[11] That may be definitionally true, but it still amounts to Americans asserting that Europe should be more like America. That advice will predictably not be heeded. Still, this does not mean that only "American-style" class actions can work. Functional substitutes may be possible for each of the three critical elements in the American model, namely, (1) an opt-out class in which any eligible class member can represent his or her fellow class members without any affirmative consent on their part, (2) contingent fees that will be judicially awarded based substantially on the size of the recovery, and (3) the "American Rule" under which the loser generally does not pay the winner's legal fees. Those ideas, established in the United States, continue to be resisted elsewhere. This chapter starts from the premise that legal rules must be fitted to the local institutional structure and culture. Nonetheless, it will assert that it is possible to design a workable (although not equivalent) substitute for the "American-style" class action.

In addition, there is reason to believe that the American-style class action would probably not work in the European (and other) contexts, even if there were no legal barriers to its implementation. Three barriers, which have generally been ignored in discussions about the transportability of the "American-style" class action, need to be faced at the outset:

1. THE ABSENCE OF JURIES. Outside the United States, civil juries are seldom used. Within the U.S. legal system, much of the power that the plaintiff's attorney possesses comes from the attorney's ability to take the case to a jury. The availability of juries in civil cases implies greater unpredictability of outcomes—and thereby increases the plaintiff's attorney's leverage. Risk-averse defendants do not know what a jury will do but can predict judges with some accuracy. Defendants can also appeal the decisions of judges more easily, while jury decisions are given greater deference by most appellate courts. In a world without juries, defendants would face less pressure to settle, and class actions in the United States are almost always resolved through settlements, not trials.

2. THE UNAVAILABILITY OF DISCOVERY. The U.S. legal system is unique in the degree to which it allows litigants to obtain discovery of confidential information—documents, e-mails, and testimony—from their adversaries. This arms the plaintiff and permits it to prove complex factual matters that could not be established in the absence of such discovery. Discovery is much less available in other legal systems, and thus private enforcement is constrained. Ultimately, even if the plaintiff's attorney could receive a contingent fee based on the size of the recovery and could escape "loser pays" fee shifting, a plaintiff's attorney still would be less effective in a "discovery-less" civil law system, and entrepreneurial litigation would thus be less threatening to defendants.

3. ADVERSARIAL VERSUS INQUISITORIAL LEGAL SYSTEMS. The U.S. legal system is fundamentally an adversarial system, with the judge's role generally restricted to that of a neutral umpire. The evidence in a case is gathered, marshaled, and presented by the plaintiff's attorney. In contrast, most European civil law systems are "inquisitorial" systems, with the judge combining, to a degree, the roles of the

judge and the prosecutor.[12] Typically, the judge conducts an investigation, hears evidence out of court, and gathers and evaluates the evidence, while the plaintiff's attorney plays a necessarily lesser role. Because the plaintiff's attorney is not the central engine driving the litigation (as he is in the United States), he cannot control the settlement process (as he can in the United States), and he correspondingly deserves (and may only receive) a lesser reward.

All these factors imply that, even if "American-style" class actions were available in Europe and other civil law systems, entrepreneurial litigation might still not take hold. U.S. judges are accustomed to and accept high-profile plaintiff's attorneys, but it is less clear that judges trained in an inquisitorial system would accord plaintiff's attorneys a similar role. But if the plaintiff's attorney does less, society needs less to reward him, and so the entrepreneurial zeal that underlies U.S. class litigation might be dampened.

None of this implies that civil law legal systems, with their different procedures and concepts of the judiciary's role, should not adopt class actions or other procedures to facilitate aggregate litigation. But it does strongly suggest the need for caution before predicting that, once the class action is transplanted to Europe (or elsewhere), it will flourish and flower as luxuriantly as it has in the United States. Rather, the private attorney general may be both economically and culturally constrained.

With this cautionary introduction, it is now time to consider the degree to which some variant of the "private attorney general" (here meaning a private party seeking to enforce public policies and pursue public law goals for private gain) can be transported to legal systems dissimilar to that of the United States. Put more simply, this chapter asks: to what extent can we have "entrepreneurial litigation" without the entrepreneur?

In overview, this chapter will conclude that the "European-style" class action will likely generate lower recoveries and less deterrence than the American-style alternative, but it still has its own distinct advantages, including a lesser vulnerability to collusion or extortion. Equally important, neither the American model nor the European model seems likely to evolve substantially in the direction of the other. In all legal environments, any mechanism for aggregate litigation has to be made compatible with existing institutional arrangements, cultures, and political values. In short, it is futile to argue that European resistance to contingent fees or concern for litigant autonomy should end; rather, it is necessary to explore what can be achieved within those constraints. Four specific issues need to be faced: (1) who should lead the class?; (2) should the class employ an Opt-In or Opt-Out rule to determine its composition?; (3) how and by whom should the class be financed?; and (4) can we adjust the "loser pays" rule to enable class litigation?

1. GOVERNANCE AND STANDING: WHO SHOULD LEAD THE CLASS ACTION?   In the United States' "opt out" class action, the class representative need not possess any special expertise but must be able to provide "fair and adequate" representation to the class.[13] Generally, courts read this requirement narrowly to mean only that the class representative not have an obvious conflict of interest. This means that the plaintiff's attorney can use as his nominal client a small claimant who will have little incentive or capacity to monitor the attorney (and who may sometimes be economically beholden to the attorney). To a degree, securities class actions are different because the position of class representative (or "lead plaintiff" in the language of the Private Securities Litigation Reform Act of 1995 [PSLRA]) will go to the volunteering class member with the largest economic stake in the action. Although this reform has worked well for securities class actions, it cannot be broadly generalized because, outside the context of securities class actions, there are seldom class members with substantial economic stakes in the action. Either the action is entirely composed of small claimants with "negative value" claims, or the large claimants have opted out, preferring to handle their claims on their own.[14] Thus, in the U.S. system, the only monitor in the typical class action for money damages will be the court, which must approve the settlement as fair and reasonable. Because the reviewing court has a strong self-interest in approving the settlement (and thereby clearing its docket), the U.S. system has long been characterized by weak monitoring of class counsel and only limited accountability.

In contrast, a common European pattern is to limit standing to bring a class action to associations that the government has approved for the purpose of bringing representative actions.[15] This approach has both obvious advantages and disadvantages. On the one hand, the government might limit approval to those associations likely to support its policies (and thereby preclude dissent). Imagine if the state of Mississippi in the 1950s could have limited standing to assert a class action raising civil rights issues to associations approved by it. Even when censorship is not the intent, a limited number of associations might become logistically constrained, thus bringing only a limited number of actions and leaving some meritorious actions unasserted. Further, competition among private enforcers may be desirable, and this approach would constrain it.

On the other hand, a key advantage of limiting standing to some form of association is that the class representative will have expertise and experience, which (with the notable exception of securities class actions) the class representative seldom has in class actions for money damages in the United States today. In fact, the United States does have considerable experience with the use of associations to organize and bring class actions. This is the basic structure of "public interest" litigation in the United States. Litigation seeking school desegregation or attacking racial discrimination was often brought by the NAACP Legal Defense Fund; similarly, the defense of civil liberties was frequently led by the American Civil Liberties Union (ACLU); and environmental class actions have regularly been brought by the Sierra Club and a number of other environmental "public interest" law firms. Under U.S. law, these bodies generally have standing to represent their members' interests.[16] Inherently, the ACLU, the NAACP Legal Defense Fund, and the Sierra Club possess great expertise and are unlikely to be overreached by a plaintiff's attorney.

Such "public interest" associations are probably at least as accountable to their members or donors as are the "lead plaintiffs" in securities class actions. Whether these members and donors enjoy voting rights or only have influence based on their donations, they represent an independent source of accountability that is largely missing in private class actions.[17] Involvement in a collusive settlement might damage a public interest organization's reputation and possibly inhibit future fund-raising. This does not deny that conflicts can arise (and in fact have arisen) in public interest litigation between the interests of the donors or stakeholders in the "public interest" entity and the class action's members.[18] But basically the interests of the class actions' members and those of the "public interest" entity's donors seem much more closely aligned than the interests of a plaintiff's attorney and the class that he or she represents. The tension is inevitable between the attorney's interest in a settlement and the class member's interest in the highest net damages recovery.

Active as public interest entities have been in class action litigation, they have usually focused only on injunctive and/or equitable relief and left money damages actions to the private bar. This parallels the contemporary European experience, where public interest groups largely bring only injunctive actions or actions for declaratory relief. What explains this restraint in the United States? The probable answer is that money damages actions are costly and beyond the means of leanly funded public interest groups. Although examples can be cited of partnerships between private firms and public entities to litigate large actions for money damages,[19] the public interest entity will generally not be able to finance costly litigation for monetary damages. Thus, if financing the litigation is the critical problem, the optimal design for the future (as later discussed) may involve a union between a public interest entity or association and a third-party litigation funder.

Given the lesser potential for conflicts of interest when a "public interest" entity will serve as the class representative, the best compromise here would be to require the use of a public interest group as the class representative, but in addition to require the court, before certifying the class, to make specific findings that the class representative had adequate experience and expertise in the field to represent the class and adequate independence to withstand the influence of any litigation funder or other interested party. This would be a substantially higher standard than prevails today in the United States.

2. OPT-IN VERSUS OPT-OUT CLASSES.   With only a few exceptions, existing European class action procedures employ an opt-in rather than an opt-out procedure.[20] This preference rests on twin pillars: (1) the normative principle that a litigant should not be bound by agents that the litigant has not authorized to act on the litigant's behalf and (2) a strong aversion to American-style entrepreneurial litigation (which is frankly not well understood in Europe). But observers in both the United States

and Europe have expressed skepticism that opt-in classes are feasible, for at least three distinct reasons: (1) participation rates will be low, with the result that neither much deterrence nor victim compensation will be generated;[21] (2) a "free rider" problem will discourage anyone from volunteering to serve as the representative plaintiff, because those who remain passive will share in the gains of the action but not in the possible losses that follow from the common European "loser pays" rule;[22] and (3) opt-in classes deny defendants the virtue of finality.[23] All these claims have some merit, but they can easily be overstated.

a. Participation Rates.   Leading U.S. scholars have estimated that the rate of opt-outs in consumer cases between 1993 and 2003 was, on average, less than 0.2 percent—less than two in a thousand.[24] But there is danger in relying on this statistic to determine the likely participation percentage in an opt-in class. Opting out makes no sense for a person holding a "negative value" claim, while opting in is entirely rational. The likelihood of rational behavior (i.e., opting in) cannot be reliably estimated by looking to the rate of irrational behavior (i.e., opting out from a "negative value" class action).

A better measure of likely participation comes from the actual experience in those European countries that have actively employed an opt-in procedure. Professor Henrik Lindblom of Sweden has surveyed the experience under his country's recent opt-in class action procedure, which was adopted in 2002.[25] As of 2007, he found nine examples, several of which are next discussed briefly.

- In a 2003 case, an airline went bankrupt after having received payments from passengers for tickets. An individual brought suit on behalf of himself and some 700 other passengers. After the court with jurisdiction over the case notified these 700 passengers, 500 opted in, and the case settled for roughly 70,000 euros.[26] Because the value of each individual action for ticket payments was modest, these were quintessential "negative value" claims.
- In a 2004 case, a nonprofit corporation was formed by prospective litigants to sue a life insurance company that transferred substantial assets to its parent, allegedly for inadequate consideration.[27] Out

of 1.2 million policy holders, some 15,000 individuals opted in and also paid membership dues of fifteen euros, allowing the nonprofit organization to amass capital of over 200,000 euros to fund the litigation.[28] Although this percentage may seem low, it must be remembered that no actual loss was experienced by these class members and that they also had to make a cash payment to opt in.

- In 2004, the Swedish consumer ombudsman brought a class action on behalf of 7,000 customers of a utility for failure to supply electricity, as agreed, under a fixed price contract.[29] This was the first public enforcement action under the Swedish class action statute.[30]
- In 2007, the residents of a suburb adjoining an airport formed a nonprofit organization, which then sued the Swedish Airports and Air Navigation Service for damages resulting from aviation noise on behalf of some 20,000 residents. At least 7,000 individuals in the area affected by the aviation noise opted into the class.[31]

Few other European countries appear to have had the same depth of experience as Sweden with opt-in class actions. But in Belgium, which at the time permitted only opt-in classes, some 5,000 minority shareholders (out of an identified total of 11,000) were convinced to opt in to a class action against a major corporation by a consumer organization and a consulting firm specializing in the representation of minority shareholders.[32] This roughly 45 percent opt-in ratio is even more impressive because many of these shareholders also had to advance legal fees to join the action.[33]

Anecdotal as this evidence is, both the Swedish examples and the Belgian case seem noteworthy because of the lack of any prior relationship or community among the class members in these cases. Commentators have opined that opt-in procedures might work only in cases where the potential class members had a preexisting relationship (such as employees in the same office in a case involving a workplace or labor dispute).[34] But customers of a utility, defrauded minority shareholders, airline passengers, insurance policy holders, or residents of a large suburb typically have little in common. Nor is it likely that most of these class members in these cases who opted in considered any of these disputes to be matters of urgent importance to them. This experience suggests that if clear notice is given individually to class members and a credible nonprofit consumer organization or public ombudsman leads the action, rates of participation in the range of one-third to over one-half are possible. Although class members rarely respond to the notices they are given in U.S. class actions, this may be in part a product of the fact that class counsel has no need to induce them to respond in an opt-out system and may even hope that they remain quietly passive. Finally, the Internet makes possible much more direct, targeted, and convincing marketing by those who truly want to reach their audience.

Some U.S. experience also shows that opt-in rates can reach or exceed 50 percent of the potential class under favorable circumstances. Several U.S. statutes—most notably the Fair Labor Standards Act (FLSA),[35] but also the Age Discrimination in Employment Act (ADEA)[36] and the Equal Pay Act[37]—employ a mandatory opt-in procedure. A 1996 study by the Federal Judicial Center calculated the opt-in rates for three FLSA cases and found them to be 39 percent, 61 percent, and 73 percent.[38] A more recent study of some twenty-one FLSA cases found the average opt-in rate to be considerably lower at 15.71 percent,[39] but it also found that if the two actions with the highest and lowest rates were excluded as outliers, this rate rose to 23.34 percent.[40] In one case, 204 out of 228 claimants, or 89.5 percent, opted in, showing that at least under some circumstances a high percentage of claimants can be induced to opt in.[41] Moreover, as plaintiff's attorneys become more adept in using websites and e-mail solicitations to reach potential class members, participation rates seem likely to rise.[42]

From a public policy perspective, this evidence can be read in different ways. Clearly, the likely participation rate for eligible claimants in an opt-in class action will be significantly below the automatic 100 percent participation rate in an opt-out class action. But, as next discussed, class members who do not opt out in an opt-out class action may still go uncompensated because they often do not file claims post-settlement; in contrast, opt-in class members, having elected to participate, are unlikely to be so indifferent.

Although opt-in participation levels will seldom approach even 50 percent of those eligible, it would be a mistake to compare such a 50 percent ceiling on the opt-in class with a 100 percent ceiling in the opt-out class. The great fallacy in contrasting the high or universal participation rate in opt-out class actions with the lower rate in opt-in actions is that this comparison looks only at the front end of the class action and ignores the back end of the proceeding. Although the opt-out class action includes everyone, relatively low percentages of the class may actually file claims after a settlement is achieved. Professors Cox and Thomas found that less than 30 percent of the highly sophisticated institutional investors in the securities class actions that they studied filed claims after a settlement had been reached.[43] In some special contexts, the rate is even lower and may fall to 1 percent or less.[44] Because institutional investors generally hold claims for significant amounts (particularly in proportion to the minimal cost of filing a claim) and because they are highly rational, this evidence suggests that proponents of the opt-out class have overstated their case. The presumed difference in participation rates may be largely meaningless if claims are not filed. In short, even if the opt-out class action automatically includes all the passive holders of negative value claims, these negative value claimants do not actually benefit from such an action when, for whatever reason, they fail to file a claim. Apathy seemingly reemerges at the back end of the opt-out class action where the need to file a claim proves to be as significant a barrier as the need to take an affirmative step at the front end of an opt-in class action.

Little is really known about why so few eligible claimants file claims.[45] In some contexts, the typically modest recovery rate may be so low that class members simply remain indifferent to what they see as only nominal compensation. Rational claimants will not expend their time to secure very small payments. Alternatively, it may sometimes be that defendants or sophisticated claimants deliberately discourage less-experienced claimants from filing by making the proof of claim process difficult (in order to maximize the recovery for themselves).[46] If the settlement precludes any reversion of the settlement fund to the defendant (as it usually does), a low claim filing rate implies that those claimants who do file will receive a higher (and conceivably even a "windfall") recovery. Whatever the reason, if our focus is on the actual compensatory benefits for small claimants, the proponents of the opt-out class action have probably oversold its advantages. Ultimately, the irony is that while European opt-in procedures fail at the front end, U.S. opt-out procedures fail similarly at the back end—in both cases because of client apathy. That is, procedures for filing claims in the United States may screen out smaller claimants as effectively as the opt-in requirements in European class actions do at the front end of litigation.

In this light, the truer advantage of the opt-out class over the opt-in class involves not any difference in compensatory benefits, but the greater deterrent threat that the opt-out class generates by aggregating more claims. Yet, even if the opt-out class is a greater deterrent, defendants may respond that this is illegitimate pressure so long as many or most of these class members will never file claims or receive any payment from the class action. Normatively, defenders of the European approach can object that the opt-out class action distorts the outcomes in litigation by generating an "extortionate" pressure to settle and sometimes even "windfall" recoveries to those class members that do file claims. Even while conceding the greater deterrent threat of the opt-out class action, Europeans may still believe that extraordinary and deliberately punitive penalties should be reserved for public enforcement, where their use is tempered by prosecutorial discretion. No attempt will be made here to resolve this debate, but it seems certain to continue.

b. Finality.   Opt-in classes do not produce finality the way that opt-out classes do. For example, if an opt-in class of one hundred or so members settles, this does not necessarily resolve the litigation, as new actions on behalf of still other opt-in class members may be filed by other attorneys. Indeed, success breeds imitation, so that the successful resolution of one opt-in class may encourage the filing of others (possibly in other countries in Europe). This may make defendants less willing to settle an opt-in class if to do so will only expose them to successive opt-in classes on behalf of other claimants.

Conversely, from a public policy perspective, this asserted disadvantage may be thought a major attraction of the opt-in class action. When there is no finality, there is also much less incentive for collusion. Defendants cannot as easily "bribe" the plaintiff's attorney to sell out the interests of the class, because the attorney only represents a much smaller group of individuals (who are also less easy to overreach because they are at least aware of the action into which they opted). Collusion is much more likely when the class action can resolve the claims of all absent class members who are defined in the complaint to be within the class (which is the pattern in an opt-out class).

To the extent finality is needed, opt-in classes can be designed so that finality is obtained by a variety of other means. For example, the statute of limitations could be adjusted and shortened so that it expired some short period (say, six months) after the resolution of an opt-in class if adequate notice is given.

3. LITIGATION FINANCE. If much of the world will not accept the contingent fee in class actions (as appears likely), the problem of funding litigation becomes central. Ideally, who should finance class litigation? In principle, the party that can best evaluate the action's prospective merits and monitor the attorney's efforts should be willing to provide more funding and at lower cost than others. In this regard, the contingent fee system of financing U.S. class actions probably has some efficiency advantages. First, attorneys have obvious expertise in evaluating the meritoriousness and settlement value of litigation, whereas other potential funders would need to hire lawyers to conduct this inquiry for them. Second, attorneys are likely to be involved in multiple lawsuits and can naturally realize the benefits of portfolio diversification; this should enable them to reach litigation decisions in a more objective, risk-neutral fashion. This point can, however, be pushed too far. Few plaintiff law firms can achieve the same level of efficient diversification as can a large hedge fund that invests in all forms of risky assets.

Conversely, when the attorney finances the action, we surrender the possibility that alternative funders might monitor the attorney's performance. Arguably, attorney-financed litigation is less efficient because class members lose the benefit of such an arm's-length party monitoring their attorney and protecting the class from collusion. To be sure, the PSLRA did respond to this monitoring problem by deliberately creating an agent (the lead plaintiff) to monitor class counsel, but this model can only be safely extended to those relatively few litigation contexts (basically, securities class actions) where individual plaintiffs are likely to hold sufficiently large stakes to induce them to monitor.

Quite apart from any efficiency arguments, much of the world has long resisted the contingent fee on ethical grounds (and only recently have there been small steps taken toward liberalizing this restriction).[47] The concern behind this resistance has been the fear that contingent fee financing compromises attorney loyalty and results in conflicts between the attorney and the client. Although American commentators believe this concern has been overstated,[48] the prevalence of this concern underlines the need to consider functional substitutes. Clearly, other potential sources of litigation finance are available. For example, hedge funds, which increasingly invest in all forms of illiquid and risky investments, and could easily fund many class actions. Indeed, as next discussed, specialized litigation funding firms with large investment portfolios have already arisen and prospered in Australia and extended their reach to the United Kingdom and Canada. Europe also appears to be welcoming this new development—far more so than the United States. Nonetheless, issues remain.

a. The Australian and British Experiences.   In Australia, which does not permit contingent fees,[49] litigation funding by private firms has become a large and accepted financial service industry—largely since 2000.[50] Some five firms dominate the Australian market, and the largest is listed on the Australian stock exchange.[51] The scale of these firms is shown by the fact that the largest held a portfolio of litigation investments (as of early 2007) with a total value of A\$1 billion.[52] Unlike U.S. funding firms (which invest almost exclusively in individual personal injury cases), the Australian firms regularly invest in class actions, and the largest regularly charges about 30 percent of the net proceeds of the case plus litigation costs—a fee that roughly approximates what U.S. plaintiff's attorneys traditionally received in class actions.[53] As of the end of 2006, the litigation funding industry in Australia was investing about A\$20 million annually to support plaintiff's litigation, and the industry seemed to be profitable.[54]

Australian litigation funders appear to take an active role in the litigation, often selecting the law firm and making important litigation decisions.[55] They justify this involvement by arguing that they do no more than do insurance companies on the defense side of the litigation.[56] In their view, the litigation funder is the functional equivalent of the insurer (although insurance companies negotiate typically with a sophisticated corporate client).

From Australia, litigation funding spread to the United Kingdom, which also restricts contingent fees, and the litigation funding industry has developed rapidly there.[57] A recent survey finds that most litigation funders charge between 20 and 40 percent of the award or settlement, and some charge even more.[58] Hedge funds also occasionally participate in the U.K. litigation funding business.[59] In both these common law countries and also in South Africa, the practice of third-party litigation funding has received judicial acceptance.[60]

b. The Early European Experience. Third parties can now fund litigation in virtually all civil law jurisdictions in Europe (with the exceptions of Greece and Portugal).[61] Even more importantly, litigation funders in Europe have begun to finance at least one type of group action: antitrust actions against cartels.[62] In a unique European variation on litigation funding, some of these funders simply purchase (or are assigned) the legal claim and do not need therefore to represent the class.[63]

In general, litigation funders appear to be very selective, accepting, according to one recent survey, only an estimated 8 percent of the claims that they review.[64] Their overall success in Europe remains uncertain, with few, if any, notable successes, and some firms have already exited the market. Although the jury is still out on the economic viability of litigation funding in Europe, two conclusions can be safely reached: (1) given the highly selective approach of litigation funders, no litigation explosion seems likely; and (2) litigation funding faces fewer legal obstacles in civil law systems than in common law systems (particularly including the United States).

c. The Issues in Third-Party Funding. On an abstract level, little distinguishes the contingency fee from funding by a third party. But separating the attorney from the litigation funder does highlight the fact that those financing the action will want some control over the litigation, particularly with respect to settlement decisions. This may be ethically problematic,[65] but it is not unprecedented, as insurance companies also regularly monitor the progress of the litigation in cases they are funding. Arguably, the ethical issues in litigation finance are even more sensitive in the case of third-party funders. First, the attorney as funder is subject to professional rules and a culture that insist on loyalty to the client.

Nothing similarly constrains a hedge fund as a source of litigation funding. Second, at least in some litigation contexts, such as environmental law, employment discrimination, and civil rights, injunctive and equitable relief may be as important to the class as money damages (or more so). Predictably, a third-party funder will be interested only in the economic return, whereas the attorney might gain reputational value from a litigation victory, even if the damages are modest. Thus, third-party funding will likely alter the balance between monetary and non-monetary relief in settlements.

Use of a third-party funder also increases the number of agents with self-interests in the case that are distinct from the client's. Is this good or bad? A plausible case can be made that, if the funder is restricted in terms of the control that it can exercise over the case, this is a less troubling relationship than having the attorney fund the case because the attorney will always have a controlling influence over litigation decisions. One can at least imagine a structure under which third-party funding is permitted, but the class counsel is instructed that all litigation decisions must be made in the interest of the class. Because class counsel would be denied a contingent fee under this structure, it might prove more loyal to the class than it is today when its economic interests and fiduciary duty sometimes point in divergent directions. The conventional wisdom about large contingent fees is that they can motivate the attorney to settle prematurely.

A third-party funder might also have such an incentive to settle prematurely, but if the attorney were paid on a noncontingent basis, it would have little, if any, incentive to settle early (and may even wish to stretch out the litigation, so long as the attorney is paid on an attractive hourly rate basis). Hence, the attorney's self-interest could counterbalance those of the litigation funder (but it is highly speculative whether the attorney could long resist pressure from the attorney's source of finance).

The litigation funding structure is necessarily complex and arguably cumbersome, as a class would have (1) a class counsel, (2) a public interest entity serving as the class representative, and (3) a separate litigation funder. Still, there may be advantages in having "agents watching agents."[66] In particular, the litigation funder would be in a position to monitor the attorney, while both the representative plaintiff (often a nonprofit organization in Europe) and the class counsel could negotiate the financial arrangement with the third-party funding firm.

4. FEE SHIFTING—WHAT TO DO WITH THE "LOSER PAYS" RULE? The "loser pays" rule creates a strong disincentive for anyone to serve as the class representative in an opt-in class action. Indeed, if simply the act of opting in made one liable for a share of the costs (or, worse yet, jointly and severally liable for all costs in the event of a loss), no rational person would ever opt in. Because the defendants' costs are likely to be greater than the plaintiffs' costs, a "loser pays" rule will generally enable the defendants to pressure the plaintiffs. Thus, to be viable, the opt-in class must find someone else to assume this potential liability. The most likely candidate is the litigation funder, who could do so contractually. The litigation funder could then insure this liability and treat its insurance cost as just another (albeit a large) cost of the litigation. To be sure, insurers might resist insuring long-shot actions, but this again can be seen as an advantage of a "loser pays" rule: that is, it tends to screen out long-shot cases. Absent insurance covering the costs that will be shifted on a defeat, the action would likely not go forward. In contrast, in the United States, the fear remains that a potentially large recovery may incentivize the plaintiff's attorney to roll the dice on a long-shot action (because it is generally safe from fee shifting).

5. PUTTING THE PIECES TOGETHER. Let us assume that Europe wishes to protect litigant autonomy and will continue to resist plaintiff's attorneys funding class litigation. (No claim is made that Europe *should* feel this way, but politically this is a safe starting point.) Two obvious means exist by which to prevent plaintiff's attorneys from dominating the class and settling the action to maximize their own interests: (1) the law could require an experienced public interest entity to serve as, in effect, the lead plaintiff; or (2) the law could permit only an opt-in class action so that those who have not consented to representation would not be bound. Nothing requires, however, that both means be used together (even if some countries may insist on both). In this light, the simplest, most direct route to the authorization of the opt-out class may be to require that it be led by a public interest entity, one resembling, say, the

Sierra Club, the ACLU, or the Legal Defense Fund. The court supervising the action could be required to find that this entity had sufficient experience and independence to provide fair and adequate representation to the class. This minimizes the danger of the unaccountable or opportunistic plaintiff's attorney by creating a responsible and competent client. If rejected, the plaintiff's attorney could still be permitted to file an opt-in class action because then the attorney would have received the individual consent of his clients.

The next step is more difficult. How do we unite either approach with litigation funding from a financial institution? In the case of the opt-out class, should the public interest entity be permitted to negotiate and approve the fee agreement (which will likely require that the litigation funder receive a percentage of the recovery—probably one-third or even more). Interestingly, in Australia, which permits opt-out class actions, the standard practice of litigation funders is to require the consent of each class member to its fee contract, which usually awards it a percentage of the recovery.[67] The litigation funder insists on this to prevent any subsequent fee dispute being raised by absent class members, but the impact has been effectively to convert opt-out classes into de facto opt-in classes in Australia. That is the trade-off: unless some means can be found to approve the fee agreement in advance, we may be stuck with the opt-in class.

To make the opt-out class politically viable, one might both (1) authorize the public interest entity serving as the class's representative to negotiate the fee contract with the litigation funder and (2) require judicial approval of the reasonableness of the fee contract, possibly at the time that the court approves the class representative. Litigation funders will be unhappy with any ex post approval requirement (which subjects them to some risk) and will want approval at the outset when the fee contract is executed. Whether that is politically feasible remains an open question.

Such a structure would essentially have three different important actors: (1) the class representative (whose expertise would have to be approved by the court), (2) a litigation funder (whose fee contract would require similar judicial approval), and (3) the plaintiff's law firm. Predictably, litigation funders will want the plaintiff's law firm to defer some of its fee until settlement (in order to ensure that the law firm has "skin in the game"). So long as this deferred fee is not based on a percentage of the recovery, it should not offend the standard prohibition on contingent fees. Such a structure is complex, but it reduces the danger of collusion. The plaintiff's attorney would also have the option of representing an opt-in class where each member would consent to the litigation funder's fee contract as a condition of admission.

The foregoing alternatives would be unlikely to yield the same kind of high-powered entrepreneurial litigation that is frequently seen in the United States. But the rest of the world may prefer a scaled-down alternative, which would permit aggregate litigation to be financed and conducted within the cultural constraints demanded by many other nations. In effect, the entrepreneurial component in the American concept of the private attorney general would be downsized. The private attorney general may be too exotic a concept for other nations to swallow in one bite.

6. A CLOUD OVER THE EUROPEAN FUTURE: THE SETTLEMENT CLASS ACTION.   The foregoing account of how Europe could import a downsized version of the private attorney general may be too optimistic. As has been stressed before, there is both an upside and a downside to the private attorney general concept, and the term can be invoked to justify dubious practices.

In particular, the class action can be used to extinguish meritorious individual claims. That possibility has surfaced in the Netherlands, with the adoption of a statutory procedure for settlement class actions.[68] Under this procedure, although a plaintiff is not permitted to sue on behalf of an opt-out class, both sides can present an out-of-court class settlement to the court for its approval. If the settlement is approved by the court, there can be no appeal, and all within the class are bound, unless they take action to opt out. As a practical matter, this means the defendant can gain finality and preclude pending or potential actions in other jurisdictions. Predictably, few "negative value" claimants will take any action and thus will be bound by the settlement.

As noted in Chapter 6, when only a settlement class is available, the result is to "disarm" the plaintiff's attorney, because the attorney loses the leverage inherent in being otherwise able to take the case to trial.[69]

Settlement classes provide defendants with a means by which to escape threatening class actions pending elsewhere (as the settlement will release all claims and preclude other pending and future actions) without exposing themselves to trial. Typically, the defendant can find an accommodating plaintiff's attorney ready to represent the settlement class, because it is a low-cost, no-risk assignment that promises a large fee award.

That seems to be the pattern that has emerged in the Netherlands. In the first significant case in which its settlement class procedure (adopted in 2005) was used, Shell Petroleum was faced with a global securities class action in the United States, which sought to represent all U.S. and foreign investors. To outflank it, Shell Petroleum reached agreement with a different group of U.S. plaintiff's attorneys. It then petitioned and received approval from the Amsterdam Court of Appeals for this out-of-court settlement, which covered an estimated 500,000 investors in one hundred jurisdictions (excluding only U.S. investors who purchased on U.S. exchanges).[70] Only 27 percent of the shares in this class appear to have been owned by class members residing in the Netherlands.[71] The plaintiff's attorneys in the U.S. action sought an injunction from the U.S. court to block the Dutch settlement, and Shell in turn sought to dismiss the U.S. action. Eventually, after much negotiation, the two sides struck a deal under which the U.S. investors settled in the U.S. action, and all other investors settled in the Dutch action (and—predictably—both teams of plaintiff's attorneys were awarded generous attorney's fees).[72] Although the terms of each settlement may have been fair, the motivation for the Netherlands action seems to have been a desire to escape the U.S. action. In effect, because of the Netherlands settlement class procedure, defendants were able to induce one team of plaintiff's attorneys to compete with another, and this likely produces underbidding.

More disturbing has been the settlement of mass tort actions under this same procedure. Some 34,000 class members (plus an unknown number of future claimants) were covered in a settlement class of diethylstilbestrol (DES) claims.[73] DES is a hormonal medication that was given to expectant mothers and is believed to have caused birth defects and other injuries. Thus, this class was exactly the type of mass tort case involving personal injuries that can no longer be certified as a class action in the United States, and it expressly covered "future claimants" (i.e., persons who have been exposed but have not manifested injury). Aggressive attempts to bind future claimants seem to have been the factor that most concerned the U.S. Supreme Court and caused it to reject mass tort settlement class actions in its *Amchem* decision.[74]

Already, there have been instances in the Netherlands of settlement classes in which those who opted out from the settlement did substantially better in their subsequent individual suits than the class did.[75] Again, this implies high agency costs in class action settlements in Europe. Also, this disparity suggests that, if opt-out classes do become feasible in Europe, the defendant's tactical response may be to file a settlement class in the Netherlands with a cooperative plaintiff's attorney. Under the Netherlands procedure, this is possible even if only a handful of the class members reside in the Netherlands. Although the Netherlands court would be unlikely to approve an obviously inadequate settlement, the settlement value of a class action is seldom obvious to third parties, and the settlement will likely only be presented to the Netherlands court if the defendants believe that it reduces their overall liability.

The irony then is that in Europe, it remains extremely difficult to certify an opt-out class action, but it is entirely feasible to gain judicial approval of exactly the type of collusion-prone settlement class action that can no longer be certified in the United States. The same battles that have been fought over settlement classes in U.S. courts seem likely to play out in Europe but possibly with a more pro-defendant result. Perhaps this should remind us that the concept of the private attorney general is a double-edged sword, and not infrequently the private attorney general turns out to be the defendant's ally.

11

CONCLUSION: TOWARD A
SEMIPRIVATE ATTORNEY GENERAL

THIS VOLUME HAS SOUGHT to present a "warts and all" portrait of the private attorney general and entrepreneurial litigation. That is an account that has long been missing in the literature, in large part because academics writing in this area either have been so ideologically committed to the private attorney general concept or so implacably opposed to it that, in either case, they have missed the divergences between theory and practice.[1] For either reason, they have disdained any empirical assessment of what entrepreneurial litigation does well (or badly). This book's assessment has been that private enforcement of law through entrepreneurial litigation does litigate complex cases well (probably better than more resource-constrained public enforcers can do) but is persistently misdirected by the tendency of plaintiff's attorneys to settle cases in their own interest. Entrepreneurial litigation does generate deterrence in some contexts, but a substantial shortfall results in the case of corporate and securities litigation because plaintiff's attorneys are indifferent to who pays the recovery, and defendants prefer to settle on a basis that passes the real costs on to others. So constructed, the resulting system benefits lawyers unduly and the public inadequately.

This assessment may sound like a prelude to proposing curbs on the private attorney general, but this book's goal has not been to bury the private attorney general, but to rehabilitate it. Entrepreneurial litigation could be redirected, but that goal ultimately requires refashioning the incentives that today invite private attorney generals to grab the low-hanging fruit, often in a manner that benefits mainly lawyers (and not their clients). If we regard the private attorney general as a public resource, it is a resource that clearly has not been well allocated in terms of its social costs and benefits. Some redeployment of this resource should be encouraged, and more accountability is needed. But how can these goals be achieved?

Let us begin with the shortcomings that we have observed and evaluate their seriousness. Here, it will quickly become evident that few universal judgments can be reached, but only context-specific ones. The standard critiques of entrepreneurial litigation (and the private attorney general by extension) fall under four basic headings: (1) overzealousness, (2) disloyalty and collusion, (3) overaggregation, and (4) lack of political accountability. A fifth (and less common) criterion also needs to be considered: symbolic justice. Law has its expressive goals; it seeks to affirm values, not simply recover financial settlements. Here, entrepreneurial litigation does poorly because it is ultimately about recovering money (or other relief) that generates fee awards. Private litigation is not geared to assigning blame or affirming principles. But is any meaningful improvement possible?

Each of these critiques needs a brief review:

1. OVERZEALOUSNESS.   This is the standard criticism made by the defense bar. In their view, plaintiff's attorneys lack discretion and judgment and will sue whenever the damages are high enough so that the case has a settlement value that covers their fees. In contrast, public enforcers, the defense bar argues, necessarily exercise prosecutorial discretion, if only because they would otherwise be overwhelmed by the volume of cases before them.

How valid is this critique? In principle, the supply of plaintiff's attorneys will rise to meet demand (that is, to exploit all profit-making opportunities that the law provides). Entrepreneurial litigation thus will tend to push the law's boundaries, sometimes into areas that public enforcers would decline to enter.[2] But, if anything is evident from the politics surrounding contemporary class action litigation, it is that persistent overzealousness can be curbed by a variety of legislative and judicial controls—and eventually will be. The Private Securities Litigation Reform Act (PSLRA) largely eliminated hastily prepared and underresearched complaints in securities class actions; the Securities Litigation Uniform Standards Act shut down the end-run tactic of bringing securities class actions in state court to avoid the PSLRA; and the Class Action Fairness Act (CAFA) denied plaintiff's attorneys access to those (relatively few) "rotten boroughs" in state courts that they had allegedly captured. Each time plaintiff's attorneys find a new stratagem to exploit, they are curbed after, at most, a few years of success. Similarly, the Supreme Court has moved in the same direction, both in its recent decisions imposing higher pleading standards that permit early dismissal of unpromising cases and in its increasingly confining decisions on class certification.[3] Viewed over the long run, if the plaintiff's bar overreaches, it will be disciplined, because defendants, once organized, enjoy far more political power (and probably more judicial empathy).

At the same time, the incentive to overreach and litigate every profitable opportunity, regardless of its merit, does demonstrably exist. Only the very best of plaintiff's attorneys have risen above this temptation. If this book has found one unassailable hero within the plaintiff's bar, it was probably Abe Pomerantz. A public citizen as well as a skilled litigator, he was, above all, a craftsman. His meticulously researched and carefully pleaded complaints were exceptional and made him a model lawyer, respected by all. But it did not make him a role model that others emulated. Instead, the dominant style of corporate and securities litigation changed some time in the late 1970s and quickly became the high-volume, instant turnaround model, perfected by Milberg, Weiss, which style was characterized by often hasty, indeed slapdash, complaints, in-house professional plaintiffs, and overnight filings in multiple courts. Milberg, Weiss was the Henry Ford of plaintiff's litigation, and it perfected the assembly-line techniques that allowed it to win control of cases and respond quickly to every opportunity. Clever and skillful as it was, its success showed entrepreneurialism besting professionalism. Ultimately, its style proved its own undoing and eventually produced the PSLRA (and some criminal convictions).

Similarly, in the current environment in which nearly every merger provokes a lawsuit, mass production and automatic case filings are again dominating individualized craftsmanship. A case's nuisance value can be its dominant asset. Again, this problem is context-specific, does not characterize all plaintiff's litigation, and may prove transitory (as reforms appear to be coming). Yet, it again demonstrates that the answer may not be legislation, as private self-help remedies are possible. Recent Delaware decisions have approved both forum selection and "loser pays" by-laws that appear more than adequate to control frivolous litigation.[4] One way or another, experience shows that reforms will come (perhaps to an excessive degree), as the plaintiff's bar does not dominate the political process. The bottom line, then, is this overzealousness can be controlled, and this critique is the one that should least concern us.

The other side of the overzealousness coin is the reality of expertise and competence. To properly balance the costs and benefits of entrepreneurial litigation, we must also recognize that at least the better plaintiff's law firms appear far more competent, proactive, and successful at handling complex litigation than are most public enforcers. Large bureaucracies, staffed by civil service lawyers, are less often characterized by overzealousness. In contrast, successful private enforcers have triumphed in a very competitive market where they developed trial skills that are largely missing on the staffs of most public enforcers. Organizationally, these private firms are equipped to handle major litigation and can mobilize the necessary staff for a large case on short notice. When necessary, they can even expand and contract their size in accordion-like fashion to staff such a case. At least as important, these firms are geared to accept risk, whereas public enforcers are not and know that they may face political criticism if they lose (which prospect inhibits them).

These characteristics are valuable assets, which public enforcement could harness. Ideally, public enforcers could handle the mundane, run-of-the-mill action and also emergency injunctive cases, but leave the major, riskier, and slower-moving complex actions that generate real deterrence to the specially retained private firm. To be sure, public enforcers could (and should) play a role in supervising such private enforcement and would be required to approve settlements, but these details can be postponed for the moment.

2. DISLOYALTY AND COLLUSION.   It is less easy, however, to dismiss the long-standing concern over whether the plaintiff's attorney will sell out the class in return for a generous fee. Although the history of class litigation compels some distrust on this point, universal judgments are again overbroad. This problem of opportunism is well controlled in some contexts but not others. For example, in securities class actions, the attorney's fee award cannot exceed a reasonable percentage of the recovery;[5] this produces a desirable incentive for the private enforcer to maximize the recovery. CAFA has also discouraged coupon settlements, which had a long history of abuse. But in the area of mass torts, because it was economically reasonable for the major asbestos industry defendants to pay fees in the $100 million range to a limited number of plaintiff's attorneys, defendants were able to secure mass tort settlements that cheaply resolved all claims of "future claimants" (i.e., persons exposed but not yet manifesting injury). Correspondingly, the tobacco industry could easily have paid billions of dollars in attorney's fees to resolve all smoking-related claims (if such a class action had been certifiable).[6]

Defenders of "mass torts" class actions still argue that these practices are not significantly different from those that occur on a smaller scale in individual mass tort litigation where plaintiff's attorneys and defendants typically resolve claims on an inventory basis. They are correct that practices are similar, but the scale is different by several orders of magnitude. Also, the plaintiff's attorney in individual litigation cannot resolve the claims of persons who have not requested that attorney's representation.

The point then is that the critical decisions in some fields, most notably mass torts litigation, affect so many and potentially so dramatically that the litigation is inherently "public" in character. Such decisions require a level of transparency and political accountability that they do not receive in private litigation. Particularly when defendants are under severe financial pressure, they may offer financial rewards to class counsel that will enrich them beyond the dreams of avarice. When these conditions are present, it is reckless to rely idealistically on the private attorney general concept. Put differently, a settlement resolving the rights of future claimants with regard to asbestos, tobacco, or any similar mass tort claim might be appropriately approved by a public agency (after much study and subject to public scrutiny), but to entrust the same decision to a conflicted plaintiff law firm (operating in a much less transparent system) invites corruption. As Lord Acton knew, power corrupts. Because class counsel has great discretionary power at the settlement stage, it is correspondingly vulnerable to corruption.

Of course, this debate over the certification of mass tort cases is now largely over, as the Supreme Court has, for all practical purposes, precluded such certification, except in rare cases. But this example illustrates that there are cases of such extraordinary size and scope that they should not be entrusted to the private attorney general and should only be resolved in a more politically accountable and "democratic" fashion. In short, entrepreneurial litigation quickly collides with the age-old problem of "who will guard the guardians." Courts alone cannot satisfactorily perform this task of guarding the guardian (both because they are too busy and because their desire for settlements can compromise their judgment). Inevitably, that leaves the public enforcer as the most logical candidate to share this burden with the court. To this end, some advisory role (possibly as an amicus curiae) needs to be structured into the settlement process for the public enforcer.

3. OVERAGGREGATION.   Weak cases can hide behind strong cases in many class actions. For example, let us assume that an employment discrimination class action covers over 10,000 persons, 70 percent of whom have valid and meritorious claims and 30 percent of whom have weak (that is, legally unsustainable) claims. If the weak can hide behind the strong, not only is the defendant compelled to pay off weak claimants to achieve a settlement, but the strong cases are subsidizing the weak ones, as, in all likelihood, the settlement was reached on a lump-sum basis. In part because of this problem, courts have greatly tightened the criteria for class certification. In so doing, recent decisions, in particular *Wal-Mart Stores v. Dukes,* may have cut off "negative value" claimants from any practical remedy.

The best answer here may be "partial" or "issue" certification, which would allow the defendant to contest its liability and raise defenses in individual actions after the major class-wide issues were resolved in the class action. To illustrate, the critical issue in a possible mass torts class that could be certified under this standard might be whether a particular drug caused a particular form of cancer. That would be the expensive issue over which experts would battle at high cost (thereby denying the negative value claimant the ability to sue outside of a class action); thus, it needs to be resolved in the class action as the key "common" issue. But once that class-wide issue was resolved or settled, many individual issues could remain that the defendant could raise in follow-on individual litigation: Did the individual plaintiff actually take the drug? Was his cancer caused instead by smoking or some genetic predisposition? Given the class settlement, individual class members could easily obtain counsel to represent them on an individual, contingent fee basis.

Partial certification seems the best answer to the overaggregation problem. It is available in theory today under Federal Rule of Civil Procedure 23, but only highly limited and infrequent use has been made of it. To be sure, there are legal, and even constitutional issues, surrounding its use, but these are better addressed in law review articles than in this summary chapter.

4. DEMOCRACY AND POLITICAL ACCOUNTABILITY. Probably the newest critique of the private attorney general has been that private enforcement is unaccountable, undemocratic, and chaotically uncoordinated.[7] Although this book rejects the broader attack by critics (such as Professor Redish) who claim that the class action is unconstitutional, it does recognize that there is merit in the narrower claim that private enforcement and public enforcement are poorly coordinated. Not only is public oversight often needed, but it might be socially desirable if the law (and public enforcers) could "nudge" plaintiff's attorneys into new fields or at least to raise different claims. For example, the extraordinary concentration of plaintiff's law firms focused on litigating "stock drop" securities cases, while ignoring other financial frauds (such as "pump and dump" schemes), seemingly represents a serious misallocation of resources. Earlier, in Chapter 7, it was noted that an estimated $17 billion

in plaintiff's attorney's fees were paid in connection with securities class actions between 1997 and 2007.[8] Had that money (or just a portion of it) instead been allocated in a more politically accountable way, it is likely that other areas of misconduct might have been pursued and litigated (e.g., employment discrimination, environmental issues, health care, etc.).

At first glance, this may sound simplistic. No federal agency has such universal jurisdiction that it can shift resources from securities litigation to environmental enforcement. The failure here is more a market failure than a political failure. Still, there are means by which such a result could be approximated if the executive branch were willing to set priorities and use its powers fully.

Before sketching such an approach to the better coordination of public and private enforcement, it must first be recognized that coordination presents politically sensitive issues. Proponents of coordination have begun to argue for a "gatekeeper" model under which private litigation by private attorney generals would have to be authorized by public enforcers (either through broad rules or narrower case-by-case decisions).[9] In effect, the public enforcer would "deputize" the private attorney general.

Interesting as this idea seems, it runs up head first against probably the central virtue of the private attorney general model, namely, its ability to protect against agency "capture." Over thirty years ago, this author referred to this as the "failsafe function" of the private attorney general: private enforcement is the last-ditch protection against political capture of the regulator.[10] Little in recent years, including the seeming passivity of the Securities and Exchange Commission (SEC) and the Department of Justice in responding to the 2008 financial crisis, lessens the force of that justification. Thus, when proponents of a gatekeeper model argue that administrative agencies should be vested with the authority to allow (or veto) private litigation on behalf of a class of persons, one can easily envision a host of anxiety-creating scenarios. Suppose, for example, the CEO of a major corporation was the leading donor and fund-raiser for the incumbent president. Would that affect whether a federal agency (led by a presidential appointee) would authorize private litigation against the CEO's company for, hypothetically, environmental damage, securities fraud, or employment discrimination? Those who are confident that partisan politics would not affect agency behavior have very different perceptions of the political world than this author.

5. SYMBOLIC JUSTICE. Law has its symbolic and expressive concerns. For many Americans, the modern high point in the "rule of law" was the Supreme Court's decision in 1954 in *Brown v. Board of Education,* to desegregate public schools—a case won by private litigants (mainly, the NAACP Legal Defense Fund). Perhaps it is unfair to ask "why have not entrepreneurial lawyers won anything like that" because entrepreneurial litigation is, by definition, a business and not a nonprofit activity. Nonetheless, it is clear that the public wants more from its champions than a financial recovery. Recently, much criticism has focused on the SEC for its "neither admit nor deny" policy that allows defendants to escape acknowledging their responsibility or accepting blame. Ultimately, the Second Circuit reversed Judge Jed Rakoff's efforts to make the SEC do more,[11] thereby enabling public and private enforcement to remain comfortable with equivocal settlements that do not establish the basic facts or assign individual responsibility. Given this failing, can we redesign the private enforcer so that it moves even marginally in these directions?

Several of the foregoing questions reduce to a common issue: are steps toward better coordination between public and private enforcement possible? Would such steps produce improvement along any of the foregoing dimensions? This book has already proposed one nonexclusive answer. Instead of giving a veto power to the administrative agency, as gatekeeper, policy planners should encourage an alliance under which the "gatekeeper" agency retains the private firm, often on a contingent fee basis. This makes coordination of public and private enforcement work through positive incentives, not negative vetoes.

What would this achieve in terms of the foregoing criteria? First, an agency like the SEC may pull its punch and not seek to identify individual culprits or to levy blame because it is resource constrained. Using private counsel would alleviate that constraint. The employer (i.e., the public agency) can instruct its agent (the private law firm) as to what it wants, and the prospect of future employment will motivate the law firm to attempt to comply. Beyond that, if we want liability imposed on individuals, and not just on the faceless corporate entity, there is one obvious incentive that the employer can use: increase the fee award for successful recoveries against individuals (even if the total amount recovered is modest). Entrepreneurial litigators respond to that signal as a dog does to Dr. Pavlov's bell.

Beyond that modest proposal, more structural reform is needed because it is sadly evident that courts are often either unable or unwilling to monitor closely the settlement process in class actions. Therefore, some additional monitor must be found, and the only logical candidates are public enforcement agencies. This means that a more formal role needs to be carved out for the public enforcer in the settlement process under which the relevant public agency would evaluate and advise the court handling the settlement of a major class action. In an earlier era, the SEC was instructed by statute to comment in an advisory role as an amicus on major bankruptcy reorganizations, and something like that role could be generalized for all federal agencies in cases involving their statutes. This would substitute informed participation by the agency at the time of settlement in place of a possibly unexplained veto by the agency at the outset.

Reasonable debate is possible over the dangers of giving a veto power to public regulators over private enforcement. In fairness, some favorable experience does exist with the use of such a veto power by public enforcers. In "qui tam" actions, the Department of Justice can veto or adopt the private plaintiff's efforts, and this approach seems to have worked reasonably well.[12] But qui tam actions largely seek to recover the government's own losses from fraud, and thus the interests of the private and public enforcer are well aligned. In contrast, in an employment discrimination, securities, or antitrust case on behalf of private parties, the government's motivation is less clear. Sometimes, the government (or, more likely, an underfunded federal agency) may not want to share credit or to risk being upstaged. At a minimum, the possibility of politically influenced decisions grows. Ultimately, there will always be the suspicion that political influence was decisive, even when it was not, thus casting the shadow of impropriety over the process.

Apart from these concerns about agency capture, other reasons also exist to doubt that public enforcers have the expertise to evaluate accurately the merits of a complex action for money damages. Pricing a lawsuit is a special talent. Although the bureaucrats within a public enforcement agency may have much experience with settling cases, they have little experience with litigating money damages actions to judgment or estimating their financial settlement value (whereas plaintiff's attorneys live and die on this ability).

Ultimately, the hardest policy question is how best to induce a redeployment of litigation resources. What would, for example, constitute a sensible reallocation? Within the plaintiff's bar, if we today identified all the plaintiff's attorneys experienced in complex federal civil litigation, it seems likely that a majority of them are today litigating corporate and securities class actions. From a social welfare perspective, this may represent an excessive investment. That brings us to the heart of the matter. Market forces often produce socially suboptimal allocations of resources across the economy. Basketball players, rock stars, and nerdy computer geeks who can design trendy computer games may make millions, while health care is underfunded. Over the short term, fads happen, and bubbles develop. Alas, that is an inevitable trait of capitalism. Similarly, the private attorney general responds to market forces, and these forces appear to make securities class litigation more profitable and less risky than, say, employment discrimination litigation (particularly after the *Wal-Mart* decision), even if the latter may produce more socially desirable results.

Given that politics and markets regularly conflict, sophisticated policy engineering must seek an accommodation. Here, the goal should be to redirect the private attorney general to serve the public interest (as that interest is democratically defined). If we think that, for the sake of argument, society needs more environmental litigation and less securities litigation, the simplest route to this end is probably for government agencies in those areas perceived to need more enforcement to hire the private attorney general on a contingent fee basis. Carrots generally work better than sticks. Toward this end, attorney fee formulas could also be adjusted (for example, courts in class actions and agencies in cases where they have retained private counsel could award higher fees for recoveries obtained from officers or secondary participants rather than from the corporate issuer).

But these are modest reforms. If a future administration were truly committed to enforcement in a particular area (hypothetically, let us say in environmental law), it could do two things: First, it could repeal (with merely a stroke of the president's pen) the existing prohibition on payment of contingent legal fees by federal agencies.[13] Second, it could specifically encourage the Environmental Protection Agency (EPA) to pay such fees in appropriate cases. Predictably, private firms would then lobby the EPA to sue on its behalf, and the EPA's enforcement capacity would thus be multiplied. Not only could the private law firms sue in the EPA's own right and name, but the EPA might also endorse specific private suits brought by the private law firm on behalf of a class, appearing at the class certification hearing as an amicus curiae. This endorsement could have an important consequence, as such "vouching" by the agency might decrease the possibility of judicial dismissal of the action and increase the prospect of class certification. In effect, the agency would be pledging its own reputation as an indication of the suit's probable merit.

To be sure, this technique could not be followed by all federal agencies across the board. Choices would have to be made, and priorities assigned. The same administration might decide not to authorize the same approach for the SEC (on the arguable premise that there was already an adequate incentive to sue under the federal securities laws). The bottom line impact of such a policy shift cannot be predicted with confidence, but presumably we would see somewhat more environmental litigation and possibly somewhat less securities litigation.

Even more could be done to influence the volume of litigation. In possibly its most controversial policy recommendation, this book has suggested that a ceiling be placed on the corporation's liability in Rule 10b-5 litigation (at least in "stock drop" cases where the corporation is not itself trading).[14] A ceiling is probably preferable to complete abolition of corporate liability in "stock drop" cases for reasons of symbolic justice. Even with a ceiling on damages, a suit could still be brought to "vindicate" the shareholders' rights, but plaintiff's attorneys would be incentivized to focus less on the corporate entity and more on secondary participants (e.g., investment banks and auditors) and corporate officers. As earlier noted, corporate recoveries are ultimately borne by the shareholders and thus generate little real compensation and only indirect and uncertain deterrence. To be sure, reducing the incentive to sue the corporation does not generate more deterrence; instead, it only makes the low-hanging fruit less attractive and redirects the private enforcer. Arguably, this proposal also closes down a contemporary Potemkin village under which counsel on both sides negotiate settlements that are largely meaningless to society (but highly remunerative to counsel on both sides).

A word of clarification is needed here. Corporate liability makes sense in most settings, even if the penalty falls on shareholders (because the fruits of the misconduct also flow to shareholders). But in the context of shareholder and securities litigation, where the victims are shareholders, it seems perversely inappropriate to impose large penalties on the corporation (and thus on the shareholders). That we do punish the victim in this fashion owes much to the fact that (1) plaintiff's attorneys find this system highly profitable and (2) defense counsel and management would prefer to see the corporation bear the penalty than individual officers. As a result, private enforcement sometimes benefits primarily the private enforcers.

Reform here is difficult. It may seem that the obvious policy response is to refocus private enforcement on individuals. Desirable as that would be, recent Supreme Court decisions have largely eclipsed the private liability of aiders and abettors. Moreover, even if secondary liability was restored, the recoveries paid by officers and directors would still largely come from directors and officers (D&O) insurance and corporate indemnification. This system is deeply entrenched in American corporate law, and even the harshest critics of D&O insurance doubt that it is politically feasible to limit liability insurance for officers and directors.[15] In this light, the most feasible, but still incomplete, reform is probably to restore "gatekeeper" liability so that secondary participants (i.e., investment banks, auditors, credit making agencies, etc.) face a higher prospect of liability.[16] If the outside gatekeepers were deterred, they could constrain corporate misbehavior—at least more effectively than they do today. But even this reform would require legislation, which is currently unlikely. In the interim, private enforcement will predictably produce settlements that are more symbolic than deterrent.

Is there any way then to generate adequate deterrence through entrepreneurial litigation? That is the key question. In retrospect, the Supreme

Court's abolition of aiding and abetting liability may have been the step that most undercut the rationale for entrepreneurial litigation. If those decisions cannot be legislatively overruled, the next best (and most feasible) reform is to design a system that effectively resurrects such liability. Here, it is essential to tie together some ideas raised earlier. A key advantage of public agencies hiring private entrepreneurial counsel to litigate on their behalf is not simply that the recoveries might increase, but that two major problems are thereby effectively sidestepped. First, the immunity that current law gives aiders and abettors from private liability would become inapplicable (as federal agencies, such as the SEC, are authorized to sue aiders and abettors).[17] Second, and even more important, indemnification would generally be barred in the case of liabilities to a public agency.[18] So repositioned, entrepreneurial litigation would have real impact. Other means to this same end are also possible.[19]

Of course it would be myopic to focus exclusively on securities and shareholder litigation. Class actions do serve valid purposes in other areas—for example, antitrust, employment discrimination, and environmental cases. But these are the areas where the class action has been most eclipsed by recent Supreme Court decisions (of which *Wal-Mart* is the most notable).[20] The ironic result is that private enforcement through entrepreneurial litigation survives primarily in the field where it achieves the least, namely, securities litigation.

Where are we left? The private attorney general and entrepreneurial litigation are deeply embedded in American culture and history. Despite recent congressional hostility and Supreme Court skepticism, they have survived—possibly by the skin of their teeth. The entrepreneurial private attorney general does offer real efficiency gains in that it often has expertise, skills, resources, and a tolerance for risk that public enforcers typically lack. Overall, the private attorney general offers four key benefits: (1) expanded resources that are independent of the budgetary process, (2) superior litigation experience, (3) better risk-bearing capacity, and (4) protection against political capture. Of these, the last may be the most important and the hardest to measure, but clearly rights without remedies wither. In a world without private enforcement and dependent on public enforcement, a change in administrations could often imply a significant change in legal rights.

With perhaps slightly less certainty, one can identify other important social benefits that follow from the institution of the private attorney general. First, entrepreneurial plaintiff's attorneys may be more innovative and willing to accept risk than attorneys within public bureaucracies. That asserted advantage can be debated (both as to its accuracy and as to its desirability), but administrative agencies, staffed with civil service attorneys, seem unlikely to be able to handle complex, long-term litigation nearly as well as the best plaintiff's law firms. Public enforcers may also decline challenging and resource-consuming large cases in very low visibility ways. Second, private enforcers are mobile, can be redeployed, and do not acquire lifetime tenure the way that civil servants usually do. Third, American society is pluralistic and decentralized, and so is private enforcement. This point goes beyond the "political capture" problem and recognizes that public enforcement tends to be centralized and slower moving. Think again of how many years more it would have taken the Department of Justice to bring the equivalent of *Brown v. Board of Education!* In principle, every constituency in society may want its own private attorney general, which means that it need not assemble or await a majoritarian political consensus before it can protect its rights.

On the other side of the ledger, the private attorney general can be corrupted, and thus in areas involving complex trade-offs (such as the treatment of "future claimants" in mass tort litigation), the private attorney general should be given much less deference than that normally accorded administrative agencies. Ultimately, this is again an argument for a closer partnership between public and private enforcement.

Across the legal landscape, closer interaction between private and public enforcement is desirable. This may be the only way that private enforcers can be sensitized to concerns about symbolic justice. For example, although some plaintiff's firms in securities litigation do focus on nonpecuniary corporate governance reforms, most do not. But more would do so if the client requested such a focus.

Even if public/private partnerships are needed, one potential reform seems clearly misconceived: giving veto power to the public agency. Conferring such a veto power to administrative agencies over private suits may screen out some frivolous or predatory actions, but it risks undercutting the independence of the private attorney general. To the extent that greater oversight is needed, the better means to this end would be for the court to ask for the administrative agency's views (as, in effect, an amicus curiae) at the settlement stage. If too many frivolous actions are being brought, the better alternative to giving a veto power to public agencies is probably a modest version of the "loser pays" rule. The screening that would produce is probably a better measure of whether the action was frivolous than an agency's possibly premature or biased prediction.

In a resource-constrained world, the challenge for the future is to both increase enforcement output and also redirect it. When public agencies retain plaintiff's counsel (as the Federal Deposit Insurance Corporation, the Federal Housing Finance Agency, and certain other financial regulators are increasingly doing), both these goals can be realized. Not only does the public enforcer "deputize" the private attorney general at the outset, but also the public enforcer maintains a continuing oversight over the case. The result is both an ex ante and ex post supervision of the private attorney general.

To its many critics, the private attorney general is a virtual pirate. Rhetorical and overstated as that claim is, it still suggests an alternative role for the private attorney general: that of the privateer. The key difference is that the pirate was an independent actor, accountable to no one and operating outside the law, while the privateer was commissioned by the Crown to wage war on its enemies. The privateer was in effect an independent contractor. Similarly, the private attorney general could be chartered and enlisted by federal agencies to litigate in specific areas where public enforcement was either weak or overtaxed. Indeed, an endorsement could be given by the federal agency to specific lawsuits (which in an ideal world would make class certification easier). In some cases, the agency could simply hire the private law firm to sue on its behalf (as some agencies now do), and this at a stroke eliminates the need for the complex and risky process of class certification.

Over the last quarter century, many have observed that the practice of law has moved from being primarily a profession to being primarily a business. Developments within the plaintiff's bar have only paralleled those within the bar generally. Where Abe Pomerantz was a politically committed and outspoken intellectual, the contemporary plaintiff's bar (while undoubtedly still liberal and left-leaning) has little difficulty in subordinating its political views to the needs of accommodating defendants and achieving mutually beneficial settlements. Precisely for this reason, greater oversight is needed. The private attorney general has not failed, but it has succeeded better at doing well than at doing good.

No single reform will correct this, and this book does not suggest that we abandon the existing model of the private attorney general as a risk-taking entrepreneur. But it does assert that additional approaches—including that of the semiprivate attorney general—should supplement that original role. The goal here is a strategy to combine entrepreneurial zeal with greater accountability and thereby to improve both public and private enforcement. It is unrealistic, even quixotic, to attempt to make the private attorney general truly virtuous, because it exists in a rough-and-tumble world. Perhaps, with greater oversight and some tweaking of the incentives, the private attorney general could do both well and good—at least marginally more than it does today.

The bottom line is that the private attorney general responds—quickly and adaptively—to the economic incentives held out for it. Unless society consciously structures those incentives to achieve its desired ends, it must anticipate that private parties will strike bargains and reach compromises that maximize their own interests and largely nullify the deterrent impact of the private attorney general. This pattern has cut across each context that this book has examined. Absent change, it will continue.

NOTES

1. LITIGATION AND DEMOCRACY

1. Tocqueville's point was not only that law could mediate political conflict in the United States, but that lawyers were trusted by its citizens as the natural protectors of democracy and the citizen's legal rights. Writing as of 1836, he observed, "When one visits America and when one studies their laws, one sees that the authority that they have given its lawyers and the influence they have allowed them to have in the government form the most powerful force against lapses of democracy." Alexis de Tocqueville, DEMOCRACY IN AMERICA 25 (Harvey C. Mansfield ed., 1992).

2. Even before Tocqueville, Edmund Burke had made this same observation that lawyers dominated "the colonies," noting that the legal profession in the United States "is numerous and powerful, and in most provinces it takes the lead." *See* Edmund Burke, *On Moving His Resolution for Conciliation with the Colonies,* March 22, 1775, *in* 2 WORKS OF THE RIGHT HONORABLE EDMUND BURKE 101, 124–125 (1886).

3. *See* Robert A. Ferguson, THE TRIAL IN AMERICAN LIFE 1 (2007).

4. Juries are guaranteed by no less than three amendments within the Bill of Rights: the Fifth Amendment protects the role of the grand jury; the Sixth assures juries in criminal cases; and the Seventh guarantees the civil jury.

5. Akhil Amar has stressed the centrality of the jury to the Bill of Rights in the U.S. Constitution, writing that "Juries stood at the center of the original Bill of Rights." *See* A. Amar, THE BILL OF RIGHTS: CREATION AND RECONSTRUCTION (1988) at 108.

6. *See* Tocqueville, *supra* note 1, at 284–285.

7. Although judges in the colonies were appointed, this practice changed by the 1840s to 1850s, with the election of state judges becoming the predominant mode.

See Lawrence Friedman, A HISTORY OF AMERICAN LAW 126–127, 371–373 (2d ed. 1985).

8. The leading decisions are *Trustees v. Greenough,* 105 U.S. 527 (1881), and *Central Railroad & Banking Co. of Georgia v. Pettus,* 113 U.S. 116 (1885); both predate the advent of the class action. In both cases, a legal action created a common fund, which benefited persons besides the named plaintiffs. In *Greenough,* the Court permitted the named plaintiff to sue the other persons benefited by the action for a share of his legal fees, and in *Pettus,* the attorneys who represented the named plaintiffs were paid first by their clients and then recovered additional fees from the others on a restitutionary rationale. For an overview, see Charles Silver, *A Restitutionary Theory of Attorneys' Fees in Class Actions,* 76 Cornell L. Rev. 656 (1991).

9. The Supreme Court first recognized the derivative action in *Dodge v. Woolsey,* 59 U.S. (18 How.) 331 (1855). Even before that date, state court decisions had given the derivative action a far broader role than it had in England, where it was restrained by a requirement that the underlying challenged action had to be not simply voidable, but void. For an overview, see Ann M. Scarletti, *Shareholder Derivative Litigation's Historical and Normative Foundations,* 61 Buffalo L. Rev. 837 (2013).

10. 347 U.S. 483 (1954) (finding de jure school segregation to violate the equal protection of the laws guaranteed by the Fourteenth Amendment). This case, involving four separate lawsuits in four states (Kansas, Virginia, South Carolina, and Delaware), was brought, coordinated, and carefully managed by the NAACP Legal Defense Fund, acting in pursuit of a long-term legal strategy. Such "public interest" litigation, while very different from the entrepreneurial litigation that is the focus of this volume, also benefited from these same nineteenth-century legal rules.

11. If private enforcement had not been available, the federal government would have at some point certainly sued to invalidate school desegregation, but that point might have been years or even a decade later, given the political costs to the two major parties if either had championed school desegregation as its cause. Similarly, the Supreme Court's equally controversial decision in *Roe v. Wade,* 410 U.S. 113 (1973), establishing a right to abortion, was also the result of private litigation, and public enforcers would have been unlikely to raise such a claim until many years later. *Roe v. Wade* was a class action brought under the liberalized procedures for civil rights class actions (i.e., Rule 23(b)(2)), discussed in Chapter 4.

12. *See, e.g., Geer v. Amalgamated Copper Co.,* 61 N.J. Eq. 364, 367, 49 Atl. 159, 161 (Ch. 1901); *Continental Sec. Co. v. Belmont,* 181 Misc. 340, 343, 144 N.Y. Supp. 801, 804 (Sup. Ct. 1913) (describing the plaintiff as "an artificer of litigation and a menace to corporate society").

13. *See* Cohen v. Beneficial Indus. Loan Corp., 337 U.S. 541, 548 (1949). Ironically, this decision held that state statutes requiring the plaintiff to post a "securities for expense" bond as a precondition to filing a derivative action applied in federal court (even though the Federal Rules of Civil Procedure had no similar rule). Nonetheless, in permitting state procedures to apply in federal court, the Court wrote,

> The remedy, born of shareholder helplessness, was long the chief regulator of corporate management and has afforded no small incentive to avoid at least grosser forms of betrayal of shareholder interests. It is argued, and not without reason, that without it, there would be little practical check on such abuses.

   Id. at 548.

14. The term was coined by Judge Jerome Frank, a leading New Deal thinker, in 1943. *See* Assoc. Indus. of New York State v. Ickes, 134 F.2d 694, 704 (2d Cir. 1943).

2. THE ORIGINS OF ENTREPRENEURIAL LITIGATION

1. *Black's Law Dictionary* defines "champerty" as "a bargain by a stranger with a party to a suit, by which such third person undertakes to carry on the litigation at his own cost and risk, in consideration of receiving, if successful, a part of the proceeds or subject sought to be recovered." BLACK'S LAW DICTIONARY (4th ed. 1968).
2. *See* Peter Karsten, *Enabling the Poor to Have Their Day in Court: The Sanctioning of Contingency Fee Contracts, A History to 1940,* 47 DePaul L. Rev. 231, 232 (1998).
3. The "frivolous suit" argument seems particularly misapplied in the English context where a "loser pays" rule has equally long been in force and should penalize frivolous actions.
4. *See* Karsten, *supra* note 2, at 234–235. James Kent, the famous Chancellor of New York, was particularly resistant to "odious" contingency fee contracts, arguing that a firm rule was necessary "to remove the temptation to imposition and abuse, for clients must apply to attorneys for assistance." *See* Arden v. Patterson, 5 Johns. Ch. 44, 48–49 (N.Y. Ch. 1821).
5. Justice Hugh Brackenbridge of the Pennsylvania Supreme Court noted that contingent fee agreements had become common as of 1818 in Pennsylvania, in his view because of the shortage of cash in common circulation, and that the "most eminent" members of the bar would not enter such agreements. *See* Karsten, *supra* note 2, at 234–235.
6. *Id.* at 239.
7. *Id.* at 240–241.
8. This is Professor Karsten's thesis. *Id.* at 244–245.
9. *See* Moore v. Trustee of Campbell, 17 Tenn. (9 Yar.) 115, 116, 118 (1836).

10. In the early nineteenth century, many state judges were appointed by either the governor or the legislature. However, by the 1840s to 1850s, the more common method was popular election of state judges. *See* Lawrence Friedman, A HISTORY OF AMERICAN LAW, 126–127, 371–373 (2d ed. 1985).

11. *See* Major's Ex'r v. Gibson, 1 Pat & H. 48, 82 (Va. 1855); Newkirk v. Cone, 18 Ill. 449, 453 (1857).

12. *See* Major's Ex'r v. Gibson, 1 Pat & H., at 82.

13. *See* Karsten, *supra* note 2, at 252. *See, e.g.,* Spaulding v. Beidleman, 160 P. 1120 (Okla. 1916).

14. *See* Randolph E. Bergstrom, COURTING DANGER: INJURY & LAW IN NEW YORK CITY, 1870–1910 88–89 (1992).

15. *See* Robert Silverman, LAW AND URBAN GROWTH: CIVIL LITIGATION IN THE BOSTON TRIAL COURTS, 1880–1900 (1981). Silverman estimates that 25 percent of tort plaintiffs in his study were low-level white-collar workers, 15 percent were skilled manual workers, 20 percent were semiskilled workers, and 10 percent were unskilled workers or domestics. *Id.* at 191.

16. *See* Karsten, *supra* note 2, at 254–255.

17. *Id.* (citing *The Contingent Fee Business,* 24 Alb. L.J. 24–27 (1881)).

18. The first contemporaneous and relatively objective reports of this new practice of "ambulance chasing" were by the Committee of Censors of the Law Association of Philadelphia. *See The Solicitation of Accident Cases,* 63 Am. L. Rev. 135 (1929). *See also Ambulance Chasing,* 20 Green Bag 145 (1908) (quoting the president of the Philadelphia Rapid Transit Company as to the increase in litigation costs that his carrier faced as a result of ambulance chasing agents of plaintiff's attorneys). For a historian's overview, see Kenneth DeVille, *New York City Ambulance Chasing in the 1920s,* 59 Historian 290 (1997).

19. John Leubsdorf, *Toward a History of the American Rule on Attorney Fee Recovery,* 47 Law & Contemp. Probs. 9 (1984).

20. *Id.* at 16.

21. *Id.* at 13–14 (noting "vast discrepancies between costs awards and usual fees" and that cost awards might amount to only "a few dollars").

22. *Id.* at 16 (citing Law v. Ewell, 15 F. Cas. 14 (C.C. D.C. 1817); Mooney v. Lloyd, 5 Serg. & Rawle 412 (Pa. 1819)).

23. *See* Arcambel v. Wiseman, 3 U.S. (Dall.) 306, 306 (1796).

24. *See* Leubsdorf, *supra* note 19, at 16 (citing cases).

25. *See* 1848 N.Y. Laws 258 (quoted and discussed in Leubsdorf, *supra* note 19, at 18–20).

26. *See* Gulf, Colorado & San Francisco Ry. v. Ellis, 165 U.S. 150 (1897).

27. *See* Act of February 26, 1853, 10 Stat. 161. If there was an appeal, additional costs could be shifted against the loser. *See* Leubsdorf, *supra* note 19, at 22.

28. *See* Leubsdorf, *supra* note 19, at 25.

29. *See, e.g.,* Note, *State Attorney Fee Shifting Statutes: Are We Quietly Repealing the American Rule,* Law & Contemp. Probs. 321 (1984).

30. In over one hundred circumstances, Congress has enacted one-way fee shifting statutes that entitle successful plaintiffs to an award of attorney's fees. Over fifty statutes primarily address the private sector, seeking to deter corporations and businesses from engaging in wrongful conduct. *See* Harold Krent, *Explaining One-Way Fee Shifting,* 79 Va. L. Rev. 2039, 2041–2042 (1993). Prominent examples include the Truth in Lending Act and Title VII of the Civil Rights Act of 1964. The use of "one-way" fee shifting became politically controversial in the early 1990s, and the first President Bush issued an executive order instructing federal agencies not to seek further such legislation. *Id.* at 2039.

31. Pub. L. No. 94-559, 90 Stat. 2641. This Act was followed by the Equal Access to Justice Act in 1980 (Pub. L. No. 96-481, 94 Stat. 2321), which further extended this policy of fostering social reform through litigation (but only certain types of litigation).

32. 421 U.S. 240 (1975).

33. Merchants and corporations could also easily obtain fee shifting in their favor by contract. Most standard form consumer contracts and leases contain such clauses entitling the successful plaintiff, suing under the contract, to its reasonable legal fees. These clauses were upheld by courts, beginning in the mid-nineteenth century, when they came into general use. *See* Leubsdorf, *supra* note 19, at 24. Because lenders, merchants, and landlords can (and do) regularly write such clauses into their contracts, the American rule is thus trivialized, as it does not apply to the world of contract litigation but is largely limited to tort litigation.

34. 105 U.S. 527, 533 (1881).

35. The Court sounded this theme, noting of the plaintiff that "He has worked for them as well as himself." *Id.* at 532.

36. *See* J. H. Guy, *Allowances by Courts of Fees to Counsel,* 13 Va. L.J. 533, 544 (1889).

37. *See* John P. Dawson, *Lawyers and Involuntary Clients: Attorney Fees from Funds,* 87 Harv. L. Rev. 1597 (1974).

38. This is Professor Leubsdorf's analysis; he relies in part on C. Fairman, JUSTICE MILLER AND THE SUPREME COURT, 1862–90 237–249 (1949). The Court in *Greenough* did not allow the individual plaintiff to receive compensation for his own time and services but only for his lawyer's time and expense. Skeptical of the client charging for his own time, the Court was more open to the lawyer charging a reasonable fee (possibly on the unstated premise that his client would monitor him).

39. 113 U.S. 116 (1885).

40. Having established this principle, the Supreme Court still found the compensation approved by the lower court in *Pettus* to be excessive and decreed that it be reduced by half. *Id.* at 127–128. Still, after *Pettus,* the client would now have little

reason to monitor the attorney's fees when the individual client was not bearing them directly but was instead shifting them to all others with a stake in the "common fund."

41. *See, e.g.,* Sprague v. Ticonic Nat'l Bank, 307 U.S. 161 (1939). The high-water mark of judicial tolerance for nonmonetary relief in the federal courts is probably *Mills v. Electric Auto-Lite Co.,* 396 U.S. 375 (1970) (awarding preliminary attorney's fees for demonstration of disclosure violations).

42. *See* George D. Hornstein, *The Counsel Fee in Stockholders' Derivative Suits,* 39 Colum. L. Rev. 784 (1939); Harry Kalven, Jr. & Maurice Rosenfield, *The Contemporary Function of the Class Suit,* 8 U. Ch. L. Rev. 684 (1941).

43. For an early decision using the percentage of the recovery method (which had a historical basis in admiralty practice), see *In re* Osofsky, 50 F.2d 925 (S.D.N.Y. 1931). Professor Hornstein was the principal academic champion of the percentage of the recovery measure for fee awards. *See* Hornstein, *supra* note 42.

44. Most commentators and most courts favor the percentage of the recovery method over the alternative method (known as the "lodestar" method), which awards attorneys the value of their time reasonably expended on the action at their normal hourly rate (if reasonable) plus some bonus for the delay and risk assumed. Judges find the percentage of the recovery method much easier to calculate but may today subject it to a "lodestar cross check" to avoid windfall fee awards in cases where little effort was expended by the attorney.

45. A simple example will illustrate this point. Assume that an individual plaintiff would be unwilling to sue under the English rule if he had only a 25 percent chance of success and a 75 percent chance of adverse fee shifting in the amount of $500,000 if the case was lost (or a discounted value of $375,000). The individual plaintiff might hold to this position even if the recovery would be $10 million if he was successful (or a $2.5 million discounted value), because he was risk averse and would be bankrupted if the case were lost. Suppose now that the plaintiff's attorney is handling twenty such cases, with, on average, the same prospective recovery under a 40 percent contingent fee agreement with each client. He should rationally view those cases as having, on average, a $2.5 million discounted recovery (and a $1 million discounted fee to him, as compared with a $375,000 discounted fee-shifting obligation—or a net positive balance, on average, of $625,000). Hence, the attorney would rationally proceed, even under the English rule. Under the American rule, the attorney would even more obviously proceed, because the attorney faces no downside (other than the loss of his own litigation costs).

46. One qualification is needed here: If the defendant is a repeat player (i.e., it is sued repetitively), it may decide to act strategically and resist settlement, even when it is cheaper to settle, in order to discourage future litigation against it. In effect, it is investing in a reputation for toughness that may pay off over the long run in

fewer suits. However, few corporate defendants are repetitively sued in class actions or derivative suits.

3. THE DERIVATIVE ACTION

1. *See* Dodge v. Woolsey, 59 U.S. 331 (1855). *Dodge* was the first Supreme Court decision to recognize the existence of the derivative action, although the decision in fact addressed only an issue of federal jurisdiction. Earlier decisions in state courts had also upheld the availability of a derivative action as a means by which a shareholder could sue corporate officers, directors, or employees who had breached their duties to the corporation in the name and right of the corporation. *See* Robinson v. Smith, 3 Paige Ch. 222 (N.Y. Ch. 1832); Taylor v. Miami Exporting Co., 5 Ohio 162, 165–168 (1831). The recovery in a derivative action goes, however, to the corporation, in whose name the shareholder is suing, and not the shareholders.

   The derivative action (much like the class action) was borrowed from English equity practice and traces back to *Charitable Corp. v. Sutton,* 26 Eng. Rep. 642 (1742) (Failure by directors to monitor loans made by charitable corporations to other directors and employees results in liability for failure to supervise.).

   The first Supreme Court decision to examine the actual requirements for a derivative action was *Hawes v. Oakland,* 104 U.S. 450 (1881). Although the U.S. courts accepted the derivative action from England as part of our legal inheritance from that country, U.S. courts never adopted the nineteenth-century English decision that largely eclipsed the derivative action in England, because it came after the time of American independence. In *Foss v. Harbottle,* 67 Eng. Rep. 189 (1843), the derivative action was effectively limited to those instances when the alleged wrong was not ratifiable by shareholders. But *Foss* was not part of the legal inheritance that the United States received from England as of the date of American independence.

2. Banks, railroads, and insurance companies were the principal exceptions to this generalization. For an overview of the growth of dispersed ownership in the United States, see John C. Coffee, Jr., *The Rise of Dispersed Ownership: The Roles of Law and the State in the Separation of Ownership and Control,* 111 Yale L.J. 1 (2001).

3. *See* Adolf Berle and Gardiner Means, THE MODERN CORPORATION AND PRIVATE PROPERTY (1932) (describing separation of ownership from control in U.S. public companies).

4. For the fullest account of his legal career, see J.A. Livingston, THE AMERICAN STOCKHOLDER 49–55 (1958).

5. *See* Note, *Extortionate Corporate Litigation: The Strike Suit,* 34 Colum. L. Rev. 1308 n.1 (1934).

6. *Id.*

7. *Id.*

8. Livingston, *supra* note 4, at 50.

9. *Id.*

10. Continental Sec. Co. v. Belmont, 144 N.Y. Supp. 801, 804 (Sup. Ct. 1913).

11. Gen. Inv. Co. v. Bethlehem Steel Corp., 102 Atl. 252, 255 (N.J. Ch. 1917).

12. Livingston, *supra* note 4, at 52.

13. *Id.* at 53.

14. Interestingly, Jerome Frank wrote this in 1933 in reviewing Adolf Berle and Gardiner Means's seminal book, THE MODERN CORPORATION AND PRIVATE PROPERTY (1933). *See* Book Review, 42 Yale L.J. 989, 992 n.6 (1933). Frank went on to observe, however, that "strike suits" did "nothing for the body of stockholders" when they were settled privately. He concluded that, in theory, the derivative suit could be replaced by public enforcement but expressed doubt that "such political agencies would be sufficiently efficient and active to constitute adequate substitutes for the minority stockholder's suit." *Id.*

15. Livingston, *supra* note 4, at 55.

16. The Depression Era marked the high water mark in judicial skepticism of business decision making. On the one hand, it was the time of the most expansive Delaware decisions on the scope of the fiduciary duties of corporate officers and directors. *See, e.g.,* Guth v. Loft, Inc., 5 A.2d 503, 510 (Del. Ch. 1939) ("[C]orporate officers and directors are not permitted to use their positions of trust and confidence to further their private interests"). Correspondingly, courts were then far more prepared to read the business judgment rule narrowly and to deem considered business decisions to have been negligent or worse. *See, e.g.,* Litwin v. Allen, 25 N.Y.S.2d 667 (N.Y. Sup. Ct. 1940).

17. *See Corporations: In the Stockholders' Interest?,* Time Mag., May 22, 1950, at 95 (profiling Abe Pomerantz).

18. Pomerantz, himself, summarized his approach to preparing derivative actions in an address before the New York City Bar Association in 1949. *See* Abraham Pomerantz, "The Preparation of Minority Stockholder Suits," Mar. 15, 1949. In it, he indicates that he did not stop with Securities and Exchange Commission filings but researched companies by going to the files of other regulators (such as public service commissions for utilities or the Interstate Commerce Commission for railroads). He also went to the findings in congressional hearings, consulted with statistical researchers, and investigated the relationships between outside directors and management.

19. This author is here relying on an interview on March 14, 2013, with Stanley Grossman, Esq., the senior partner in the Pomerantz firm, who was a longtime colleague and protégé of Mr. Pomerantz. He joined the "Pomerantz firm" in 1969 as its seventh lawyer.

20. As of late 2014, the website for the Pomerantz firm shows that it has still remained relatively small, with only twelve partners, fourteen associates, and five special counsel (for a total of thirty-one lawyers). In comparison, the largest plaintiff's firm specializing in class actions, which is much younger than the Pomerantz firm, is Robbins Geller Rudman & Dowd LLP. An outgrowth of the old Milberg, Weiss firm, its website shows some 173 attorneys (including sixty-seven partners) as of late 2014, making it more than five times larger than the Pomerantz firm. For more with respect to the growth of the Milberg, Weiss firm, see text accompanying notes 27–38, *infra* Chapter 4.

21. Franklin Wood, N.Y. Chamber of Commerce, SURVEY AND REPORT REGARDING STOCKHOLDERS' DERIVATIVES SUITS (1944). This study covered all derivative actions filed in two New York State courts in New York City and in federal court in the Southern District of New York.

22. *Id.* at 112.

23. *Id.* at 57.

24. *Id.* at 78–82.

25. *Id.* at 42.

26. *Id.* at 75.

27. *Id.* at 42.

28. For discussions of the role of the professional plaintiff, see Douglas Branson, *The American Law Institute Principles of Corporate Governance and the Derivative Action: A View from the Other Side,* 43 Wash. & Lee L. Rev. 399, 418 (1986). For the estimate that Harry Lewis has filed between 300 and 400 actions, see Elliott L. Weiss & John S. Beckerman, *Let the Money Do the Monitoring: How Institutional Investors Can Reduce Agency Costs in Securities Class Actions,* 104 Yale L.J. 2053, 2059 n.28 (1995).

29. *See In re* Revlon, Inc. S'holder Litig., 990 A.2d 940, 944 n.3 (Del. Ch. 2010).

30. For the estimate that institutional investors serve as the plaintiff in roughly one-third of all derivative actions, see Jessica Erickson, *Corporate Governance in the Courtroom: An Empirical Analysis,* 51 Wm. & Mary L. Rev. 1749, 1766–1767 (2010). She also finds that a new generation of professional plaintiffs has arisen in derivative actions. *Id.* at 1768.

31. *See* Alfred Conard, *A Behavioral Analysis of Directors' Liability for Negligence,* 1972 Duke L.J. 895, 901 n.21 (1972); George D. Hornstein, *The Death Knell of Stockholders' Derivative Suits in New York,* 32 Cal. L. Rev. 123, 127–128 (1944).

32. As of 2002, some sixteen states still had security-for-expenses statutes. *See* Deborah A. DeMott, SHAREHOLDER DERIVATIVE ACTIONS: LAW AND PRACTICE § 3.2 (2003). New York, itself, abandoned the "security for expenses" bond in 1973, possibly because it had become ineffective, as multiple plaintiffs could easily aggregate their stock to exceed the $50,000 ceiling.

33. *See* Cohen v. Beneficial Ind. Loan Corp., 337 U.S. 541 (1949). *The reasoning in Cohen was artful*. It would have been difficult for the Court to read a state statute to modify federal procedural rules (as the Supreme Court had long resisted allowing state law to modify federal procedural law in order to assure uniformity in federal court procedures), but the Court's decision in *Cohen* subtly read the federal rule to be inapplicable. This result appears to have been driven by the desire to deter "strike" suits (or at least to defer to a strong state law policy seeking to discourage such suits).

34. Because the New York statute expressly permitted plaintiffs to avoid posting a bond if they could secure enough other shareholders to join the suit to exceed either the $50,000 or the 5 percent threshold, plaintiff's attorneys learned to respond to a defendant's request for a bond by seeking a shareholder list so that they could communicate with other shareholders. This was a valid request under the state law of most jurisdictions. Not wanting plaintiff's attorneys communicating with their shareholders and alleging fraud, corporate counsel usually withdrew their demand for a bond. However, when a bond was required, plaintiff's attorneys, including even Pomerantz, were so undercapitalized that they almost always dropped the suit.

35. *See* text accompanying notes 2–10, *infra* Chapter 5.

36. *See* Thomas M. Jones, *An Empirical Examination of the Resolution of Shareholder Derivative and Class Action Lawsuits*, 60 B.U. L. Rev. 542 (1980).

37. *See* Bryant Garth, Ilene H. Nagel, & S. Jay Plager, *The Role of Empirical Research in Assessing the Efficacy of the Shareholders' Derivative Suit: Promise and Potential*, 48 Law & Contemp. Probs. 137, 146–147 (1985).

38. *See* Roberta Romano, *The Shareholder Suit: Litigation without Foundation?*, 7 J. Law, Econ. & Org. 55 (1991).

39. *See* Jessica Erickson, *Corporate Governance in the Courtroom: An Empirical Analysis*, 51 Wm. & Mary L. Rev. 1749, 1798–1803 (2010). This author finds that 43 percent of the derivative actions in federal court that she surveyed were involuntarily dismissed, while another 25 percent were voluntarily dismissed. *Id.* at 1789–1792. Only one action in her survey resulted in a money judgment after trial, while about 30 percent were resolved through settlement. *Id.* at 1794–1795 and 1798. Focusing at length on these settlements, she concludes that the "vast majority of shareholder derivative suits do not benefit the corporations on whose behalf the suits are brought." *Id.* at 1830.

40. *See* Aronson v. Lewis, 473 A.2d 805, 808 (Del. 1984).

41. *See* Erickson, *supra* note 39, at 1782 (finding demand not to be made on directors in approximately 80 percent of the derivative actions surveyed). Even when demand is made, this action may be accompanied by a parallel action in which demand is not made, in order to cover all the litigation bases.

42. *See* White v. Panic, 783 A.2d 543, 551 (Del. 2007). Mere conclusory allegations are insufficient.

43. Where there is no clear property right to a valuable asset (such as the right to control a class or derivative action), a "tragedy of the commons" can occur; that is, individuals tend to deplete "common pool" assets inefficiently and suboptimally. In medieval times, when all had access to the "common" pasture, overgrazing resulted (thereby resulting in the classic "tragedy of the commons" as the land was used inefficiently and reduced in value). *See generally* Garrett Hardin, *The Tragedy of the Commons*, 162 Science 1243 (1968). In the case of class and derivative actions, the absence of a clear property right may lead to multiple actions being filed and a race to settle the action prematurely and at a reduced amount.

44. The most recent empirical survey confirms this long-standing pattern of rare monetary recoveries. *See* Erickson, *supra* note 39, at 1798–1802. She found only four "public company" settlements based exclusively on financial relief (or 9.5 percent of her sample). Another 40.5 percent of the settlements involved only corporate governance reforms, and 42.9 percent involved a mixture of governance reforms and limited monetary compensation. *Id.* at 1798–1799. To every generalization, however, there is at least one prominent exception. In 2011, the Delaware Chancery Court awarded a record $2.031 billion recovery to plaintiffs in a "squeeze-out" merger case. *See In re* S. Peru Copper Corp. S'holders Derivative Litig., 30 A.2d 60 (Del. Ch. 2011), *aff'd sub nom* Ams. Mining Corp. v. Theriault, 51 A.3d 1213 (2012). The subject company was, however, controlled by a dominating foreign parent, did not have an independent board, and did not conform to customary U.S. practices.

45. This chart was prepared by my colleague Professor Jeffrey Gordon. *See* Jeffrey Gordon, *The Rise of Independent Directors in the United States, 1950–2005: Of Shareholder Value and Stock Market Prices,* 59 Stan. L. Rev. 1465, 1474 (2007).

46. For such a representative view, see Kenneth B. Davis, Jr., *The Forgotten Derivative Suit,* 61 Vand. L. Rev. 387, 389 (2008); *see also* Robert B. Thompson & Randall S. Thomas, *The Public and Private Faces of Derivative Litigation,* 57 Vand. L. Rev. 1747, 1749 n.6 (2004) (noting that the derivative action has been pronounced "dead" by many).

47. The information for this table was provided to this author by the Delaware Court of Chancery in May 2013, and the generous assistance of Justice Jack Jacobs of the Delaware Supreme Court in gathering this data is acknowledged.

48. *See* Erickson, *supra* note 39, at 1758–1759.

49. Approximately 30 percent of the derivative actions in the Erickson study settled, with the rest being either involuntarily or voluntarily dismissed. *Id.* at 1794–1795. This is lower than the settlement rate in securities class actions, which is over 50 percent (and is discussed in Chapter 4). However, some of the voluntary dismissals may have been the product of private settlements that were not disclosed to the court, as required under Rule 23.1 of the Federal Rules of Civil Procedure. Thus, the settlement rate may be somewhat higher (although these additional settlements may have violated the Federal Rules).

50. *Id.* at 1806 (median fee award was "slightly less than $1 million").

51. Both forms of misconduct require a brief explanation. Stock option backdating gives the recipient of the option a free ride if the stock price was lower (as it always is) on the date to which the grant of the option is backdated. The holder of the stock option is not profiting as an investor but as the recipient of a gift to the extent of this built-in appreciation. Literally, hundreds of companies engaged in backdating during the late 1990s. Market timing "is a trading strategy that exploits time delays in mutual funds daily valuation systems." *See* Janus Capital Grp. Inc. v. First Derivative Traders, 131 S. Ct. 2296, 2300 n.1 (2011). This tactic grew as U.S. mutual funds invested increasingly in foreign stocks. If a savvy investor knows that stock prices closed six hours earlier on a foreign exchange and that subsequent developments after the close of the market have increased the value of certain companies listed there, he may wish to buy U.S. mutual funds that are known to be invested in that stock, because their price will be determined based on the out-of-date price on the foreign market, and thus the investor can buy the mutual fund at an undervalued price. As Eliot Spitzer once explained, this is "like allowing betting on horse races after they have crossed the finish line." *See* Jerry W. Markham, *Mutual Fund Scandals—A Comparative Analysis of the Role of Corporate Governance in the Regulation of Collective Investment,* 3 Hastings Bus. L.J. 67, 88 (2006). The practice unfairly diluted the value of the shares held by the existing mutual fund investors.

52. For example, stock option backdating may not significantly affect the value of the corporation's shares; thus, a securities class action would yield little damages. In contrast, a derivative action could seek to cancel or revise the stock option. A number of derivative actions did succeed in this regard, forcing their holders to surrender some (or all) of the option's value.

53. In 2012, more than 50 percent of the securities class actions that settled in that year were accompanied by a derivative action filing. *See* Ellen M. Ryan & Laura E. Simmons, SECURITIES CLASS ACTION SETTLEMENTS: 2012 REVIEW AND ANALYSIS 16 (2012). This was up from an average of 30 percent for the years between the passage of the Private Securities Litigation Reform Act in 1995 and 2011. *Id.* Correspondingly, the most recent empirical study of derivative actions finds that a majority of the derivative actions directed at public companies were accompanied by a parallel securities class action. *See* Erickson, *supra* note 39, at 1776.

54. The fact that "tagalong" derivative actions are more likely in cases involving large securities class action settlements supports this interpretation that one of the defendant's purposes in settling the derivative action is to prevent relitigation of the securities class action claims, dressed up as derivative claims.

55. With regard to the paucity of monetary recoveries in derivative actions, see sources cited *supra* notes 35–38. Even when there are monetary recoveries, the ubiquity of D&O insurance, which virtually all public companies carry in ample amounts, makes plain that the cost of the recovery is ultimately borne by

shareholders who bear the cost of the insurance premiums paid by the corporation on such insurance. The prospect of an uninsured recovery against directors is very low. Empirical studies have found very few examples where liability has been actually imposed on outside directors. *See* Bernard S. Black, Brian P. Cheffins & Michael D. Klausner, *Outside Director Liability,* 58 Stan. L. Rev. 1055 (2006) (empirical study of outside director liability finding almost no out-of-pocket payments by outside directors). Thus, from a deterrent perspective, the derivative action represents a monetary threat only when the recovery might exceed the level of D&O insurance, and this is very rare.

56. The Private Securities Litigation Reform Act of 1995 did this by giving presumptive control of the securities class action to the plaintiff with the largest stake in the action. *See* Section 21D(a)(3)(B)(iii) of the Securities Exchange Act of 1934. Its provisions and impact will be discussed in Chapter 4.

57. *See* Erickson, *supra* note 39, at 1769.

58. *Id.* Professor Erickson finds that only two firms appeared on both the "top ten" list for derivative actions and the similar list for securities class actions. Specifically, she first identified the ten most common plaintiff's firms in derivative actions (which firms collectively appeared in over 75 percent of the derivative actions she surveyed in 2006 and 2007), and then she compared that list to the top ten lists for law firms handling securities class actions in 2006, 2007, or 2008. *Id.* The leading common firm to both lists was Coughlin, Stoia, Geller, Rudman & Robbins, which was the successor firm to the California side of Milberg, Weiss. Today, that firm, now known as Robbins, Geller, Rudman & Dowd, is the largest plaintiff's law firm in the nation. Different divisions within this firm appear to play different litigation roles.

59. *See* Cohen v. Beneficial Indus. Loan Corp., 337 U.S. 541, 548 (1949).

60. This greater vulnerability to collusion follows from a basic difference between the derivative action and the class action. In the derivative action, the corporation pays the fees of the successful plaintiff's attorney (whereas in the class action, the plaintiff's attorney's fee comes out of the settlement fund and is thus borne by the class). As a result, in derivative actions, the defendant's legal fees are indemnified by the corporation; the plaintiffs are legally entitled to a fee award from the corporation (if the court finds a "benefit" from the action), and the damages, if any, are usually covered by D&O insurance, on which the corporation pays the insurance premiums. All these costs are ultimately borne by the shareholders and produce a uniquely "bloodless" and circular form of litigation.

4. THE EMERGENCE OF THE CLASS ACTION

1. *See* Stephen C. Yeazell, FROM MEDIEVAL GROUP LITIGATION TO THE MODERN CLASS ACTION (1987). Other historians trace the class action back to

seventeenth-century English Chancery Court practice. The Supreme Court first adopted a procedural rule (Rule 48) to address class actions in 1842.

2. Joseph Story was the American champion of equity, and because the class action in England arose in equity, he endorsed it as well. In *West v. Randall,* 29 F. Cas. 718, 722 (C.C.D.R.I. 1820), and later and more importantly in *Beatty v. Kurtz,* 27 U.S. 566 (1829), he wrote decisions that permitted some individuals in a preexisting group to sue on behalf of the larger group.

3. Justice Story saw group litigation as an outgrowth of the English practice involving "bills of peace," which sought to prevent a multiplicity of suits and avoid unnecessary litigation. *See* 2 Joseph Story, COMMENTARIES ON EQUITY JURISPRUDENCE 148 (1836). Both *West v. Randall* and *Beatty v. Kurtz* can be so viewed in this fashion. *West* involved whether one heir could sue on behalf of all the heirs, and *Beatty* involved a congregation of Lutherans that sought to sue, through their representatives, to protect their church and cemetery. In both cases, Story permitted the representatives to sue on behalf of the group to avoid unnecessary additional litigation.

4. This remained the views of legal academics well into the twentieth century. *See* Zechariah Chafee, *Bills of Peace with Multiple Parties,* 45 Harv. L. Rev. 1297 (1932) (stressing the desirability of avoiding a multiplicity of suits from the standpoint of judicial economy). Looking backward, it is astonishing that a scholar of Chafee's originality and iconoclasm would have been satisfied with this narrow a rationale for the class action or could have failed to recognize the broader potential of the class action as a means for enabling persons to obtain access to the courts who otherwise could not.

5. 8 U. Chi. L. Rev. 684 (1941). The authors never used the term "private attorney general" because that term was only coined in a 1943 discussion by Judge Jerome Frank. *See* Associated Indus. of New York State v. Ickes, 134 F.2d 694, 704 (2d Cir. 1943). Nonetheless, their article was the first clear articulation of the concept.

6. Charles Clark, a former dean of the Yale Law School and then a judge on the Second Circuit Court of Appeals, chaired the drafting committee that wrote the Federal Rules of Civil Procedure and was assisted by James W. Moore, later also a professor at Yale and the author of the first major treatise on the Federal Rules. The Federal Rules of Civil Procedure essentially sought simplification and flexibility, and, to that end, relaxed many of the procedural and pleading barriers of earlier law, presumably with a view to increasing access to the courts.

7. Congress's instruction to this effect was set forth in the Rules Enabling Act (see 28 U.S.C.A. § 2072(b)).

8. The Supreme Court had clearly recognized that such cases could be asserted as class actions in its nineteenth- and early twentieth-century decisions. *See* Smith v. Swormstedt, 57 U.S. 288 (1853) (dispute between factions of Methodist Church over pension rights); Supreme Tribe of Ben-Hur v. Cauble, 255 U.S. 356 (1921) (dispute within fraternal organization over proposed reorganization).

9. Professor Moore explained this tripartite division of class actions in Rule 23 in a contemporaneous law review article as based on the history of class actions. *See* James Moore, *Federal Rules of Civil Procedure: Some Problems Raised by the Preliminary Draft*, 25 Geo. L.J. 551 (1937). If the boundaries between these three categories were unclear, so was the tangled case law that Rule 23 was attempting to restate and codify.

10. For a fuller discussion of the hopeless ambiguities surrounding the "spurious" class action, see Charles Alan Wright, Arthur R. Miller & May Kay Kane, FEDERAL PRACTICE AND PROCEDURE: CIVIL 3D § 1752 (2005). A number of cases indicated that a judgment in a spurious class action would not bind absent parties under the usual principles of *res judicata*. *See* Nagler v. Admiral Corp., 248 F.2d 319, 327 (2d Cir. 1957); Hurd v. Illinois Bell Tel. Co., 234 F.2d 942, 944 (7th Cir. 1956); Kainz v. Anhaeuser-Busch, Inc., 194 F.2d 737, 742 (7th Cir. 1952). It was less certain, however, whether such a judgment would carry collateral estoppel effect with regard to the specific findings made.

11. For early cases certifying antitrust class actions, see *Union Carbide & Carbon Corp. v. Nisley*, 300 F.2d 561 (10th Cir. 1962); *Nagler v. Admiral Corp.*, 248 F.2d 319 (2d Cir. 1957). As discussed in the text, the antitrust class action matured before the securities class action for two distinct reasons: First, the Department of Justice's aggressive campaigns against price fixing in the early 1960s produced a host of follow-on private actions, some of them class actions. Second, the cause of action for securities fraud under Rule 10b-5 did not fully develop until the end of that decade. *See infra* note 19.

12. For an overview, see Gilbert Geis, "The Heavy Electrical Equipment Antitrust Cases of 1961," in Marshall B. Clinard & Richard Quinney, CRIMINAL BE-HAVIOR SYSTEMS: A TYPOLOGY (1967).

13. This is Table 52 (minus some footnotes) from the 1972 REPORT OF THE PROCEEDINGS OF THE JUDICIAL CONFERENCE OF THE UNITED STATES 187 (1972).

14. Defendants feared that corporate executives might have to be deposed in hundreds of cases. All feared that critical early decisions might be made by remote district courts based on an inadequate record in poorly litigated cases, which would then bind other courts. An American Bar Association (ABA) study found that there were a total of 2,233 private antitrust actions brought against defendants in the electrical equipment conspiracy. *See* ABA SECTION OF ANTITRUST LAW MONOGRAPH, THE TREBLE DAMAGES REMEDY 13 (1986).

15. The consolidation is only for pretrial purposes, and ultimately litigants can escape back to their home forum. However, the judge so assigned becomes as a practical matter the supervisor of settlement negotiations (and may see his role as to encourage such settlements). For descriptions of the formation of the coordinating committee and its evolution into the JPML, see Mark Herrmann &

Pearson Bownas, *The Problem of Multidistrict Litigation: An Uncommon Focus on Common Questions*, 82 Tul. L. Rev. 2297 (2008) and Richard Marcus, *Cure-all for an Era of Dispersed Litigation? Toward a Maximalist Use of the Multidistrict Litigation Panel's Transfer Power*, 82 Tul. L. Rev. 2245 (2008).

16. In time, defendants learned that they could exploit overlapping class actions and even solicit low bidders, because the first case to settle would cut off all rival actions on behalf of the same class. The more that one team of plaintiff's attorneys worked hard and refused to settle cheaply, the more that defendants were incentivized to find a different team of plaintiff's attorneys with whom to settle. If necessary, both parties to the settlement could agree to expand the boundaries of their class action to maximize its overlap with others and thus its preclusive impact. Later, in Chapter 8, we will see that this search would mature into a phenomenon known as the "reverse auction" in which defendants structure an auction among rival plaintiff's counsel and settle with the lowest-bidding plaintiff's team.

17. Harold Kohn was probably the leading plaintiff's antitrust lawyer of the twentieth century and is another plaintiff's attorney whose pioneering role in antitrust class actions deserves book-length treatment. For a review of one of his many colorful and controversial cases, see Connie Bruck, *Harold Kohn against the World*, Am. Law., January 1982, at 28. David Berger's firm, Berger & Montague, remains one of the leading firms in antitrust class action litigation. As discussed in Chapter 7, Professor Milton Handler of the Columbia Law School was also a principal architect of the plaintiff's litigation strategy in these cases but thereafter shifted to the defendant's side in antitrust litigation.

18. *See, e.g.,* Escott v. Barchris Const. Corp., 340 F.2d 731 (2d Cir. 1965); Harris v. Palm Springs Alpine Estates Inc., 329 F.2d 12, 16 (9th Cir. 1964); Cherner v. Transitron Electr. Corp., 221 F. Supp. 48 (D. Mass. 1963). One of the earliest of these cases was *Speed v. Transamerica, Corp.,* 99 F. Supp. 808, 833, *modified and aff'd,* 235 F.2d 369 (3d Cir. 1956).

19. Although Rule 10b-5 (the SEC's principal antifraud rule) was adopted by the SEC in 1942, it was primarily used as a weapon of public enforcement. The first case to recognize a private cause of action under it was *Kardon v. National Gypsum Co.,* 73 F. Supp. 798 (E.D. Pa. 1947), but *Kardon* and other early cases generally involved face-to-face transactions and not trading in the open market. Particularly unclear at the time was whether the Rule 10b-5 authorized private litigation against a corporate issuer that had made a materially false statement but had not, itself, traded. That Rule 10b-5 reached these "stock drop" cases was only resolved in favor of liability in the Texas Gulf Sulphur litigation at the end of the 1960s. *See* SEC v. Texas Gulf Sulphur Co.; 401 F.2d 833 (2d Cir. 1968) (en banc).

20. For a review of these problems and the inconsistent judicial response to them in civil rights cases, see Charles Alan Wright, Arthur S. Miller & May Kay Kane, FEDERAL PRACTICE AND PROCEDURE: CIVIL 3D § 1752, at 26–27 (2005).

21. For an overview of the drafting of Rule 23, see Arthur S. Miller, *Of Frankenstein Monsters and Shining Knights: Myth, Reality and the "Class Action Problem,"* 92 Harv. L. Rev. 664 (1979).

22. *See* 1972 REPORTS OF THE PROCEEDINGS OF THE JUDICIAL CONFERENCE OF THE UNITED STATES 187.

23. *Id.* at 189, tbl. 54.

24. *Id.*

25. *See* 1973 REPORTS OF THE PROCEEDINGS OF THE JUDICIAL CONFERENCE OF THE UNITED STATES 155. As of June 30, 1972, some 588 class actions were then pending in the Southern District of New York, while a number of other districts had only one or none. *See* 1972 REPORTS OF THE PROCEEDINGS OF THE JUDICIAL CONFERENCE OF THE UNITED STATES 188.

26. 283 F. Supp. 643 (S.D.N.Y. 1968).

27. For a fuller description of the case and Mr. Weiss, see Patrick Dillon & Carl M. Cannon, CIRCLE OF GREED: THE SPECTACULAR RISE AND FALL OF THE LAWYER WHO BROUGHT CORPORATE AMERICA TO ITS KNEES 59–60 (2010). As a matter of full disclosure, the author notes that he has met both Mr. Weiss and Mr. Lerach (and other partners at Milberg, Weiss) on a number of occasions and has worked as an expert witness with both their law firms.

28. *Id.* at 60.

29. Elsewhere, this author has described in detail an actual such political convention, which was used to organize a large antitrust class action, but it broke down and produced much publicized mudslinging by the rival sides. *See* John C. Coffee, Jr., *Rescuing the Private Attorney General: Why the Model of the Lawyer as Bounty Hunter Is Not Working,* 42 Md. L. Rev. 215 (1983).

30. According to the Administrative Office of the U.S. courts, securities class action filings peaked at 305 in 1974 and then declined to a low of 67 in 1980. As noted above, this data may not be fully accurate because of data handling problems, but a decline of this magnitude (after increases throughout the early 1970s) strongly suggests that the class action procedure was not yet fully accepted or its prerequisites generally agreed upon. Similarly, the same Administrative Office reports show that antitrust class actions peaked at 237 in 1977 and then also declined (to 112 in 1980). This decline could partly be a reaction to the *Eisen* decision's imposition of the cost of notice on the plaintiffs (as next discussed), but that is mere speculation.

31. 417 U.S. 156, 178–179 (1974).

32. 524 F.2d 861 (9th Cir. 1975). *See also* Note, *The Fraud-on-the-Market Theory,* 95 Harv. L. Rev. 1143 (1982).

33. It was also argued for plaintiffs by David Berger of the Philadelphia Bar.

34. *See* Panzirer v. Wolf, 663 F.2d 365 (2d Cir. 1981).

35. *See* Basic Inc. v. Levinson, 485 U.S. 224 (1988). In 2014, with some misgivings and three dissents, the Court reaffirmed its adherence to the "fraud-on-the-market"

doctrine in *Halliburton Co. v. Erica P. John Fund, Inc.*, 134 S. Ct. 2398 (2014), which case is discussed at the end of this chapter.

36. *See* Dillon & Cannon, *supra* note 27, at 2. The $45 billion figure was for recoveries between the time of Milberg's formation and 2010. For the 50 percent figure, see Laura E. Simmons & Ellen M. Ryan, CORNERSTONE RESEARCH, SECURITIES CLASS ACTION SETTLEMENTS: 2006 REVIEW AND ANALYSIS 16 (2006).

37. *Id.* at 3.

38. *See* Blue Chip Stamps v. Manor Drug Stores, 421 U.S. 723, 739 (1975).

39. *See* Dillon & Cannon, *supra* note 27, at 4 (describing efforts of L. John Doerr).

40. *Id.* at 370. Lerach not only opted out, but threatened to sue class counsel (Bernstein, Litowitz, Berger & Grossmann and Barrack, Rodos & Bacine, a prominent Philadelphia plaintiff's firm) for malpractice on behalf of his clients. *Id.* at 369. Mel Weiss particularly saw this threat as disloyal to Milberg.

41. *Id.* at 376. After the convictions of Weiss and Lerach, both firms dropped the name of their founding partners. Milberg, Weiss is now known as Milberg, and the Lerach firm, which is now the largest of the plaintiff's law firms nationwide, reorganized and is now known as Robbins Geller Rudman & Dowd.

42. *Id.* at 378.

43. *See* Ellen M. Ryan & Laura E. Simmons, SECURITIES CLASS ACTIONS: 2012 REVIEW AND ANALYSIS 2 (2013). This decline in the number of settlements has been relatively steady, falling from 119 in 2005, to ninety in 2006, rising to 108 in 2007, then falling again to ninety-seven in 2008, ninety-nine in 2010, and sixty-five in 2011. *Id.*

44. The total settlement dollars paid in 2012 increased by over 100 percent from 2011, from $1.405 billion in 2011 to $2.901 billion in 2012. As next discussed, this reflects the growing importance of "megasettlements."

45. Table 4.2 is a simplified version of the table set forth in Ryan & Simmons, *supra* note 43, at 2.

46. *Id.* at 2.

47. In 2013, Cornerstone Research reports that the total amount paid in securities class action settlements was $4.77 billion (a 46 percent rise over 2012), and the total number of settlements was sixty-seven (up from fifty-seven in 2012, but well under the 199 in 2005). *See* Laarni Bulan, Ellen M. Ryan & Laura E. Simmons, SECURITIES CLASS ACTION SETTLEMENTS—2013 REVIEW AND ANALYSIS 1–3 (2014).

48. One reason that aggregate recoveries are unlikely to again reach their 2006 peak is that the law has changed adversely to plaintiffs. In particular, legal changes have made it more difficult to sue secondary participants. Because both Enron and WorldCom were bankrupt (and thus could not be sued), the record recoveries in those two cases were largely obtained from the investment banks that

served them. Today, they would be far harder to sue in the wake of the Supreme Court's decisions in *Stoneridge Inv. Partners, LLC v. Scientific-Atlanta, Inc.,* 552 U.S. 148 (2008) and *Janus Capital Group, Inc. v. First Derivative Traders, Inc.,* 131 S. Ct. 2296 (2011).

49. In 2013, the average securities class action settlement was $71.3 million (up from $55.5 million, on an inflated-adjusted basis, in 2012), while the median settlement in 2013 was $6.5 million (down from $8.3 million average on an inflated-adjusted basis over 1996 to 2012). *See* Bulan, Ryan & Simmons, *supra* note 47, at 1. This large disparity between the median and the average settlement reflects the two-track character of securities litigation discussed in the text.

50. *Id.* at 1.

51. *Id.* In 2006, megasettlements (i.e., those over $100 million) accounted for 18 percent of all settlements and 95 percent of settlement dollars. In 2012, they accounted for only 11 percent of all settlements, but 74 percent of settlement dollars, and in 2013, this percentage rose to 84 percent. With the exception of 2011, megasettlements have accounted for over 50 percent of all settlement dollars in every year from 2003 through 2012. *See* Ryan & Simmons, *supra* note 43, at 4.

52. *See* Bulan, Ryan and Simmons, *supra* note 47, at 1.

53. For securities class actions settled between 2007 and 2011, the median duration from filing until settlement was 3.3 years. But larger cases take longer to reach settlement. In 2012, the median settlement for cases settling within two years of filing was $2.9 million, as compared with a median settlement of $18 million for cases settling after two years. *See* Ryan & Simmons, *supra* note 43, at 5. Cases recovering $100 million or more may require four years or more to settle, and smaller plaintiff's firms may not be able to afford carrying a major (and thus costly) case this long on a contingent fee basis.

54. *See* Ellen M. Ryan & Laura E. Simmons, SECURITIES CLASS ACTION SETTLEMENTS: 2011 REVIEW AND ANALYSIS 17 (2012). The three firms were Robbins Geller Rudman & Dowd (which handled 35 percent of the settlements in that year), Labaton Sucharow (which handled 13 percent), and Bernstein Litowitz Berger & Grossmann (which handled 10 percent). Ryan and Simmons's 2012 study does not provide updated information on this point.

55. 133 S. Ct. 1184 (2013).

56. 134 S. Ct. 2398 (2014).

57. *Id.* at 2414–2417. The defendant will have the burden of proof at this hearing but will presumably seek to rely on event studies showing that any stock price decline at the time of the corrective disclosure was not statistically significant and so does not confirm any price impact. Much law remains to be made here, and this volume will not make predictions on the precise standard that will emerge.

58. Studying some 726 securities class actions between 2000 and 2003, Michael Klausner and Jason Hegland found that of this number, 443 (or 61 percent)

settled, 249 (or 34 percent) were dismissed, and thirty-four (or 5 percent) remained unresolved. *See* Michael Klausner & Jason Hegland, *When Are Securities Class Actions Dismissed, When Do They Settle, and for How Much?— Part II*, 23 PLUS Journal 1 at Fig. 1 (2010). On this basis, an estimate of a 60 percent survival rate seems conservative.

59. No authoritative database is available on the performance of opt-outs, as these cases typically settle on a confidential basis (because they are not class actions and are not subject to judicial approval). Still, public pension funds that opt out do typically report their recoveries. In the AOL Time Warner class action, several institutional plaintiffs have reported that they did between seven and twenty-four times better than if they had stayed in the class. For a detailed comparison by this author, see John C. Coffee, Jr., *Litigation Governance: Taking Accountability Seriously*, 110 Colum. L. Rev. 228, 312–313 (2010).

60. Between 2003 and 2012, median settlements as a percentage of estimated damages ranged between a high at 3.3 percent (in 2003) and an all-time low of 1.8 percent in 2012. *See* Ryan & Simmons, *supra* note 43, at 8. In 2013, this percentage was 2.1 percent. *See* Bulan, Ryan & Simmons, *supra* note 47, at 8. The factor that most determines the percentage of the damages recovered is the size of the estimated damages, as the percentage declines as the estimated damages increase. *See* Ryan & Simmons, *supra* note 43, at 8. In addition to the size of the estimated damages, other factors also influence the percentage recovered, including whether there was a parallel SEC enforcement action or an accounting restatement.

61. *See* Coffee, *supra* note 59, at 312 (citing examples of recoveries in the 70 percent range or higher and noting that CalPERS recovered $117.7 million in one case where it opted out based on estimated losses of $129 million, thus implying a 90 percent recovery).

62. Some defendants are seeking to obtain class certification at an earlier moment before the settlement is announced, as class members must opt out within a short period after the class is certified. Their hope is that rationally apathetic shareholders will do nothing at this stage and will later have no opportunity to opt out once the settlement is announced. Rule 23 was revised to permit the court to give a second opportunity to plaintiffs to opt out at this later, settlement approval stage, but courts may not be motivated to exercise that opportunity, as they may prefer that class members remain within the class.

63. Most settlement agreements in securities class actions contain a "blowout" provision under which the defendants can rescind the settlement agreement if more than a specified percentage (usually 10 percent) of the class opts out. The problem with this provision is that if it is exercised, it leaves the defendant facing an undesired trial on the merits. Until recently, this provision was never exercised (although it may have sometimes led to renegotiation of the settle-

ment's terms). In at least one recent securities class action, however, the blowout provision has been exercised, but this has little impact on the opt-outs and can only lead to either a reduced recovery in the class action (to reflect the unexpected level of opt-outs) or a trial.

64. ATP Tour Inc. v. Deutscher Tennis Bund, 91 A. 3d 554 (Del. 2014).

65. *Id.* at 560. Delaware law traditionally provides that corporate powers may not be used for an "improper purpose." *See* Schnell v. Chris-Craft Industries, 285 A. 2d 437 (Del. 1971).

66. This author testified before the SEC's Investor Advisory Committee on October 9, 2014, and described these developments in more detail. *See* "Fee-Shifting Bylaws: Can They Apply in Federal Court?—The Case for Preemption" (Testimony of Professor John C. Coffee, Jr.), *available at* http://ssrn.com/abstract=2508973.

67. *See* Section 173 ("Claims against Corporation") of the Amended and Restated Memorandum and Articles of Association of Alibaba Group Holding Limited, which is incorporated in the Cayman Islands. For a fuller description, see Coffee, *supra* note 66, at 1.

68. In Globus v. Law Research Service, Inc., 418 F. 2d 1276 (2d Cir. 1969), the Second Circuit held that, at least in cases where the violation involved scienter, indemnification of such liabilities was against the public policy expressed in the federal securities laws and so was prohibited. *See also* Heizer Corp. v. Ross, 601 F. 2d 330, 334 (7th Cir. 1979). Similarly, the SEC has long refused to accelerate registration statements containing mandatory arbitration provisions that barred shareholders from suing in court. For a brief review, see Note, *In a Bind: Mandatory Arbitration Clauses in the Corporate Derivative Context,* 28 Ohio St. J. on Disp. Resol., 737, 745 (2013). In this author's judgment, there is no valid conceptual difference between mandatory arbitration and mandatory fee-shifting provisions, which can each be preclusive.

5. MERGER AND ACQUISITION CLASS ACTIONS

1. This heightened standard dates back to at least 1983 and Delaware's seminal decision in *Weinberger v. UOP, Inc.,* 457 A.2d 701 (Del. 1983), which placed the burden on a majority shareholder to prove the "entire fairness" of a squeeze-out merger. *See also* Kahn v. Lynch Commc'n Sys., Inc., 638 A.2d 1110 (Del. 1994).

2. There has been a wealth of recent scholarship on this topic. *See,* in particular, John Armour, Bernard Black & Brian Cheffins, *Delaware's Balancing Act,* 87 Indiana L.J. 1345 (2012); John Armour, Bernard Black & Brian Cheffins, *Is Delaware Losing Its Cases?,* 9 J. Empirical Legal Stud. 605 (2012); Matthew D. Cain & Steven M. Davidoff, *A Great Game: The Dynamics of State Competition and Litigation* (Jan. 2013), *available at* http://ssrn.com/abstract=1984758; Brian

Cheffins, John Armour & Bernard Black, *Delaware Corporate Litigation and the Fragmentation of the Plaintiff's Bar*, 2012 Colum. Bus. L. Rev. 427 (2012); John C. Coffee, Jr., *The Delaware Court of Chancery: Change, Continuity—and Competition*, 2012 Colum. Bus. L. Rev. 387 (2012); Robert M. Daines & Olga Koumrian, SHAREHOLDER LITIGATION INVOLVING MERGERS AND ACQUISITIONS (2013); Sean J. Griffith & Alexandra D. Lahav, *The Market for Preclusion in Merger Litigation* (Oct. 1, 2012), *available at* http://ssrn.com/abstract=2155809; Leo E. Strine, Jr., Lawrence A. Hamermesh & Matthew C. Jennejohn, *Putting Stockholders First, Not the First-Filed Complaint*, 69 Bus. Law. 1 (2013).

3. *See* Cheffins, Armour & Black, *supra* note 2.

4. *See* Strine, Hamermesh & Jennejohn, *supra* note 2, at 57–66. These authors note that Delaware never treated the "first to file" rule as "ironclad." But, even if the Delaware courts did not grant automatic priority to the first filed action, Delaware counsel may have done so. The law firms bringing these cases were generally not based in Delaware and thus had to find a Delaware firm to move to allow it to appear (with the Delaware firm) on a *pro hac vice* basis. One particular Delaware law firm long performed this role for out-of-state plaintiff's firms, and it gave priority to the first out-of-state firm to retain it. This system has now also come unglued, as there are today multiple Delaware plaintiff's firms willing and able to serve out-of-state counsel as their local counsel.

5. *Id.* at 88. *See In re* Citigroup Inc. S'holder Derivative Litig., 964 A.2d 106, 117 (Del. Ch. 2009); Ryan v. Gifford, 918 A.2d 341, 349 (Del. Ch. 2007); Biondi v. Scrushy, 820 A.2d 1148, 1158–59 (Del. Ch. 2003).

6. On a few and rare occasions, Delaware courts have taken control of a case away from a plaintiff's firm that the court decides is doing nothing. *See In re* Revlon S'holders Litig., 990 A.2d 940 (Del. Ch. 2010). This is unusual in the polite culture of Delaware, but it also does not solve the defendant's problem, as the case now becomes more likely to settle outside Delaware.

7. Probably the first article to notice this trend toward fleeing Delaware appeared in 2007 and was written by a very experienced practitioner. *See* Theodore Mirvis, *Anywhere but Chancery: Ted Mirvis Sounds an Alarm and Suggests Some Solutions*, 7 M&A J. 17 (2007). In short, by 2007 the trend was already established.

8. *See* Cheffins, Armour & Black, *supra* note 2, at 439.

9. *See* C.N.V. Krishnan et al., *Shareholder Litigation in Mergers and Acquisitions*, 12 (Vanderbilt Law & Econ. Research Paper No. 10–37 (2012)), *available at* http://ssrn.com/abstract=1722227.

10. *See* Daines & Koumrian, *supra* note 2, at 1, fig. 1.

11. *Id.* at fig. 2.

12. *Id.* at 2, fig. 3.

13. *See* Browning Jeffries, *The Plaintiffs' Lawyer's Transaction Tax: The New Cost of Doing Business in Public Company Deals*, 11 Berkeley Bus L. J. 55, 58–60, 2014; *see*

also Cain & Davidoff, *supra* note 2. Of course, when the action is filed before the proxy statement is released, it cannot challenge at this point the adequacy of the disclosures made therein, but it is generally amended once the proxy statement is released to contest its contents and the settlement is generally based on revised proxy disclosures.

14. *See In re* Revlon S'holders Litig., 990 A. 2d 940, 945 (Del. Ch. 2010).

15. Daines & Koumrian, *supra* note 2, at 5, fig. 6.

16. *See* text and note accompanying note 58, *supra* Chapter 4.

17. *See* Cain & Davidoff, *supra* note 2, at 17, 37–38. This study covers the years 2006 through 2012.

18. *See* Daines & Koumrian, *supra* note 2, at 9.

19. *Id.* at 9, fig. 9.

20. The term "reverse auction," which is widely used, was originally coined by this author in a different litigation context. *See* John C. Coffee, Jr., *Class Wars: The Dilemma of Mass Tort Class Action,* 95 Colum. L. Rev. 1343, 1370–1371 (1995) ("[The] 'reverse auction' [is] a jurisdictional competition among different teams of plaintiff's attorneys in different actions that involve the same underlying allegations. . . . The practical impact of this approach is that it allows the defendants to pick and choose the plaintiff team with which they will deal. Indeed, it signals to the unscrupulous plaintiff's attorney that by filing a parallel shadow action in state court, it can underbid the original plaintiff's attorney team.").

21. *See* Matsushita Elec. Indus. Co. Ltd. v. Epstein, 516 U.S. 367 (1996) (holding that a Delaware court settlement could block even claims under federal law over which the Delaware court lacked subject matter jurisdiction). Due process of law requires that, before "full faith and credit" is given to a judgment or settlement, there must be a finding that the class members received "adequate representation" in the proceeding that is to be given finality, but this issue of adequate representation can rarely be collaterally attacked. Delaware will also defer to a final judgment in a different jurisdiction involving a Delaware corporation.

22. For such a vivid example and the use of the term "reverse auction" by Judge Richard Posner, see *Reynolds v. Beneficial Nat'l Bank,* 288 F.3d 277, 282 (7th Cir. 2002). There, plaintiffs in several states had certified class actions and were approaching trials in which some were seeking hefty awards of punitive damages. Fearful of the outcome in those trials, defendants approached some plaintiff's attorneys in Chicago and invited them to settle a nationwide class action in federal court to block those trials. At the time they were approached to settle, the plaintiff's attorneys did not appear to have any pending action (or probably any clients), but they found some quickly.

　　True "reverse auctions" occur less frequently in the M&A context, because no plaintiff's attorney in this context has a realistic chance of enjoining the action or securing a large money judgment. Defense counsel would usually prefer that all (or most) of the competing plaintiff's attorneys join in a global settlement (in order to avoid lengthy hearings in which the settlement is attacked as collusive or inadequate), but this requires that all the plaintiff's attorneys join in the settlement and share what is usually a modest fee to begin with. As a result, negotiations are slow and frequently break down.

6. THE MASS TORT CLASS ACTION

1. *See* text accompanying notes 2–5, *supra* Chapter 4. This desire to avoid repetitive litigation was also the function of the "bill of peace" in early equity practice.
2. One qualification needs to be recognized here. Class aggregation may benefit claimants who have a low prospect of success at trial (for example, because of the lack of scientific evidence). In this setting, aggregation can force a settlement because the defendant cannot risk trial of a multibillion dollar class action. This risk that an "immature" mass tort could gain leverage at the class level, even though the individual claims could not succeed, was addressed at an early point by courts, which refused to certify a litigation class in this context. *See In re* Rhone-Poulenc Rorer, Inc., 51 F.3d 1293 (7th Cir. 1995) (granting mandamus and reversing certification of nationwide class action of hemophiliacs infected by the AIDS virus because too little evidence supported this "immature" mass tort). Thus, although it is true that plaintiffs with weak claims on the merits can benefit from class certification, those cases are often not certifiable.
3. Some toxic products, most notably asbestos, have a long latency period during which injuries (most notably, mesothelioma) can manifest themselves as much as forty or more years after the end of the exposure. Thus, even after a product has been removed from the market, the producer can expect continuing claims to be asserted. As a result, the significance of these future claims may vastly outweigh present claims made against the producer. In *Amchem Products, Inc. v. Windsor,* 521 U.S. 591, 598 (1997), the Court cited estimates (made in 1991) that as many as 265,000 asbestos-caused deaths might result by 2015.
4. The asbestos industry's largest producer, Johns-Manville Corporation, filed for bankruptcy and transferred 80 percent of its ownership to a bankruptcy trust in 1988. Two years later, that trust was effectively insolvent. By the end of 1994, some 240,000 claims had been filed against this trust, and several hundred thousand more claims were expected. Judge Jack Weinstein orchestrated an effort to obtain additional funds from the reorganized Manville Corporation to fund the payments by the trust. *See In re* Joint E. & S. Dist. Asbestos Litig., 129 B.R. 710 (E.&S.D.N.Y. 1991), *vacated on other grounds,* 982 F.2d 721 (2d Cir. 1992), *modified sub nom. In re* Findley, 993 F.2d 7 (2d Cir. 1993). This experience may have frustrated the asbestos industry, convincing it that bankruptcy reorganizations

did not provide final relief, because it could be reopened if the funds initially contributed proved inadequate. In any event, at least fifteen major asbestos producers filed for bankruptcy reorganization between 1982 and the filing of the first global asbestos class action. *See* John C. Coffee, Jr., *Class Wars: The Dilemma of the Mass Tort Class Action,* 95 Colum. L. Rev. 1343, 1386 n.163 (1995).

5. For the best of these articles, see David Rosenberg, *The Causal Connection in Mass Exposure Cases: A "Public Law" Vision of the Tort System,* 97 Harv. L. Rev. 851 (1984); *see also* David Rosenberg, *Class Actions for Mass Torts: Doing Individual Justice by Collective Means,* 62 Ind. L.J. 561 (1987).

6. *Amendments to Rules of Civil Procedure,* 39 F.R.D. 69, 103 (1966). The chief draftsman of the 1966 revision of Rule 23, Harvard Professor Benjamin Kaplan, has also described the intent of Rule 23(b)(3) as limited and not designed to reach mass accidents. *See* Benjamin Kaplan, *Continuing Work of the Civil Committee: 1966 Amendments to the Federal Rules of Civil Procedure,* 81 Harv. L. Rev. 356, 386, 391–393 (1967).

7. *See* Deborah R. Hensler & Mark A. Peterson, *Understanding Mass Personal Injury Litigation: A Socio-Legal Analysis,* 59 Brook. L. Rev. 961 (1993). The phenomenon of higher rates of "claiming" dates back to the 1960s and probably relates to the development of mass media and other informational networks. In any event, between 1961 and 1984, federal court tort filings nearly doubled. *See* John G. Fleming, THE AMERICAN TORT PROCESS 34 (1988).

8. *See, e.g., In re* N. Dist. of Cal. "Dalkon Shield" IUD Prods. Liab. Litig., 521 F. Supp. 1188 (N.D. Cal.), *modified,* 525 F. Supp. 887 (N.D. Cal. 1981), *vacated,* 693 F.2d 847 (9th Cir. 1982). The Ninth Circuit vacated a litigation class in this decision, but later the Fourth Circuit upheld a "settlement class." *See infra* note 16. The Dalkon Shield was an intrauterine birth control device.

9. *In re* "Agent Orange" Prod. Liab. Litig., 818 F.2d 145 (2d Cir. 1987), *cert. denied,* 484 U.S. 1004 (1988) (upholding Judge Jack Weinstein's certification of a settlement class).

10. *See In re* Federal Skywalk Cases, 93 F.R.D. 415 (W.D. Mo.), *rev'd,* 680 F.2d 1175 (8th Cir.), *cert. denied,* 459 U.S. 988 (1982).

11. In both the above *Dalkon Shield* case and in the *Federal Skywalk* case, class certification was denied when the plaintiffs sought to certify a litigation class for trial but later granted when the parties agreed to a "settlement only" class action. *See also* Harrigan v. United States, 63 F.R.D. 402, 407 (E.D. Pa. 1974) (rejecting class certification in a personal injury mass tort class action against the Veterans Administration for negligent surgery on veterans).

12. 782 F.2d 468 (5th Cir. 1986).

13. *Id.* at 473.

14. *See In re* Asbestos School Litig., 104 F.R.D. 422 (E.D. Pa. 1984), *aff'd in part,* 789 F.2d 996 (3d Cir.) (reversing non–opt-out provision, but otherwise allowing

a permissive class certification for property damages), *cert. denied,* 479 U.S. 852 (1986).

15. *In re* "Agent Orange" Prod. Liab. Litig., 818 F.2d 145 (2d Cir. 1987), *cert. denied,* 484 U.S. 1004 (1988).

16. *See In re* A.H. Robins Co., 880 F.2d 709 (4th Cir.), *cert. denied,* 493 U.S. 959 (1989). Earlier, the Ninth Circuit had denied certification of a litigation class. *See supra* note 8. But between 1983, when the Ninth Circuit denied certification, and 1989 (the date of the Fourth Circuit's decision approving a settlement class), defendants may have come to realize that a settlement class was their best protection against unending individual litigation.

17. *See* Francis E. McGovern, *Resolving Mature Mass Tort Litigation,* 69 B.U. L. Rev. 659, 660 (1989). The early flood of asbestos litigation came from jurisdictions in which World War II naval shipyards were located. Although many industries used asbestos, it was comparatively simple for plaintiff's attorneys to screen workers in these shipyards and develop a large number of cases. Unions sometimes assisted in this process. The Eastern District of Texas included a number of Gulf Coast shipyards.

18. *See* Deborah R. Hensler & Mark A. Peterson, *Understanding Mass Personal Injury Litigation: A Socio-Legal Analysis,* 59 Brook. L. Rev. 961 (1993).

19. Deborah R. Hensler, *Reading the Tort Litigation Tea Leaves: What's Going on in the Civil Liability System?,* 16 Just. Sys. J. 139, 147 (1993). The rate began to fall soon afterward and was down to a still sizable 57 percent of new products liability cases by 1991. *Id.*

20. *See* Georgine v. Amchem Prods. Inc., 157 F.R.D. 246, 265 (E.D. Pa. 1994) (citing report prepared by the Ad Hoc Committee on Asbestos Litigation appointed by Chief Justice Rehnquist).

21. *See* Cimino v. Raymark Indus., 751 F. Supp. 649, 652 (E.D. Texas 1990). Other courts in nonasbestos mass tort cases have made similarly frustrated findings. *See In re* Bendectin Prods. Liab. Litig., 102 F.R.D. 239, 240 & n.3 (S.D. Ohio 1984) (estimating that trial of the mass tort cases involving Bendectin would take 21,000 trial days or 105 judge years).

22. *See* Thomas E. Willging, TRENDS IN ASBESTOS LITIGATION 15 (1987) (estimating that 40 percent of asbestos filings in late 1970s and early 1980s were in those three district courts, and 52 percent were in the First and Fifth Circuits).

23. The ubiquity of the use of asbestos in ship construction appears to have made it cost efficient for plaintiff's attorneys to pay for wholesale screening of former shipyard workers, assisted by their unions. In some cases, this "screening" seems to have involved significant fabrication of claims.

24. Richard B. Sobol, BENDING THE LAW: THE STORY OF THE DALKON SHIELD BANKRUPTCY 106 (1991).

25. Peter H. Schuck, AGENT ORANGE ON TRIAL: MASS TOXIC DISASTERS IN THE COURTS 205 (1986).

26. For a fuller description of the "mass tort cycle" from "immature" to "mature" phases, see Coffee, *supra* note 4, at 1359–1363. These terms did not originate with this author. *See* Francis E. McGovern, *Toward a Functional Approach for Managing Complex Litigation,* 53 U. Chi. L. Rev. 440, 482 (1986) (describing normal cyclical evolution of a mass tort).

27. For a fuller discussion of this point, see Coffee, *supra* note 4, at 1359–1361. The basic distinction is that in much recurring litigation (automobile accidents or medical malpractice), the issues are highly fact specific. Mass tort cases, in contrast, turn on common scientific issues of causation. Evidence that wins in one case will be heard again in the next case.

28. *See* Hensler & Peterson, *supra* note 18, at 966.

29. *Id.; see also* Morton Mintz, AT ANY COST: CORPORATE GREED, WOMEN, AND THE DALKON SHIELD 4 (1985).

30. As asbestos litigation surged in the 1980s, the principal producers organized into a defense consortium to pursue common defenses and employ common counsel. *See* Coffee, *supra* note 4, at 1365–1366.

31. JUDICIAL CONFERENCE OF THE UNITED STATES, REPORT OF THE JUDICIAL CONFERENCE AD HOC COMMITTEE ON ASBESTOS LITIGA-TION 2 (Mar. 1991). For a fuller discussion of this report, see Coffee, *supra* note 4, at 1363–1364 and 1389.

32. JUDICIAL CONFERENCE OF THE UNITED STATES, *supra* note 31, at 3.

33. For a fuller description, see Coffee, *supra* note 4, at 1389–1390. This petition followed an earlier, but unsuccessful, attempt by ten federal district judges to form an "ad hoc nationwide coordinating committee" to resolve asbestos litigation.

34. *See In re* Asbestos Prods. Liab. Litig., 771 F. Supp. 415 (J.P.M.L. 1991). Symptomatically, Philadelphia (i.e., the Eastern District of Pennsylvania) was the district court that then had the most asbestos cases on its civil docket (5,703). *See* Coffee, *supra* note 4, at 1390 n.183.

35. This letter from Judge Robert M. Parker, Chief Judge of the Eastern District of Texas, to Judge Charles R. Weiner, dated August 1, 1991, was also sent to a number of other federal judges active in asbestos litigation, including Judge Jack Weinstein of the Eastern District of New York, who filed it with the clerk of the district court for the Eastern District of New York. For a fuller description, see Coffee, *supra* note 4, at 1390–1391.

36. *See* Coffee, *supra* note 4, at 1391.

37. *Id.* Indeed, a majority of the thirteen-member plaintiffs' steering committee filed a motion with the JPML, asking it to dissolve the multi-district litigation proceeding and transfer the cases back to their original courts. *Id.* at 1391 n.186.

38. *Id.* at 1392. These two firms had very larger inventories of cases and were targeted by defendants precisely because they would benefit the most from inventory settlements. Ness, Motley, Loadholt, Richardson & Poole of South Carolina was

generally regarded to have been the most active firm in asbestos litigation with the largest inventory, and the Greitzer & Locks firm had the largest inventory of cases in the Philadelphia region.

39. *See* Coffee, *supra* note 4, at 1393. The case became known as *Georgine v. Amchem Products, Inc.,* 157 F.R.D. 246 (E.D. Pa. 1994).

40. This was expressly set forth in the stipulation of settlement. Coffee, *supra* note 4, at 1392.

41. *Id.* at 1393.

42. Judge Lowell A. Reed, Jr., of the same district court, was appointed by Judge Weiner to conduct the fairness hearing on the settlement. Elaborate hearings were held, at which this author testified on a pro bono basis (receiving no payment, other than travel expenses) for the objectors.

43. Coffee, *supra* note 4, at 1393.

44. Georgine v. Amchem Prods., 83 F. 3d 610 (3d Circ. 1996), vacating 157 F.R.D 837 (CE.D. Pa. 1995).

45. Only a few plaintiff's firms did object, and these were plaintiff's firms that tended to specialize in trials rather than large inventory settlements. This was another division in the plaintiff's bar: the split between "trial" lawyers and "settlers." At the fairness hearing the trial lawyers were led (effectively) by the late Fred Baron of Baron & Budd, a Texas firm specializing in individual asbestos litigation. On appeal they were represented by Harvard Law Professor Laurence Tribe.

46. Under most inventory settlements and bankruptcy reorganizations, those who had asbestos-related symptoms received compensation for their lesser injuries, but not under *Georgine.* Indeed, under the Johns-Manville settlement, a person with asbestos disease could receive up to $300,000, depending on the degree of disability, but, even if disabled, this same person would receive only between $5,800 and $7,500 under *Georgine. See* Coffee, *supra* note 4, at 1396.

47. *Id.* at 1394.

48. *Id.* at 1394–1395 (quoting testimony of Dr. Christine Oliver of the Harvard Medical School testifying for objectors to the settlement).

49. *Id.* at 1396–1397.

50. Under the *Georgine* settlement, the amounts to be received by a future claimant (if the claimant was not blocked by the "case flow maximums" limiting the number of cases to be compensated per year) was fixed for the first ten years without any inflation adjustment. *Id.* at 1399. Thereafter, the parties could negotiate an inflation adjustment. but this was not mandatory and would probably require that the plaintiffs trade something else in return.

51. Ahearn v. Fibreboard Corp., 162 F.R.D. 505 (E.D. Tex. 1995), *modified, In re Asbestos Litig.,* 90 F.3d 963 (5th Cir. 1996).

52. *See* Coffee, *supra* note 4, at 1400. This number later rose to over 200,000 asbestos-related claims by the time the proposed settlement was finalized.

53. *Id.*
54. *Id.*
55. *Id.* at 1400–1401.
56. *Id.* at 1401. This was the same date (September 9, 1993) as the *Ahearn* class action was filed. Obviously, Judge Parker wasted no time. As in *Georgine,* the class was nearly exclusively composed of future claimants.
57. *Id.*
58. *Id.* The *Ahearn* class action notice to the class disclosed that approval of the global class action settlement "will operate to trigger payments in excess of $300 million" to present claimant clients of class counsel. *Id.* at 1401 n.328.
59. *Id.* at 1402. This small amount apparently came from other insurance resources.
60. *Id.* The guardian ad litem appointed by the Court to protect the future claimants found that, once its asbestos liabilities were removed, Fibreboard's market value might be $250 to $300 million. Other experts placed it in the range of $230 to $240 million. It seems unusual that such a company could escape in this fashion, paying no more than $10 million to obtain releases that made it worth somewhere in the $200 to $300 million value. Again, this may reflect the lack of adversarial bargaining.
61. *Id.*
62. *Id.* at 1403. This ruling was based on Judge Parker's finding that Fibreboard's insurance assets (which were obtained through a parallel settlement with its insurers) were a "limited fund," which would be exhausted before all the individual claimants could be paid. Historically, Rule 23(b)(1)(B) was used in "limited fund" cases (for example, a specific asset to which various claimants asserted rights), but here the fund was "limited" only by the agreement of the parties.
63. Georgine v. Amchem Prods., Inc., 83 F.3d 610 (3d Cir. 1996).
64. Amchem Prods., Inc. v. Windsor, 521 U.S. 591, 597 (1997).
65. *Id.* at 606.
66. *Id.* at 626.
67. *Id.* at 621.
68. *Id.* at 620.
69. *Id.* at 627.
70. *Id.* at 628.
71. *Id.*
72. 527 U.S. 815 (1999).
73. *Id.* at 838–839.
74. *Id.* at 845.
75. One much cited estimate is that transaction costs consume $.61 of each asbestos litigation dollar (of which $.37 is attributable to defendants' litigation costs). *See* Cimino v. Raymark Indus., 751 F. Supp. 649, 651 (E.D. Tex. 1990). *See also* Alvin

B. Rubin, *Mass Torts and Litigation Disasters,* 20 Ga. L. Rev. 429, 434 (1986) (discussing studies that show that the majority of payments in product liability cases are for legal services).

76. For recent analyses of this settlement, see Nancy J. Moore, *Symposium: Lawyering for Groups: Civil Rights, Mass Torts and Everything in Between: Ethical Issues in Mass Tort Plaintiff Representation: Beyond the Aggregate Settlement Rule,* 81 Fordham L. Rev. 3233, 3236 (2013); Howard M. Erichson & Benjamin C. Zipursky, *Consent Versus Closure,* 96 Cornell L. Rev. 265, 279–292 (2011).

77. These provisions in the Vioxx settlement may arguably violate ABA Model Rule 1.8(g) (the "Aggregate Settlement Rule"). For the debate, see the sources cited *supra* note 76.

78. For a good analysis of these problems, see Charles Silver & Geoffrey P. Miller, *The Quasi–Class Action Method of Managing Multi-District Litigations: Problems and a Proposal,* 63 Vand. L. Rev. 107 (2010). For the opposite perspective, see Linda S. Mullenix, *Dubious Doctrines: The Quasi–Class Action,* 80 U. Cinn. L. Rev. 389, 390 (2012) (asserting that the quasi-class action is "an unfortunate drift into further lawlessness in administering aggregate claims.").

79. *See* Silver and Miller, *supra* note 78.

80. The best known of these cases is *In re* Zyprexa, 433 F. Supp. 2d 268 (E.D.N.Y. 2008); *see also* Jack Weinstein, *The Democratization of Mass Actions in the Internet Age,* 45 Colum. J. L. & Soc. Probs. 451 (2012).

III. THE SEARCH FOR REFORM

1. This pattern of modest settlements (in percentage terms) and high fee awards has changed only slightly over the last decade. As of 2000, the data showed that securities class actions yielded recoveries of under 5 percent of the potential damages but paid fee awards of 31–33 percent. *See* John C. Coffee, Jr., *Litigation Governance: A Gentle Critique of the Third Circuit Task Force Report,* 74 Temple L. Rev. 805, 806 (2001). Since that time, the size of the average recovery has risen, the percentage of the loss recovered has fallen, and fee awards as a percentage of the recovery have declined—all marginally. This is all consistent with the standard observation that fee awards are a declining percentage of the recovery.

2. Virtually all publicly held corporations have adopted a provision in their certificate of incorporation that eliminates (or at least sharply curtails) directorial liability for monetary damages for breach of the duty of care. The first state to adopt such a provision was Delaware. *See* Delaware General Corporation Law § 102(b)(7). Almost all the other states have adopted a corresponding provision. These charter amendments do not apply to breaches of the duty of loyalty or actions not in good faith.

3. On this theme of the stratification of the plaintiff's bar and the recent growth in size of the leading firms, see Morris Ratner, *A New Model of Plaintiff's Class Action Attorneys*, 31 Rev. Litig. 757, 773–781 (2012) (listing the size of the major plaintiff's firms). Some practices, such as "copy cat" complaints, are, he suggests, more associated with the smaller "bottom feeder" firms. Hopefully, larger plaintiff's firms may acquire a greater interest in developing and protecting reputational capital.

7. A PRELUDE TO CLASS ACTION REFORM

1. 483 U.S. 224 (1988). This doctrine remains, however, subject to attack.
2. The leading such decision was *Castano v. American Tobacco Co.,* 84 F.3d 734 (5th Cir. 1996) (rejecting a nationwide class action on behalf of tobacco victims). Unlike the asbestos cases, this decision did not involve a settlement class and was fiercely fought by defendants. *See also In re* Rhone-Poulenc Rorer, Inc., 51 F.3d 1293 (7th Cir. 1995) (refusing to certify a class in the case of an immature mass tort) (Posner, J).
3. The PSLRA's provisions are set forth further in sections 21D and 21E of the Securities Exchange Act of 1934.
4. *See* text accompanying notes 43–54, *supra* Chapter 4.
5. *See* Securities Litigation Uniform Standards Act of 1998, Pub. L. No. 105-353, 112 Stat. 3227 (codified in various sections of 15 U.S.C.).
6. For the defendant's side of this story, see Victor E. Schwartz et al., *Asbestos Litigation in Madison County, Illinois: The Challenge Ahead,* 16 Wash. U.J.L. & Pol'y 235 (2004). Several counties in Texas and Alabama were generally considered close rivals to Madison County.
7. For a description of "drive-by certification," see Stephen B. Burbank, *The Class Action Fairness Act of 2005 in Historical Context: A Preliminary View,* 156 U. Pa. L. Rev. 1439, 1507–1509 (2008).
8. 131 S. Ct. 2541 (2011).
9. *Id.* at 2547.
10. *Id.* at 2554.
11. *Id.* at 2552.
12. *Id.* (citing *General Telephone Co. of Southwest v. Falcon,* 457 U.S. 147, 157–158, for the proposition that the class must "have suffered the same injury" as the class representative).
13. 131 S. Ct. 1740 (2011).
14. *See* Stephanie Strom, *When "Liking" a Brand Online Voids the Right to Sue,* N.Y. Times, Apr. 16, 2014, at B-1. Joining a Facebook "community" relating to Cheerios also triggered the mandatory arbitration provision (or so General Mills asserted).

15. *See* Richard Frankel, *The Arbitration Clause as Super Contract,* 91 Wash. U. L. Rev. 531 (2014) (describing ways in which the Court has uncharacteristically overridden state law to favor arbitration as a policy).

16. 133 S. Ct. 1426 (2013). Lower federal courts appear to be resisting *Comcast* and permitting individualized damage hearings. *See* Butler v. Sears Roebuck & Co., 727 F.3d 796 (7th Cir. 2013) (Posner); *In re* Whirlpool Corp. Front-Loading Washer Products Liab. Litig., 722 F.3d 838 (6th Cir. 2013). It is premature to predict how successful this resistance will prove (although Judge Posner's decision for the Seventh Circuit is highly persuasive).

17. *See* Halliburton Co. v. Erica P. John Fund, Inc., 134 S. Ct. 2398 (2014). This case was discussed in Chapter 4.

18. One qualification is needed here: many courts might still certify a settlement class on these facts. This would be in defiance of the Court's holding in *Ortiz v. Fibreboard Corp.,* 527 U.S. 815 (1999) (requiring litigation and settlement classes to meet the same standards), but passive disobedience to that decision continues.

19. Rule 23(b)(3)(D) requires that, prior to certification, the Court consider "the likely difficulties in managing a class action." This is known as the manageability requirement and would be contestable on these facts.

20. The Fraud-on-the-Market Doctrine, first announced in *Basic, Inc. v. Levinson,* 485 U.S. 224 (1988), spares plaintiffs from any obligation to prove individual reliance, but it only applies to securities trading in an efficient securities market.

21. *See* Halliburton Co. v. Erica P. John Fund, Inc., 134 S. Ct. 2398 (2014).

22. Among recent Supreme Court decisions that could have greatly curtailed the class action's availability (but did not) are the following: Shady Grove Orthopedic Assocs., P.A. v. Allstate Ins. Co., 130 S. Ct. 1431 (2010); Erica P. John Fund, Inc. v. Halliburton Co., 131 S. Ct. 2179 (2011); and Amgen Inc. v. Connecticut Retirement Plans and Trust Funds, 133 S. Ct. 1184 (2013). Space does not permit discussion of these cases, but they collectively negate the claim that the Court is racing in an unbroken line of decisions to end the modern class action.

23. *See* Milton Handler, *The Shift from Substantive to Procedural Innovations in Antitrust Suits—The Twenty Third Annual Antitrust Review,* 71 Colum. L. Rev. 1, 9 (1971). This author should note that he knew Milton Handler late in the latter's life and always found him a penetrating legal mind, even in his nineties.

24. *See* Henry J. Friendly, FEDERAL JURISDICTION: A GENERAL VIEW 120 (1973) (citing Handler, *supra* note 23).

25. *See In re* Rhone-Poulenc Rorer, Inc., 51 F.3d 1293, 1299–1300 (7th Cir. 1965) (Posner) (decertifying class to protect defendants from extortionate pressure to settle).

26. *See, e.g.,* Bruce L. Hay & David Rosenberg, *"Sweetheart" and "Blackmail" Settlements in Class Actions: Reality and Remedy,* 75 Notre Dame L. Rev. 1377, 1378 (2000) (finding risk of extortionate pressure overstated); *see also* David Rosen-

berg, *Mass Tort Class Actions: What Defendants Have and Plaintiffs Don't*, 37
Harv. J. on Legis. 393, 430 (2000) (expressing "doubt" that class actions "exert
systematic blackmail pressure against defendants").

27. *See* Thomas E. Willging et al., EMPIRICAL STUDY OF CLASS ACTIONS IN
FOUR FEDERAL DISTRICT COURTS: FINAL REPORT TO THE ADVISORY
COMMITTEE ON CIVIL RULES 61 (1996).

28. *See* Handler, *supra* note 23, at 7–10. For a careful assessment of the differences
between the views of Milton Handler, Henry Friendly, and others on this issue of
extortion, see Charles Silver, *"We're Scared to Death:" Class Certification and
Blackmail*, 78 N.Y.U. L. Rev. 1357 (2003).

29. *See* Federal Rule of Civil Procedure 23(f) (authorizing permissive interlocutory
appeals of class certification). This provision, adopted in 2001, was expressly
intended to protect defendants from excessive pressure. *See* Silver, *supra* note 28,
at 1358.

30. *See* Friendly, *supra* note 24, at 119–120. Rather than focusing on providing
compensation to small claimants, he believed that "the important thing is to stop
the evil conduct." *Id.* at 120.

31. *See In re* Rhone-Poulenc Rorer Inc., 51 F.3d 1293, 1299–1300 (7th Cir. 1995). Judge
Posner stressed, however, that pressure alone was not sufficient to constitute
extortion and that the benefits of creating a remedy for "negative value" claimants justified the class action. *Id.* at 1298. The key fact to him in *Rhone-Poulenc*
was that in individual trials, plaintiffs had lost twelve out of thirteen trials,
suggesting that these were large claimant cases (not negative value cases) that
were viable as individual actions but had little legal merit.

32. Many commentators have long asserted that the combination of class actions and
treble damages is toxic. Some states have responded. For example, New York
State precludes a class action that seeks a penalty (including treble damages).
Thus, damages under the New York State antitrust law (the Donnelly Act) cannot
be brought in a class action filed in New York State Court. *See* N.Y.C.P.L.R.
§ 901(b).

33. *See* Wal-Mart Stores Inc. v. Dukes, 131 S. Ct. 2541, 2552 (2011).

34. *Wal-Mart*'s new theory of "commonality" was actually unnecessary. More
logically, the Court could have first found that the *Wal-Mart* class could not be
certified under Rule 23(b)(2) because money damages were not available under
that provision (as the Court did eventually find) and then turned to the "predominance" requirement of Rule 23(b)(3), which was even more clearly not dissatis-
fied. Instead, by inventing a new definition for the "commonality" requirement of
Rule 23(a)(2), the Court fashioned a far broader rule that will also apply to bar
future injunctive or equitable actions under Rule 23(b)(2).

35. This same problem is equally prevalent in inventory settlements and "quasi-class
actions" where defendants are similarly required to make an "all or nothing"

choice on a large group of cases. Thus, the potential for extortion would survive the death of the class action.

36. This author has advanced this thesis several times (but never as a basis for abolishing the class action). *See* John C. Coffee, Jr., *The Unfaithful Champion: The Plaintiff as Monitor in Shareholder Litigation,* 48 Law & Contemp. Probs. 5 (1985).

37. Sections 2(a)(2)(A) and 2(a)(3)(A) of CAFA announce Congress's finding that unfair class action settlements have undercut respect for law and have awarded lucrative fees to attorneys, "while leaving class members with . . . little or no compensation." *See also* S. Rep. No. 108-123, at 16–18 (2003) (listing examples).

38. For a highly readable expose of the abuses of coupon settlements, see J. Brendan Day, *My Lawyer Went to Court and All I Got Was This Lousy Coupon! The Class Action Fairness Act's Inadequate Provision for Judicial Scrutiny over Proposed Coupon Settlements,* 38 Seton Hall L. Rev. 1085 (2008) (finding that the problem has still not been satisfactorily resolved).

39. *See Boeing v. Van Gemert,* 444 U.S. 472 (1980) (permitting plaintiff's attorney fee to be paid on the total recovery, even though much of it went unclaimed and reverted to defendant).

40. *In re* Baby Products Antitrust Litig., 708 F.3d 163, 174 (3d Cir. 2013) (stating that a *cy pres* recovery should be limited to a small portion of the total recovery).

41. This may explain why some institutional investors serve as lead plaintiffs. That is, they may have learned that, even though the total recovery in a class action is a small percentage of the total market loss, only a low percentage of the claimants will file claims and those who do file will ultimately receive a disproportionate recovery. In other words, the recovery to the class could be 2 percent of the total loss, but the recovery to those that file could be 20 percent of their individual losses.

42. For a discussion of "professional" objectors and the means used by plaintiff's attorneys to combat them, see John E. Lopatka & D. Brooks Smith, *Class Action Professional Objectors: What to Do about Them?,* 39 Fla. St. U. L. Rev. 865 (2012).

43. Long ago, Judge Henry Friendly explained that the key fact about class and derivative litigation is that the interests of the class and the plaintiff's attorney "are by no means congruent." *See* Saylor v. Lindsley, 456 F.2d 896, 900 (2d Cir. 1972). Typically, the plaintiff's attorney has more at stake and a stronger interest in settlement than the class members. Even earlier, he observed that "[o]nce a settlement is agreed, the attorneys for the plaintiff shareholders link arms with their former adversaries to defend their joint handiwork." Allegheny Corp v. Kirby, 333 F. 2d 327, 347 (2d Cir. 1964). In his view, this pattern necessitated closer scrutiny of settlements by the court in the class action context. As usual, Judge Friendly was entirely correct, but the problem remains of how to bell this cat.

44. 753 F. 3d 718 (7th Cir. 2014).

45. *Id.* at 721.

46. *Id.* at 725–726.

47. *Id.* at 726–727.

48. *See* Joseph A. Grundfest, "Damages and Reliance under Section 10(b) of the Exchange Act," Rock Center for Corporate Governance, Working Paper Series No. 150, at 1 (Aug. 28, 2013), *available at* http://ssrn.com/abstract=2317537 (relying on data compiled by Cornerstone Research).

49. *Id.*

50. Various estimates exist. A study by NERA in 1995 found that in securities class actions where officers or directors were named as defendants, 68.2 percent of the settlement was paid by liability insurers and 31.4 percent was paid by the defendant corporation, leaving only 0.4 percent to be paid by others (which would include the accountants, underwriters, and officers and directors). *See* Frederick C. Dunbar et al., RECENT TRENDS III: WHAT EXPLAINS SETTLE-MENTS IN SHAREHOLDER CLASS ACTIONS? 9 (1995). Testimony before Congress has estimated that 96 percent of settlements are within the policy range of the D&O insurance policy, with the insurance liability usually being the sole source of the settlement funds. *See* James Cox, *Making Securities Fraud Class Actions Virtuous,* 39 Ariz. L. Rev. 497, 512 (1997).

51. One study of the 3,230 federal securities class actions that were filed between 1991 and 2004 attempted to contact all the participants in these cases, including counsel for both sides, D&O insurers, and others. Based on this elaborate effort, it was able to identify only thirteen settlements "since 1980 in which outside directors made out-of-pocket payments." *See* Bernard Black, Brian Cheffins & Michael Klausner, *Outside Director Liability,* 58 Stan. L. Rev. 1055, 1068 (2006). For the fullest study finding that managers seldom pay in securities litigation, see Tom Baker & Sean J. Griffith, ENSURING CORPORATE MISCONDUCT: HOW LIABILITY INSURANCE UNDERMINES SHAREHOLDER LITIGA-TION 134–136 (2010). For a similar view (by an experienced scholar and practitioner) that "individual defendants almost never contribute to settlements," see Janet Alexander, *Rethinking Damages in Securities Class Actions,* 48 Stan. L. Rev. 1487, 1497 (1996).

52. *See* Baker & Griffith, *supra* note 51, at 201–203 (finding that D&O insurance is not priced to risk and thus the insured firm "does not have an adequate incentive to take care to control insured losses from the underlying risk").

53. For evidence of large reputational penalties as a result of SEC enforcement actions, see Jonathan H. Karpoff, D. Scott Lee & Gerald S. Martin, *The Cost to Firms of Cooking the Books,* 43 J. Fin. & Quantitative Analysis 581 (2008). These authors find that the decline in the present value of future cash flows is in excess of 7.5 times the average financial sanction paid to the SEC. *See also* Brian Carson McTier & John K. Wald, *The Causes and Consequences of Securities Class Litigation,* 17 J. Corp. Fin. 649 (2011). In a related study, Karpoff, Lee and Martin

find that corporate managers identified as responsible for false statements swiftly lose their jobs. *See* Jonathan H. Karpoff, D. Scott Lee & Gerald S. Martin, *The Consequences to Managers for Financial Misrepresentation,* 88 J. Fin. Econ. 193, 201–208 (2008). Even if public enforcement works (as this evidence suggests), other scholars argue that private enforcement adds little of significance to deter securities fraud. *See* Amanda M. Rose, *The Multienforcer Approach to Securities Fraud Deterrence: A Critical Analysis,* 158 U. Pa. L. Rev. 2173 (2010).

54. *See* Lynn Bai, James D. Cox & Randall S. Thomas, *Lying and Getting Caught: An Empirical Study of the Effect of Securities Class Action Settlements on Targeted Firms,* 158 U. Pa. L. Rev. 1877 (2010).

55. For another study also finding that, in the wake of fraud, the long-run stock price and operating performance of the company did not differ significantly from that of a matched set of firms that did not engage in fraud, see Dalia Marciukaityte et al., *Governance and Performance Changes after Accusations of Corporate Fraud,* 62 Fin. Analysts J. 32 (2006). In short, reputational penalties appear to be the exception, not the rule.

56. *See* James D. Cox & Randall S. Thomas, *Mapping the American Shareholder Litigation Experience: A Survey of Empirical Studies of the Enforcement of the U.S. Securities Law,* 6 Eur. Company & Fin. L. Rev. 164 (2009); Stephen P. Ferris & Adam C. Pritchard, *Stock Price Reactions to Securities Fraud Class Actions under the Private Securities Litigation Reform Act,* Mich. L. & Econ. Research Paper No. 01-009 (2001), *available at* http://ssrn.com/abstract_id = 288216. These studies find both an initial stock decline on the filing of corrective disclosure and a second decline on the filing of the class action.

57. This term "circularity" is widely used and was coined by this author. *See* John C. Coffee, Jr., *Reforming the Securities Class Action: An Essay on Deterrence and Its Implementation,* 106 Colum. L. Rev. 1534, 1556 (2006). In essence, the term means that investors are paying themselves.

58. *See* Lawrence E. Mitchell, *The "Innocent Shareholder": An Essay on Compensation and Deterrence in Securities Class-Action Lawsuits,* 2009 Wisc. L. Rev. 243, 287–290 (2009). Professor Mitchell argues that shareholders are ultimately responsible for managerial malfeasance and that holding the corporation liable deters shareholder shirking or passivity.

59. Cox and Thomas make this argument also. *See* Cox & Thomas, *supra* note 56, at 172.

60. The typical class period in a securities class action is now under a year. It is shrinking because of the obligation imposed on plaintiffs by the Supreme Court in *Dura Pharmaceuticals, Inc. v. Broudo,* 544 U.S. 336 (2005), to demonstrate "loss causation" (i.e., that the misstatement or omission caused the shareholder's loss). The longer the class period is, the harder it is to satisfy this burden, and so plaintiffs are prudently alleging shorter class periods than in the past.

61. *See* James D. Cox & Randall S. Thomas, *Letting Billions Slip through Your Fingers: Empirical Evidence and Legal Implications of the Failure of Financial Institutions to Participate in Securities Class Action Settlements,* 58 Stan. L. Rev. 411 (2005).

62. Section 21D(a)(6) ("Restrictions on Payment of Attorneys' Fees and Expenses") of the Securities Exchange Act of 1934 restricts plaintiff's attorney's fees and expenses, providing that they may "not exceed a reasonable percentage of the amount of any damages and prejudgment interest actually paid to the class." *See* 15 U.S.C. § 78u-4(a)(6). This provision was added by the PSLRA in 1995 to discourage reversionary (or "claims made") settlements, because any amount returned to the defendant cannot be used to justify an award of attorney's fees.

63. If an institutional investor has suffered a loss of $1 million and the total loss to all investors was $1 billion and the settlement fund is $100 million, the institutional investor should, on a proportionate basis, receive one-tenth of 1 percent of the fund, or $100,000. But if only 10 percent of the claimants file claims totaling only $100 million, the institutional investor will receive his entire loss (because the settlement fund can cover the losses of all claimants). The institutional investor should be happy with this recovery, but it is the product of apathy by retail investors.

64. *See* Globus v. Law Research Servs., Inc., 418 F.2d 1276, 1287–1289 (2d Cir. 1969) (finding federal law to preempt state indemnification law where indemnification would be inconsistent with the policies of the federal securities laws).

65. Corporate liability under Rule 10b-5 for misleading statements to the market dates back at least to *SEC v. Texas Gulf Sulphur Co.,* 401 F.2d 833 (2d Cir. 1968) (en banc). This rule is entirely judge-made law. This author has argued elsewhere that placing liability on the nontrading corporation may have been a policy mistake, as it entices private enforcers away from suing the culpable actors. *See* Coffee, *supra* note 57. In any event, aiders and abettors were liable for misleading statements until the Supreme Court's decision in *Central Bank of Denver v. First Interstate Bank of Denver,* 511 U.S. 164 (1994) (holding that Rule 10b-5 does not apply to aiders and abettors, but only to the makers of the statement). This restriction largely protects auditors, lawyers, investment bankers, and other "gatekeepers" from liability under the federal securities laws, and otherwise they would be the persons most easily deterred.

66. *See* Martin H. Redish, WHOLESALE JUSTICE: CONSTITUTIONAL DEMOCRACY AND THE PROBLEM OF THE CLASS ACTION LAWSUIT (2009). Even those who find Professor Redish's views challenging and provocative still characterize him as a "bomb thrower." *See* Richard Marcus, *Bomb Throwing, Democratic Theory, and Basic Values—A New Path to Procedural Harmonization?* 107 Nw. L. Rev. 475, 476 (2013) (reviewing Redish's position and describing him as a longtime "bomb thrower").

67. This issue comes down to the constitutionality of the Rules Enabling Act (REA), which delegates judicial rulemaking to the Supreme Court, which in turn

delegates it to an advisory committee on the Federal Rules. In *Shady Grove Orthopedic Associates P.A. v. Allstate Insurance Co.,* 130 S. Ct. 1431 (2010), the Court recently analyzed the REA at length and does not seem inclined to find it unconstitutional.

68. Redish asserts that litigant autonomy is a central value to our democratic system. Redish, *supra* note 66, at 136. Individuals, he argues, can only waive their rights by informed consent, not by the operation of a rule that deems them to consent if they do not object. He also restates this argument as a quasi–First Amendment argument, claiming that individuals have a right to be free from any association with the class. *Id.* at 159–162.

69. Opting out is not expressly authorized with respect to class actions under Rule 23(b)(1) or Rule 23(b)(2), but these are not the provisions used to certify class actions seeking money damages. Some courts permit opting out even under these provisions.

70. Under the American Law Institute's standards, claimants in aggregate litigation can commit themselves by contract to accept a settlement that receives a supermajority vote from similar claimants. *See* A.L.I., PRINCIPLES OF THE LAW OF AGGREGATE LITIGATION § 3.17 (2010). The ALI's proposal is controversial, and some see it as creating a more "lawyer-driven" system of aggregate litigation.

71. Defense counsel can negotiate a settlement under whose terms the plaintiff's counsel must decline to represent any individual claimants (including existing clients) who reject the proposed group settlement. This was precisely what the Vioxx settlement required, although it is arguable that this violated the ABA's Model Rules. *See* text accompanying notes 75–79, *supra* Chapter 6.

72. For a concise explanation of bankruptcy reorganization as it might apply to mass torts, see Troy McKenzie, *Toward a Bankruptcy Model for Non-Class Aggregate Litigation,* 87 N.Y.U. L. Rev. 960, 999–1010 (2012). Under standard bankruptcy practice, tort claimants could be grouped into a single class, and the class would have to approve the plan of reorganization by a supermajority vote. If it did not, the plan could still be implemented under the "cram down" provisions of the Bankruptcy Act. *See* 11 U.S.C. § 1129(b)(1). Again, individual consent is not necessary. Only in the class action is there an unqualified right to opt out.

73. *See* Redish, *supra* note 66, at 176–225.

74. In *Amchem Products, Inc. v. Windsor,* 521 U.S. 591, 628 (1997), the Court implied, but did not hold, that adequate notice could not be given to future claimants, thus precluding class certification.

75. For example, a special guardian ad litem, with no connection to the settling parties, could be appointed to examine and contest the settlement. No specific proposal is, however, here advanced.

76. Although the private attorney general is not authorized by statute, federal law does occasionally address who can perform this function. An example is the

"lead plaintiff" provision of the PSLRA. *See* 15 U.S.C. § 78u-4(a)(3)(B). This shows at least implicit congressional consent to the private attorney general concept in the context of securities class actions.

77. Once private enforcement is authorized, only a new legislative majority (and probably only a supermajority) can amend the legislation to delete private enforcement. This is far more unlikely than a change in policy by the administrative agency authorized to enforce the law. For a fuller development of this theme, see Sean Farhang, THE LITIGATION STATE: PUBLIC REGULATION AND PRIVATE LAWSUITS IN THE U.S. 19–59 (2010).

78. Similarly, Professor Marcus, reviewing Professor Redish's proposals, observes that "Americans are not necessarily willing to leave the enforcement of public policy to public officials." Marcus, *supra* note 66, at 500. He is correct, but his formulation significantly understates the matter.

8. THE NEEDED REFORMS

1. 516 U.S. 367 (1966).
2. *See* Epstein v. MCA, Inc., 50 F.3d 644 (9th Cir. 1995).
3. *See* Amchem Prods. Inc. v. Windsor, 521 U.S. 591 (1997). The Court reiterated this position in *Ortiz v. Fibreboard Corp.*, 527 U.S. 815 (1999). Essentially, these cases held that a settlement class could not be certified where a litigation class was uncertifiable, because plaintiff's counsel was handcuffed when it could only settle. *Matsushita* deals with the slightly different fact pattern of state court counsel who also can only settle but not litigate the federal claims. Suffice it to say that the decision has been much criticized. *See* Marcel Kahan & Linda Silberman, *Matsushita and Beyond: The Role of State Courts in Class Actions Involving Exclusive Federal Claims,* Sup. Ct. Rev. 1996, 219 (1997).
4. In the absence of congressional legislation, individual states could create a functional equivalent to the JPML by entering into an interstate compact. A potential problem here is article I, section 10 of the U.S. Constitution (the "Compact Clause"), which requires congressional approval of such interstate compacts. In recent years, however, the Supreme Court has only invalidated interstate compacts when they "encroach" upon federal supremacy. *See* U.S. Steel Corp. v. Multistate Tax Comm'n, 434 U.S. 452 (1978). That would not appear to be an issue here. Still, few states, other than Delaware, are likely to have any incentive to enter into such a compact, as their jurisdictions would probably lose a net flow of litigation to Delaware.
5. The so-called Delaware carve out is set forth in section 28(f)(3) of the Securities Exchange Act of 1934, and it exempts from that section's ban on securities class actions in state court those actions that arise under the statutory or common law of a corporation's jurisdiction of incorporation and that have certain other

characteristics. This exemption will typically apply to class actions in state court challenging mergers. *See* 15 U.S.C. § 78bb(f)(3). Passed as a part of SLUSA, it was intended to preserve the jurisdiction of the Delaware Chancery Court (and other state courts) to continue to make the law of fiduciary duties. But its unintended impact has been to permit multi-forum litigation.

6. *See* Boilermakers Local 154 Retirement Fund v. Chevron Corp., 2013 Del. Ch. LEXIS 154 (Del. Ch. June 25, 2013).

7. *Id.* at 16 (quoting the clause used by Chevron).

8. The economic logic here is that, in the absence of clear property rights, individuals tend to deplete common pool assets inefficiently. In medieval times, when all had access to certain common lands, overgrazing and a "tragedy of the commons" resulted. *See* Garrett Hardin, *The Tragedy of the Commons*, 162 Science 1243 (1968).

9. A Third Circuit Task Force concluded in 2001 that almost all "traditional" means of selecting class counsel are preferable to the auction. *See* Eleanor W. Myers (Associate Reporter), *Third Circuit Task Force Report on the Selection of Class Counsel*, 74 Temple L. Rev. 689, 704 (2002). Space constraints preclude further consideration of this interesting, but now dated, procedure.

10. This is the pattern in the antitrust context, where there are often large claimants. Their marked tendency has been to opt out and settle on an individual basis. *See* John C. Coffee, Jr., *Accountability and Competition in Securities Class Actions: Why "Exit" Works Better than "Voice,"* 30 Cardozo L. Rev. 407, 433–435 (2008) (discussing behavior of large claimants in antitrust class actions).

11. 133 S. Ct. 1426 (2013). Securities class actions appear at present to be alone safe from *Comcast*'s requirement of a common damages model because of the relative ease with which securities prices (and hence damages) can be calculated. Again, Judge Richard Posner has criticized and sought to narrow *Comcast*'s scope. *See* Butler v. Sears Roebuck & Co., 737 F.3d 796 (7th Cir. 2013). Whether his resistance will change, or only slow, the outcome remains to be seen.

12. Rule 23(c)(4) ("Particular issues") provides that, "When appropriate, an action may be brought or maintained as a class action with respect to particular issues." Different circuits have very different views on when "partial" certification is "appropriate." Compare *McReynolds v. Merrill Lynch, Pierce, Fenner & Smith*, 672 F.3d 482 (7th Cir. 2012) (approving partial certification in Title VII employment discrimination) and *In re Nassau County Strip Search Cases*, 461 F.3d 219 (2d Cir. 2006) (approving partial certification) with *Castano v. American Tobacco Co.*, 84 F.3d 734, 735 n. 21 (5th Cir. 1996) (broadly disapproving of partial certification).

13. In the parlance of the law, this is known as "issue preclusion" or "collateral estoppel": the defendant cannot relitigate facts fully adjudicated in an earlier trial. Indeed, even nonclass members may be able to use these findings adjudicated in the class action trial to estop the defendant from denying them in their actions. *See* Parklane Hosiery Inc. v. Shore, 439 U.S. 322 (1979).

14. The simplest remedy for the class action attorneys is either to represent the class members in the individual actions at a reduced fee (in order to assure that the individual recovery is taxed for their class fee) or to find attorneys for the individual claimants in those jurisdictions where they cannot appear and enter into contractual agreements with those attorneys. Also, most cases settle, and if the class action settles, the class attorneys can bargain for the defendants to pay their fees, even though no recovery may be paid at this point to the class members. As always, there is some potential for collusion in this latter course.

15. The constitutional issue here involves the application of the Seventh Amendment (which guarantees a "jury trial" in cases at common law) to the context of partial certification. Partial or "issue" certification contemplates a second trial on a limited issue. The Reexamination Clause of the Seventh Amendment to the U.S. Constitution, however, provides that "no fact tried by a jury should be otherwise re-examined in any Court of the United States than according to the common law." Several decisions dealing with mass tort litigation have found this clause to be a barrier to partial certification where the lines between the issues resolved by the jury in the class action trial and those to be resolved by jury in the individual trial (or by the court) are not clear-cut (with the result that the same actual factual or legal issues may be present in both proceedings and thus subject to arguable "re-examination" in the second proceeding). *See In re* Rhone Poulenc-Rorer Inc., 51 F.3d 1293 (7th Cir. 1995); Cimino v. Raymark Indus., Inc., 151 F.3d 297, 313–315 (5th Cir. 1998). *See also* Allison v. Citgo Petroleum Corp., 151 F.3d 402, 422–426 (5th Cir. 1998) (finding a similar violation in an employment discrimination class action). The Supreme Court has to date found a violation of the Reexamination Clause only when the issues overlap sufficiently that there would be "confusion and uncertainty." *See* Gasoline Prods. Co. v. Champlin Ref. Co., 283 U.S. 494, 500 (1931). For a fuller and incisive treatment of this issue, see Patrick Woolley, *Mass Tort Litigation and the Seventh Amendment Reexamination Clause,* 83 Iowa L. Rev. 499 (1998). Professor Woolley argues persuasively that there is no constitutional barrier to the same evidence being presented in two proceedings, but only to the relitigation of specific findings reached by a jury. Thus, for example, if a jury in the class action determined that exposure to a specific substance for a specific minimum duration could cause cancer (i.e., the general causation issue), a second jury could determine that a specific individual in the class had been so exposed for the requisite period and that the exposure caused his specific injury (the proximate causation issue). It is not here contended that all issues split cleanly between the class trial and an individual trial, but many do. To give the clearest example, a jury hearing a class action trial in a nonsecurities consumer fraud case could find that the defendant acted with scienter and misrepresented material information, and the jury hearing the follow-on individual case could resolve the remaining issue of

individual reliance. In this way, partial certification solves some of the problems posed by an aggressive reading of the predominance requirement.

16. The SEC has taken the position that indemnification of securities law liabilities is contrary to the policies of the federal securities laws and thus preempted. *See* Globus v. Law Research Service, Inc., 418 F. 2d 1276 (2d Cir. 1969); Heizer Corp. v. Ross, 601 F. 2d 330, 334 (7th Cir. 1979). Similarly, the SEC could assert that disproportionate fee shifting was also precluded by the federal securities laws. Here, the case for preemption is strengthened by the fact that section 21D(c)(3) of the Securities Exchange Act of 1934 makes fee shifting the presumptive penalty in securities class actions if either party violates Rule 11 of the Federal Rules of Civil Procedure. This favors fee shifting but preconditions it on a judicial finding of culpable conduct and is thus far from automatic. The topic of preemption is beyond the scope of this book, but federal courts have found that state anti-takeover statutes that precluded any "meaningful opportunity for success" were preempted by the Williams Act (a provision of the Securities Exchange Act of 1934 that regulates tender offers). *See* City Capital Associates v. Interco, Inc., 696 F. Supp 1551 (D. Del. 1988); BNS Inc. v. Koppers Co., 683 F. Supp. 458, 469 (D. Del 1988). A similar standard could apply here; that is, the penalty would be enforceable up to the point at which it would preclude future meritorious actions. In determining preemption, some weight should also be given to who adopted the provision (the board or the shareholders). Provisions adopted by public shareholders deserve greater deference.

17. Rule 11 requires the plaintiff's attorney to represent only that its claims "are warranted by existing law or by a nonfrivolous argument for extending, modifying, or reversing existing law or establishing new law" and that its "factual contentions have evidentiary support . . . or will likely have evidentiary support after a reasonable opportunity for further investigation or discovery." *See* Federal Rules of Civil Procedure 11(b)(2) and (3). This is frankly a very generous and permissive standard.

One qualification is needed here. In federal securities litigation, section 21D(c) of the Securities Exchange Act of 1934 does mandate fee shifting for a violation of Rule 11(b) of the Federal Rules of Civil Procedure. This makes fee shifting against the loser marginally more likely, but in practice fee shifting is still the exception and not the rule.

18. Rule 11 of the Federal Rules of Civil Procedure does authorize the court to award "reasonable expenses, including attorney's fees, incurred for the motion" to the party bringing a motion for sanctions "if warranted." *See* Federal Rules of Civil Procedure 11(c)(2). But this is an additional amount.

19. *See* ATP Tour, Inc. v. Deutscher Tennis Bund, 91 A. 3d 554 (Del. 2014).

20. Some twenty-four companies have adopted such a provision in just the first four months after the Delaware Supreme Court's decision. This author has examined

these provisions in recent testimony before the SEC's Investor Advisory Committee on October 9, 2014. *See* John C. Coffee, Jr., "Fee-Shifting Bylaws. Can They Apply in Federal Court? The Case for Preemption," *available at* http://ssrn.com /abstract=2508973. Federal courts could find such provisions to be inconsistent with (and thus preempted by) either Rule 11 of the Federal Rules of Civil Procedure or the PSLRA (which makes fee shifting against the loser depend on the court's specific finding). The PSLRA would apply only in securities class actions, but that is a major category. For a brief discussion of the preemption issue, see text and note *supra* at note 16.

21. The key decision is *Central Bank of Denver v. First Interstate Bank of Denver,* 511 U.S. 164 (1994). Prior to *Central Bank,* as Justice Stevens pointed out in his dissent, all federal circuits recognized aiding and abetting liability under Rule 10b-5. *See id.* at 192.

22. Others have made similar proposals, and Canada has adopted such a system (*see infra* note 26). *See* Donald C. Langevoort, *Capping Damages for Open Market Securities Fraud,* 38 Ariz. L. Rev. 639 (1996). It must be emphasized that this proposal would revise only Rule 10b-5 and not affect sections 11 or 12 of the Securities Act of 1933. Both of these latter sections apply only when the corporation is selling securities, and in those cases there is less circularity of the payments. Instead, those who benefitted from the alleged fraud are paying those who lost from it.

23. *See* 18 U.S.C. § 2. This statute dates back to 1909. *See* 35 Stat. 1152 (Act of Mar. 4, 1909). In the civil law, the Restatement of Torts has also long made the aider and abettor liable for injuries caused in part by its knowing assistance. *See* Restatement (Second) of Torts, § 876(b) (1977).

24. This liability was based on a "scheme to defraud" theory; that theory was subsequently rejected by the Supreme Court in *Stoneridge Investment Partners LLC v. Scientific Atlanta,* 552 U.S. 148 (2008). As here contemplated, both theories (which are closely related) would be restored.

25. In testimony before a subcommittee of the Senate Committee on the Judiciary, at the request of Senator Arlen Specter, this author presented a specific proposal at a time when restoration of aiding and abetting liability was under active consideration. It used a 10 percent test set at the greater of the issuer's average annual income over its last three years, its audited net worth, or its year-end market capitalization. *See* Testimony of John C. Coffee, Jr., before the Subcommittee on Crime and Drugs of the United States Senate Committee on the Judiciary, Sept. 17, 2009 (Hearings on S.1551: The Liability for Aiding and Abetting Securities Violations Act of 2009).

26. The Ontario Securities Act places a ceiling on damages that may be imposed on the issuer in open market trading cases (i.e., where the corporation is not itself selling securities). It is set at the greater of (1) 5 percent of the subject company's

market capitalization or (2) $1 million. *See* Ontario Securities Act, R.S.O., 1990 c. S.5, sec. 138.7.

27. 134 S. Ct. 2398 (2014).

28. *See, e.g.,* Donald C. Langevoort, *Basic at Twenty: Rethinking Fraud on the Market,* 2009 Wisc. L. Rev. 151 (2009); William W. Bratton & Michael L. Wachter, *The Political Economy of Fraud on the Market,* 160 U. Pa. L. Rev. 69 (2011). The presumption of reliance can be both overinclusive and underinclusive. It is overinclusive because some investors are "indexed" and thus do not rely on firm-specific information, while other investors are searching for misvalued stocks and do not assume that the information in the corporation's financial statement is accurate. *See* Grigori Erenburg et al., *The Paradox of "Fraud-on-the Market" Theory: Who Relies on the Efficiency of Market Prices?,* 8 J. Empirical Leg. Studies 260 (2011). It is also underinclusive for reasons explained in the text.

29. *See* Blackie v. Barrack, 524 F.2d 891, 906 n.22 (9th Cir. 1975).

30. 485 U.S. 224, 245 (1988) ("The presumption of reliance employed in this case is consistent with, and, by facilitating Rule 10b-5 litigation, supports the Congressional policy embodied in the 1934 Act"). This may have been the last time the Court suggested that "facilitating Rule 10b-5 litigation" was desirable.

31. The trade-off is that defendants gain an opportunity to convince the court on the merits at class certification that the alleged misrepresentation or omission caused no damages, while plaintiffs may be able to exploit the doctrine's presumption of reliance even in the case of stocks traded in thinner markets.

32. For a fuller statement of this rationale, see Zohar Goshen & Gideon Parchomovsky, *The Essential Role of Securities Regulation,* 55 Duke L.J. 711, 771–780 (2006).

9. PUBLIC ENFORCEMENT AND THE PRIVATE ATTORNEY GENERAL

1. This table was prepared by Max W. Berger, Esq., the senior partner of Bernstein Litowitz Berger & Grossman, the largest plaintiff's law firm in New York City.

2. Jed S. Rakoff, *The Financial Crisis: Why Have No High-Level Executives Been Prosecuted?,* New York Rev. of Books, Jan. 9, 2014. Judge Rakoff has refused to approve two major SEC settlements on the grounds that they were inadequate. *See* SEC v. Citigroup Global Mkts., 827 F. Supp. 2d 328 (S.D.N.Y. 2011), rev'd, 2014 U.S. App. LEXIS 10516 (2d Cir. June 4, 2014).

3. For a well-known example, see David Dayen, *The SEC Nails a Minnow While the Whales Go Free: Why Wasn't Goldman Sachs on Trial Alongside Fabrice Tourre?,* New Republic, Aug. 6, 2013, *available at* http://www.newrepublic.com/article /114188/fabrice-tourre:goldman-sachs-trial-sec-nails-minnow. Even when the agency does sue, it has been less successful than in the past. *See* Peter S. Henning, *SEC's Losing Streak in Court Puts Agency in Spotlight,* N.Y. Times, Feb. 10, 2014.

4. Lehman's "Repo 105 transactions" involved purely financial exchanges on the last day of each quarter that Lehman employed to disguise its leverage (and then unwound the next day). By characterizing these transactions as sales, rather than as loans, each of these transactions "shaved $38.6 billion from Lehman's debt in the fourth quarter of 2007, and $49.1 billion in the first and second quarters of 2008, respectively." *See* David A. Skeel, Jr. & Thomas H. Jackson, *Transaction Consistency and the New Finance in Bankruptcy*, 112 Colum. L. Rev. 152, 164 (2012). Anton Valukas, the former U.S. attorney in Chicago and now the senior partner at Jenner & Block, prepared a 2,000-page report that asserted that Lehman officials could be held liable for cooking the books and materially misrepresenting their financial position. *See* Cate Long, *Robert Khuzami; Master Distracter,* Reuters:MuniLand Blog, Jan. 17, 2013, *available at* http://blogs.reuters.com /muniland/2013/01/17/robert-khuzami-master-distracter. For a description of the SEC's decision not to sue Lehman's executives, see William Alden, *How the SEC Threw in the Towel on Lehman,* N.Y. Times, Sept. 9, 2013 (reporting that SEC Chairman Mary Schapiro pushed for an enforcement action but met resistance from George Canellos, then the director of the Enforcement Division).

5. *See Conclusions of the Financial Crisis Inquiry Commission, available at* http:// www.fcic-static.law.stanford.edu/cdn-media/fcic-report-conclusions.pdf.

6. It is important to understand that the SEC is not authorized to sue for compensatory damages (i.e., the losses suffered by all injured investors), but only for disgorgement (the gains received by the alleged wrongdoer). Thus, one reason that the private recoveries in class actions may be larger than SEC settlements is that the potential damages are greater. Although this is possible, SEC settlements do not generally seem to have approached the disgorgement ceiling; rather, SEC penalties seem more to be determined by comparison to other settlements (i.e., a basically precedent-driven approach).

7. This well-known quotation from Mr. Buffett comes from the 2001 Chairman's Letter of Berkshire Hathaway. *See* http://www.berkshirehathaway.com/2001or /2001letter.html.

8. Plaintiff's law firms have an accordion-like ability to expand quickly. When confronted with major discovery or document review demands, they can hire "contract attorneys" as short-term employees to meet this need. Although defendant firms are also able to use such contract attorneys, their cultures may inhibit them from hiring outside the traditional associate hiring process.

9. For lists of recent SEC losses, see Henning, *supra* note 3, and Jean Eaglesham, *SEC Tries to Stem Defeats at Trials,* Wall St. J., Feb. 14, 2014 at C1. It would take a chapter to recite all the recent SEC failures. To be sure, the SEC did win in the Fabrice Tourre case, but he was a low-ranking Goldman Sachs employee. *See* Dayen, *supra* note 3. When the SEC sued Citigroup, the only individual defendant named was Brian Stoker, a mid-level executive. In its action against JPMorgan,

the SEC named Edward Steffelin, who did not work at JPMorgan, but rather at an associated consulting firm. The case against Stoker resulted in a jury acquittal (and the jury in an unusual move issued a statement asking the SEC to bring more actions against senior officials but not against lower-ranking "scapegoats"). *See* Peter Lattman, *SEC Gets Encouragement from Jury that Ruled Against It,* N.Y. Times, Aug. 3, 2012. In the Steffelin case, the SEC agreed to a dismissal in late 2012 with prejudice—an admission that it had mishandled the case. *See* James B. Stewart, *Another Fumble by the SEC on Fraud,* N.Y. Times, Nov. 16, 2012. In its fraud case against Bruce Bent and his son Bruce Bent II, who together ran the Reserve Primary Fund—the money market fund that "broke the buck" in 2008, a federal jury in 2012 found for the defendants on all the fraud charges. *See* Nathaniel Popper & Jessica Silver-Greenberg, *Money-Market Pioneer and Son Cleared of Fraud,* N.Y. Times, Nov. 12, 2012. In another embarrassing litigation defeat, a federal jury found for Mark Cuban in an insider trading case in 2013. *See* Henning, *supra* note 3. In all likelihood, these losses have made the SEC more risk averse about suing senior officials.

10. Because most conservative congressmen favor a tough "law and order" approach, they rarely threaten to cut the Department of Justice's budget.

11. In fiscal year 2012 (which ended on October 31, 2012), the SEC filed 734 enforcement actions and settled 714 cases (up from 670 in 2011 and its highest total since 2007). *See* Jorge Baez, James Overdahl & Elaine Buckberg, *SEC Settlement Trends: 2012 Update* (NERA Economic Consulting, Jan. 14, 2013), *available at* http://www.nera.com/67_7974.htm.

12. The composition of SEC cases has changed significantly since 2008, with increased emphasis on smaller cases involving frauds by individual brokers. *See* Baez, Overdahl, and Buckberg, *supra* note 11; David Marcus & Sara Gilley, *The Changing Nature of SEC Enforcement Actions,* Cornerstone Research (Oct. 8, 2013). Any percentage increase in one category of cases implies a corresponding decrease elsewhere, and the category that has recently shrunk the most is that of actions against public companies. According to the study by Baez, Overdahl, and Buckberg, *supra* note 11, fiscal year 2011 was the fourth straight year of decline in securities cases brought by the SEC against public companies, with only eleven actions against public companies, themselves, having been brought by the SEC in that fiscal year. *Id.* An even more recent study of SEC enforcement actions by Morvillo & Abramowitz, a prominent "white collar" defense firm, shows that of the 526 cases filed by the SEC between January 1, 2013, and September 30, 2013, only twenty-eight cases (or 9 percent) were "public issuer disclosure cases" (the category that once included the SEC's suits against Enron and WorldCom). *See* Morvillo & Abramowitz, *SEC Enforcement Data Analyses: Analysis of Cases Filed between January 1, 2013 and September 30, 2013* 1, *available at* http://www.maglaw.com/events/speaking-engagements/00076/_res/id=Attachments/index=0/MAGIA%20SEC%20Report.pdf.

13. *See* Jean Eaglesham, *SEC Pads Case Tally With Easy Prey,* Wall St. J., Oct. 17, 2013 at 1; Joshua Gallu, *SEC Boosts Tally of Enforcement Successes with Routine Actions,* Bloomberg (Feb. 22, 2013), *available at* http://www.bloomberg.com/news /2013-02-22/sec-boosts-tally-of-enforcement-successes-with-routine-actions.html) (noting high level (31 percent) of administrative cases in SEC's total number of cases).

14. For a summary of the many criticisms of this policy, see Lynndon Groff, *Is Too Big to Fail Too Big to Confess? Scrutinizing the SEC's "No-Admit" Consent Judgment Proposals,* 54 B.C.L. Rev. 1727, 1728–1729 (2013).

15. In early 2013, Attorney General Eric Holder suggested in substance that the adverse economic consequences of prosecuting large banks might make them "too big to jail." He expressly noted that "the size of some of these institutions becomes so large that it does become difficult for us to prosecute them . . . if we do bring a criminal charge—it will have a negative impact on the national economy, perhaps even the world economy." *See* Andrew Ross Sorkin, *Realities behind Prosecuting Big Banks,* New York Times: Dealbook Blog (Mar. 11, 2013), *available at* http://dealbook.nytimes.com/2013/03/11/big-banks-go-wrong-but -pay-a-little-price.

16. For this statistic and other recoveries by federal agencies, see Margaret H. Lemos & Max Minzner, *For-Profit Public Enforcement,* 127 Harv. L. Rev. 853, 854–855 (2014). They similarly report that the Department of Justice and Health and Human Services jointly recovered $3 billion in health care fraud actions in 2012. *Id.* at 855. In short, these numbers show that funds are available (if they can be tapped) that would pay for a high level of public enforcement by retained private counsel.

17. Under section 308(a) of the Sarbanes-Oxley Act of 2002 (which is known as the "Fair Funds for Investors" provision), the SEC may distribute the civil disgorgement that it receives in enforcement actions to investors. *See* 15 U.S.C. § 7246. For an overview, see Barbara Black, *Should the SEC Be a Collection Agency for Defrauded Investors?,* 63 Bus. Law. 317 (2008). Otherwise, penalties paid to the SEC do not remain with the agency but go into the federal treasury.

18. *See* Leah Godesky, *State Attorneys General and Contingency Fee Arrangements: An Affront to the Neutrality Doctrine?* 42 Colum. J.L. & Soc. Probs. 587, 588 (2008–2009). A few states, including New York and Virginia, did not use private counsel or refused to enter contingency fee agreements, but they were a small minority. *Id.*

19. Rhode Island, Oklahoma, and several counties in California have brought such actions on a contingency fee basis. *Id.* at 589.

20. *See* Federal Deposit Insurance Corporation, MANAGING THE CRISIS: THE FDIC AND RTC EXPERIENCE 473–474 (1998), *available at* http://www.fdic.gov /bank/historical/managing/contents.pdf.

21. *Id.* at 482. The FDIC asked firms for discounts off their normal fees and appears to have regarded the contingency fee as a cost-saving technique.

22. *See* Federal Deposit Insurance Corporation, OUTSIDE COUNSEL DESKBOOK (June 1, 2005), *available at* http://www.fdic.gov/buying/legal/outside [hereinafter Deskbook]. *See also* FEDERAL DEPOSIT INSURANCE CORPORATION, OVERVIEW OF FDIC PROCESS FOR RETAINING OUTSIDE COUNSEL (Mar. 4, 2009), *available at* http://www.fdic.gov/buying/legal/ocbrochure/over view.htm.

23. Deskbook, *supra* note 22, at 10.

24. *Id.* at 10.

25. *See* Karen Weise, *The FDIC Claims an IndyMac Victory,* Bloomberg Business-week, Dec. 10, 2012.

26. Michael Perry, the former CEO of IndyMac, settled with the FDIC for $1 million but succeeded in having all fraud claims brought by the SEC dismissed. *See* Edvard Pettersson, *Ex-IndyMac CEO Michael Perry Settles with SEC for $80,000,* Bloomberg Personal Finance (Oct. 1, 2012), *available at* http://www.bloomberg .com/news/2012-10-01/ex-IndyMac-ceo-michael-perry-settles-with-SEC-for -80,000-1-html.

27. *See* Cornerstone Research, *Characteristics of FDIC Lawsuits against Directors and Officers of Failed Financial Institutions* (Sept. 2013), at Report Summary and 1, *available at* https://www.cornerstone.com/getattachment/a6315fce-2429-43fd-a0bb -aedd86f72e71/Characteristics-nbsp;of-FDIC-Lawsuits-against-Dire.aspx.

28. *Id.*

29. *Id.*

30. *See* Press Release: FHFA Announces $5.1 Billion in Settlements with JPMorgan (Oct. 25, 2013), *available at* http://www.fhfa.gov/webfiles/25649/FHFAJPMorgan Settlement Agreement.pdf.

31. Estimates vary. *See* David Dayen, *FHFA Will Secure Up to $28 Billion from Banks in Its MBS Lawsuit,* Naked Capitalism Blog (Nov. 12, 2013), *available at* http:// www.nakedcapitalism.com/2013/11/david-dayen-fhfa-will-secure-up-to-28 -billion-from-banks-in-its-mbs-lawsuit.html; Nela Richardson, *JPMorgan Settlement Implies Billions for Others,* Bloomberg Insight (Nov. 12, 2013), *available at* http://www.scribd.com/doc/183458491/JPMorgan-Settlement-Implies-Billions -for-Others-BGOV-Insights-Nov1202013-pdf (estimating $23 billion from other banks).

32. *See* Alison Frankel, *Quinn Emanuel Is Not Riding an MBS Wave; It Triggered a Tsunami,* REUTERS (Sept. 2, 2011), *available at* http://blogs.reuters.com/alison .frankel/2011/09/02/quinn-emanuel-is-not-riding-an-mbs-wave-it-triggered-a -tsunami/.

33. *See* Letter from William A. DeSarno Inspector General to Representative Darrell Issa, Chairman of House Committee on Oversight & Gov't Reform (Feb. 6, 2013), *available at* http://www.ncua.gov/about/leadership/CO/OIG/Documents/0162013 0206IssaResponse.pdf.

34. *See* 31 U.S.C. § 3729.

35. *See* 31 U.S.C. § 3730.

36. *See* 31 U.S.C. § 3730(d).

37. *See* Gibson, Dunn & Crutcher LLP, 2011 YEAR-END FALSE CLAIMS ACT UPDATE 1 (Jan. 5, 2012), *available at* http://www.gibsondunn.com/publications /Documents/2011YearEndFalseClaimsActUpdate.pdf.

38. *See* Gibson, Dunn & Crutcher LLP, 2012 YEAR-END FALSE CLAIMS ACT UPDATE 1 (Jan. 8, 2013), *available at* http://www.gibsondunn.com/publications /Documents/2012YearEnd-FalseClaimsActUpdate.pdf.

39. *See* Gibson, Dunn & Crutcher, *supra* note 37, at 1–2 ; Gibson, Dunn & Crutcher, *supra* note 38, at 1.

40. *See* Gibson, Dunn & Crutcher, *supra* note 38, at 3.

41. This was the phrase used by Assistant Attorney General Tony West in 2011. *See id.*

42. Vermont Agency of Natural Res. v. United States ex rel Stevens, 529 U.S. 765 (2000) (finding that respondent relator had standing to sue on behalf of the United States but dismissing action on other unrelated grounds because a state could not be a defendant in such an action).

43. *See* Martin H. Redish, *Private Contingent Fee Lawyers and Public Power: Constitutional and Political Implications,* 18 S. Ct. Econ. Rev. 77 (2010). This is a polar and exaggerated position, with which few would agree and which probably follows from Professor Redish's view that the class action is itself unconstitutional. It also gives no weight to the Supreme Court's decision to uphold the qui tam action, where large contingent fees are common. *See* text accompanying *supra* note 42. Finally, since the time of Professor Redish's article, the Supreme Court has decided *Filarsky v. Delia,* 133 S. Ct. 1657 (2012), in which it recognized that during the nineteenth century "private citizens were actively involved in government work" and "private lawyers were regularly engaged to conduct criminal prosecutions on behalf of the state." *Id.* at 1663. In light of this recognition, use of private counsel by public agencies would seem to have little vulnerability if minimum safeguards are observed.

44. *See, e.g.,* Santa Clara v. Superior Court, 74 Cal. Rptr. 3d 842 (Ct. App. 2008); State v. Hagerty, 580 N.W. ad 139 (N.D. 1998); State v. Lead Indus. Ass'n, 951 A.2d 428 (R.I. 2008); Kinder v. Nixon, 2000 WL 684860 (Mo. Ct. App. May 30, 2000).

45. That is, if the expected recovery of $1 billion is discounted by a 10 percent chance of success, this produces an expected recovery of $100 million. If the contingent fee on this expected recovery were one-third, a risk-neutral attorney might invest up to $33 million in time and expenses to recover an expected $33.3 million—a rational, but very risky, gamble.

46. This point has been independently stressed to this author by several prominent plaintiff's counsel, including Max Berger and Stephen Susman, in describing how

they make litigation decisions. This does not mean to imply that no plaintiff's attorneys take long-shot actions, but the good ones do not (and those are the ones that a responsible public agency would retain).

47. *See* Executive Order No. 13,433, 3 C.F.R. 13,433 (2007).

48. Agencies can avoid the requirement if they obtain the permission of the Attorney General and notify the Office of Management and Budget of any such fee arrangement.

49. Executive Order No. 13,433 covers executive agencies as defined in 5 U.S.C. section 105, which cover executive departments, government corporations, and "an independent establishment."

50. For Mr. Canellos's role in the decision not to sue Lehman executives, see Alden, *supra* note 4 (reporting that Canellos resisted pressure from the SEC chair to bring such an action).

51. *See* John C. Coffee, Jr., *SEC Enforcement: What Has Gone Wrong?,* Nat'l L.J., Dec. 3, 2012.

52. *See* Robert S. Khuzami & George S. Canellos, *Unfair Claims, Untenable Solution: Professor John Coffee Does Not Do the SEC's Enforcement Record Justice,* Nat'l L.J., Jan. 14, 2013. For an independent third party's view of this exchange, see Editorial, *Professor Coffee Hits a Nerve at SEC,* Corp. Crime Rep., Jan. 15, 2013.

53. Khuzami & Canellos, *supra* note 52.

54. *Id.*

55. *See, e.g.,* Margaret H. Lemos, *Aggregate Litigation Goes Public: Representative Suits by State Attorney Generals,* 126 Harv. L. Rev. 486 (2012); *see also* Deborah R. Hensler, *Goldilocks and the Class Action,* 126 Harv. L. Rev. F. 56 (2012). Their point is that elected officials will serve their voters more than class members (and particularly any out of state class members).

56. An obvious example of this conflict is the multistate tobacco settlement in which some $246 billion was paid by the tobacco industry, but relatively little went to smoking victims, while much more went to fund ordinary state purposes, such as highway pothole repairs. In the case of federal public agencies, provisions such as section 308(a) of the Sarbanes-Oxley Act (the "fair funds for investors" provision) already establish a structure for directing compensation received by the agency to victims. *See* text and note *supra* note 17.

10. THE GLOBALIZATION OF THE CLASS ACTION

1. When Rule 23 of the Federal Rules of Civil Procedure was revised in 1966, Rule 23(b)(2) was crafted to facilitate class actions seeking injunctive or equitable relief (which actions often challenged segregated schools and facilities).

2. *See* Deborah R. Hensler, *The Future of Mass Litigation: Global Class Actions and Third Party Litigation Funding,* 79 Geo. Wash. L. Rev. 306, 309 (2011). Quebec

authorized class actions in 1973, but class actions did not become prevalent in Canada until the 1990s, when the number of securities class actions exploded in Ontario. *See* Tanya J. Monestier, *Is Canada the New Shangri-La of Global Securities Class Actions?*, 32 Nw. J. Int'l L. & Bus. 305 (2012). Australia adopted a federal class action rule in 1992, but it was not until the late 1990s that the actions came to be used frequently. Israel had various class actions as of 2000, but did not adopt a transsubstantive class action rule applicable to all causes of action until 2006.

3. For a discussion of these statutes, see Rachael Mulherin, *The Case for an Opt Out Class Action for European Member States: A Legal and Empirical Analysis,* 15 Colum. J. Eur. L. 409 (2009); Stefaan Voet, *Cultural Dimensions of Group Litigation: the Belgian Case,* 41 Geo. J. Int'l & Comp. L. 433 (2013). The special case of the Netherlands and its settlement class procedure is discussed at the end of this chapter. In a number of European countries, representative organizations or other interest groups can bring a collective action to enforce specified laws but generally only to obtain injunctive or declaratory relief (and not monetary damages). *See* Rhonda Wasserman, *Transnational Class Actions and Interjurisdictional Preclusion,* 86 Notre Dame L. Rev. 313, 348–349 (2011).

4. Perhaps the most important example of this type is the German "Capital Markets Model Case Law" (or "KapMuG"). Adopted originally in 2005 and now extended to 2020, this statute facilitates the resolution of securities fraud claims through a "test case" procedure that binds only those who have, in effect, opted into the case, but the action only resolves the common question presented to the court (and not other issues, such as damages). *See* Wasserman, *supra* note 3, at 365–368.

5. *See* Hensler, *supra* note 2, at 309.

6. For overviews of the "Securities-Related Class Action Act" in South Korea, see Dae Hwan Chung, *Introduction to South Korea's New Securities-Related Class Action,* 30 J. Corp. L. 165 (2005); Ye Kyowng Kim, *A Study on the Securities Class Action Lawsuit System,* 29 Korea Int'l Acct. Rev. 3 (2009) (noting first class action in 2009); Ok-Rial Song, IMPROVING CORPORATE GOVERNANCE THROUGH LITIGATION: DERIVATIVE SUB AND CLASS ACTIONS IN KOREA (2008).

7. *See* Chung, *supra* note 6, at 171.

8. *See* Ching-Ping Shao, *Representative Litigation in Corporate and Securities Laws by Government-Sanctioned Nonprofit Organizations: Lessons from Taiwain,* 15 Asian-Pac. L. & Pol'y J. 58, 82 (2013).

9. *See* Hensler, *supra* note 2, at 307 (listing Argentina, Australia, Brazil, Bulgaria, Canada, Chile, China, Denmark, Finland, Indonesia, Israel, Italy, Netherlands, Norway, Poland, Portugal, South Korea, Spain, Sweden, Taiwan, and the United States). Other nations, most notably Germany, have authorized forms of class actions since then.

10. *Id.*

11. *See* Samuel Issacharoff & Geoffrey P. Miller, *Will Aggregate Litigation Come to Europe?*, 62 Vand. L. Rev. 179 (2009).

12. The central difference between the two systems is the active investigatory role played by the court in continental "inquisitorial" systems. In an adversarial system, the parties gather and present the evidence to the court; in contrast, in an inquisitorial system, the court takes responsibility for gathering the evidence and may do so outside the courtroom, relying on its assistants, not the parties. Rather than a continuous trial, continental procedure may contemplate a series of hearings where the court announces findings and receives input from the parties. *See* McNeil v. Wisconsin, 501 U.S. 171, 181 n.2 (1991) (describing the key criterion of an inquisitorial system to be that the judge conducts the factual and legal investigation himself). For a fuller description, see Amelia D. Kessler, *Our Inquisitorial Tradition: Equity Procedure, Due Process, and the Search for an Alternative to the Adversarial,* 90 Cornell L. Rev. 1181, 1188 (2005).

13. This is the language of Rule 23(a)(4) of the Federal Rules of Civil Procedure.

14. Such opting out by large claimants has become extremely common in securities and antitrust cases. *See* John C. Coffee, Jr., *Accountability and Competition in Securities Class Actions: Why "Exit" Works Better than "Voice,"* 20 Cardozo L. Rev. 401, 425–429 (2008).

15. *See* Deborah R. Hensler, *The Globalization of Class Actions: An Overview,* 622 Annals 7, 14 (2009).

16. Hunt v. Wash. State Apple Cider Adver. Comm'n, 432 U.S. 333, 343 (1977); Int'l Union, United Auto. Aerospace & Agric. Implement Workers of Am. v. Brock, 477 U.S. 274, 290 (1986).

17. To be sure, a major public pension fund also has reputational capital that might be damaged by involvement in a scandal, but the likelihood of stigma is much lower.

18. For a discussion of the potential conflicts between class members and the entity, see Derrick A. Bell, Jr., *Serving Two Masters: Integration Ideals and Client Interests in School Desegregation Litigation,* 85 Yale L.J. 470, 505–511 (1976). *See also* William B. Rubenstein, *Divided We Litigate: Addressing Disputes among Group Members and Lawyers in Civil Rights Campaigns,* 106 Yale L.J. 1623 (1997).

19. For example, in *Wal-Mart Stores Inc. v. Dukes,* 131 S. Ct. 2541 (2011), a combination of private law firms and public interest law firms joined together to litigate that case (unsuccessfully, however) to the Supreme Court.

20. *See* Christopher Hodges, THE REFORM OF CLASS AND REPRESENTATIVE ACTIONS IN EUROPEAN LEGAL SYSTEMS: A NEW FRAMEWORK FOR COLLECTIVE REDRESS IN EUROPE 119 (2008).

21. *See* Issacharoff & Miller, *supra* note 11, at 203–206.

22. *Id.* at 203–204.

23. *Id.* at 206–207.

24. *See* Eisenberg & Miller, *The Role of Opt-Outs and Objectors in Class Action Litigation: Theoretical and Empirical Issues,* 57 Vand. L. Rev. 1529, 1532 (2004).

25. *See* Henrik Lindblom, THE GLOBALIZATION OF CLASS ACTIONS: GROUP LITIGATION IN SWEDEN (Dec. 6, 2007), *available at* http://www.law.stanford .edu/display/images/dynamic/events_media/Sweden_National_Report.pdf.

26. *Id.* at 21–22 (discussing *Bo Aberg v. Kefalas Elfeterios ("Air Olympic"),* Stockholm District Court, case number T 3515 (2003)).

27. *Id.* at 22–33 (discussing *Grupptalan mot Skandia v. Forsakringsaktiebolaget Skandia,* Stockholm District Court, case number T 97 (2004)).

28. *Id.* at 22.

29. *Id.* at 23–24 (discussing *The Consumer Ombudsman v. Kraftkommission i Sverige AB,* Umel District Court, T 5416 (2004)).

30. *Id.* at 23.

31. *Id.*

32. *See* Matthias E. Storme & Evelyne Terryn, BELGIAN REPORT ON CLASS ACTIONS 6 (Dec. 13, 2007), *available at* http://www.law.stanford.edu/display /images/dynamic/events_media/Belgium_National_Report.pdf. Of these 5,000 shareholders that did opt in, some 2,000 were members of the consumer organization Test-Aankoo, and the rest were clients of the consulting firm Deminor.

33. The consumer organization had greater success in convincing its members to join the action because its members did not have to bear legal fees, which were advanced by their organization. In contrast, the clients of Deminor were required "to advance a limited sum to cover the costs of the proceeding." *Id.* Thus, although the overall opt-in rate was slightly over 45 percent (i.e., 5,000 out of 11,000), only about one-third of the clients of Deminor ultimately authorized the firm to represent them in the action. *Id.* This disparity suggests that any obligation to advance legal costs will deter opt-ins even more than the tendency of small claimants to be rationally apathetic. It also underscores the obvious utility of using consumer organizations in the role of lead plaintiff in jurisdictions that forbid contingency fees, at least to the extent that such organizations are willing to bear all or most of the litigation's expenses.

34. *See* Issacharoff & Miller, *supra* note 11, at 204–205 (describing workplace litigation as a "specialized context" where "class members have many opportunities to communicate with one another about the litigation"). But see *infra* note 39 (suggesting that the opt-in rate in workplace litigation could be unrepresentatively low because of deterrent effect of employer-employee relationship).

35. *See* 29 U.S.C. § 216(b) (2006) (specifying opt-in requirement for FLSA).

36. *See* 29 U.S.C. § 626(b) (similar opt-in requirement for ADEA).

37. *See* 29 U.S.C. § 216(d) (mandating that opt-in procedure for the FLSA also apply to the Equal Pay Act).

38. *See* Thomas Willging et al., EMPIRICAL STUDY OF CLASS ACTIONS IN FOUR FEDERAL DISTRICT COURTS: FINAL REPORT TO THE ADVISORY COMMITTEE ON CIVIL RULES 54 (1996).

39. *See* Andrew C. Brunsden, *Hybrid Class Actions, Dual Certification, and Wage Law Enforcement in the Federal Courts,* 29 Berkeley J. Emp. & Lab. L. 269, 294 (2008) (discussing low opt-in rate of 15.71 percent in FLSA cases).

40. *Id.* at 294 n.129.

41. *Id.* at 293 (showing opt-in rate of 89.5 percent in *Lindsay v. Gov't Employees Ins. Co.*).

42. Attorneys at the Texas law firm of Starzyk & Associates, P.C., which specializes in FLSA cases, have advised this author that they use a website for each FLSA action to alert employees of a defendant company and that they send e-mails to all employees in the relevant job descriptions that are the subject of the FLSA litigation. They also alerted me to one recent California class action in which 256 out of the 364 persons eligible to participate in a "wage and hour" settlement elected to do; this represents a 70.33 percent participation rate. *See* "Declaration of Monica Balderrama in Support of Motion for Final Approval of Class Action Settlement," 16, ¶ 52 (Sept. 14, 2008), in *Winzelberg v. Liberty Mutual Co.,* Case No. CV 07-460 GAF (C.D. Cal.) (copy on file at Columbia Law Review). In this light, historic participation rates in the 15 to 23 percent range, as discussed in the text, may understate the potential for the opt-in class when Internet solicitation techniques are utilized.

43. *See* James D. Cox & Randall S. Thomas, *Letting Billions Slip through Your Fingers: Empirical Evidence and Legal Implications of the Failure of Financial Institutions to Participate in Securities Class Action Settlements,* 58 Stan. L. Rev. 411, 413 (2005).

44. Extremely low participation rates have been reported in the case of coupon settlements, where the rate appears to fall below 1 percent. *See* James Tharin & Brian Blockovich, *Coupons and the Class Action Fairness Act,* 18 Geo. J. Legal Ethics 1443, 1448 (2005). For recent examples, see *Yeagley v. Wells Fargo & Co.,* 2008 U.S. Dist. LEXIS 5040 at *5 (N.D. Cal. Jan. 18, 2008) (finding that less than 1 percent of the class responded to the settlement notice); *Figueroa v. Sharper Image,* 517 F. Supp. 2d. 1292, 1327 (S.D. Fla. 2007) (rejecting proposed settlement, in part because "very low numbers of class members" expressed interest in the $19 coupon, which was the principal component of the proposed settlement).

45. Of course, an obvious hypothesis is that class counsel in opt-out class actions is not motivated to pay for, or accept the delay incident to, the use of more costly notice procedures that will elicit higher participation rates. Because some federal circuits base the fee award on the settlement size and not the portion of the settlement actually paid out, the plaintiff's attorney in these circuits has little economic incentive to encourage class members to file claims. *See* Masters v. Wilhelmina Model Agency, Inc., 473 F.3d 423, 437 (2d Cir. 2007) (favoring fee award based on total settlement fund). Another possible explanation for low

participation rates is that institutional investors have little interest in funds being expended to attract retail investors to participate and thus share the recovery with them. The lead plaintiff may thus have a conflict with smaller class members. I have discussed this issue of participation rates with the professional "claims administrators" of class action settlements (including the largest of these, which is the Garden City Group, Inc.) and have been advised that participation rates are highly variable, often falling below 10 percent, but can reach much higher percentages when individual class members will receive a cash payment of several hundred dollars or more. Nonpecuniary relief, such as a coupon settlement, elicits much lower levels of participation.

46. If unclaimed amounts in the settlement fund revert to the defendant, then it has a clear incentive to make the claims process arduous to maximize this reversion. Such "claims made" settlements used to be common but are today less so. *See* Geoffrey P. Miller & Lori S. Singer, *Nonpecuniary Class Action Settlements,* Law & Contemp. Probs. 97, 106 (1997). In cases where the settlement contains no reversionary provision, all of the settlement goes to those class members who do file, and they thus have a similar incentive to discourage others from filing to maximize their own recovery. Reverter clauses are today disfavored in the United States because sophisticated courts have come to recognize that they produce illusory settlements in which the settlement fund can be largely returned to the defendant.

47. England and Wales have allowed the "conditional fee," which allows the attorney to waive attorney's fees if the action is not successful and permits an enhanced fee if the action is successful. But this fee is not based on a percentage of the recovery. This change was largely motivated by a desire to finance personal injury litigation, not class actions. For an overview, see Richard Abel, *An American Hamburger Stand in St. Paul's Cathedral: Replacing Legal Aid with Conditional Fees in English Personal Injury Litigation,* 51 DePaul L. Rev. 253 (2001). Sweden also permits "risk agreements" between the representative plaintiff and the class counsel. In one recent case, this agreement provided that class counsel would be paid twice its usual hourly fee if successful and only one-half that fee if the case was lost. Lindblom, *supra* note 25, at 21–22. This is a far milder enhancement or reduction than is common in the United States, where the fee is fully contingent on success and may sometimes exceed 30 percent of the recovery.

48. Cf. Issacharoff & Miller, *supra* note 11, at 197–202 (highlighting usefulness of contingent fee system). This author tends to agree that this criticism has often been overstated but also believes that there is a case for insulating the class attorney, as the key professional, from the conflicts of interest that arise when the attorney finances the litigation.

49. Under Australian law, an attorney can receive a normal fee plus an agreed uplift (which is a percentage of its normal fee that is contingent on winning the case). Recent legislation has capped this uplift at 25 percent in most Australian

jurisdictions. *See* Stuart Clark & Christina Harris, *The Push to Reform Class Action Procedure in Australia: Evolution or Revolution?*, 32 Melb. U. L. Rev. 775, 789 (2008).

50. For overviews, see Susan Lorde Martin, *Litigation Financing: Another Subprime Industry That Has a Place in the United States Market,* 53 Vill. L. Rev. 83, 107–112 (2008).

51. *See id.* at 107–108. The largest, Bentham IMF, went public in 2001 and is listed on the Australian Stock Exchange.

52. *Id.* at 107.

53. *Id.* For the comparable percentage fees charged by U.S. plaintiff's attorneys in securities cases, see Denise M. Martin et al., *Recent Trends IV: What Explains Filing and Settlements in Shareholder Class Actions,* 5 Stan. J. L., Bus. & Fin. 121, 141 (1999) (finding 32 percent to be the average fee award during the 1990s).

54. Martin, *supra* note 50, at 109. Professor Martin estimates that the largest Australian litigation funding firm (now called Bentham IMF) earned A$8 million between 2002 and 2006, or a roughly 7 percent return per annum on its capital. *Id.* at 108.

55. *See* Martin, *supra* note 50, at 109 (noting that in Australia "litigation funders provide the same services as insurance companies," who typically make key litigation decisions for defendants).

56. *Id.*

57. *Id.* at 112–113.

58. The first firm to enter the U.K. market in a significant way was IM Litigation Funding, which was founded in 2002. It charged fees of between 25 percent and 50 percent. *Id.* at 113. IM Litigation Funding appears, however, to be no longer operating. The current major litigation funders in the United Kingdom— Harbour, Calunius Capital, and Vannin Capital—charge fees in the 20 percent to 40 percent range. *See* Cento Veljanovski, *Third Party Litigation Funding in Europe,* 8 J.L., Eco., & Pol'y 405, 424 (2012).

59. *See* Martin, *supra* note 50, at 113 (noting that in the United Kingdom, both hedge funds, insurers, and private investors were funding litigation).

60. The leading Australian decision is *Campbells Cash & Carry Pty. Ltd. v. Fostif Pty. Ltd.,* 229 A.L.R. 58 (2006). *See* Lee Aitken, *Before the High Court—"Litigation Lending" after Fostif: An Advance in Consumer Protection or a Licence for "Bottomfeeders"?,* 28 Sydney L. Rev. 171, 171 (2006) (describing potential problems with allowing litigation funding). In the United Kingdom, the Civil Justice Council, an advisory public body, has concluded that litigation funding provides a necessary role in assuring access to justice. *See* Martin, *supra* note 50, at 112. The Supreme Court of South Africa in 2004 upheld a litigation funding agreement against the claim that it was contrary to public policy. *See* Price Waterhouse Coopers, Inc., et al. v. Nat'l Potato Co-op Ltd., 2004 (6) SA 66 (SCA) at 79–80; see also Martin, *supra* note 50, at 113–114 (analyzing decision).

61. *See* Cento Veljanovski, *Third Party Litigation Funding in Europe*, 8 J.L., Econ. & Pol'y 405, 406 (2012).

62. *Id.* at 428 (noting that litigation funders have entered this field "largely on the back of the European Commission's aggressive cartel protection program"). The Cartel Damages Group, based in Brussels, is probably the leading European litigation funder in the area of group actions, where it has been active in this area since 2001. *Id.* at 430.

63. *Id.*

64. *Id.* at 436.

65. In the United States, client control of the litigation remains ethically required. *See* Julia H. McLaughlin, *Litigation Funding: Charting a Legal and Ethical Course*, 31 Vt. L. Rev. 615 (2007). The major litigation funding firms in the United States entered into a settlement with the New York Attorney General in 2005, which establishes a number of protections for the consumer/litigant. *Id.* at 654–655; *see also* Martin, *supra* note 50, at 109 (noting that in the United States, "litigation funders agree not to make any decisions about the lawsuits").

66. Some corporate governance scholars argue that this is a desirable structure, because the self-interest of the agents motivates them to watch each other. *See* Bernard S. Black, *Agents Watching Agents: The Promise of Institutional Investor Voice*, 39 UCLA L. Rev. 811, 817–818 (1992) (assessing potential for oversight of corporate managers by institutional money managers).

67. *See* Hensler, *supra* note 15, at 24.

68. The Dutch Act on the Collective Settlement of Mass Claims ("Wet collective afwikkeling massaschade" or, more popularly, WCAM) was adopted in 2005. For detailed reviews, see Franziska Weber & William H. Van Boom, *Dutch Treat: The Dutch Collective Settlement of Mass Damage Act (WCAM 2005)*, 1 Contratto e Impresa/Europa 69 (2011), *available at* http://ssrn.com/abstract=1872363 (June 25, 2011) and Karen Jelsma & Manon Cordewenner, *The Settlement of Mass Claims: A Hot Topic in the Netherlands*, Int'l L.Q. 13–20 (2011).

69. This was the Supreme Court's conclusion in *Amchem Products Inc. v. Windsor*, 521 U.S. 591, 621 (1997). That is, if a plaintiff can only settle, but not sue, he is "disarmed" and cannot provide adequate representation to the class.

70. Hensler, *supra* note 2, at 313–314. The total settlement amount came to $352,600,000. *Id.*

71. *Id.* at 314.

72. *Id.* at 317–318. Professor Hensler reports that the total legal fees to all the U.S. lawyers in the two rival actions were $107 million. *Id.* at 318. At this price, it should not be hard to reach peace.

73. *Id.* at 313.

74. *See Amchem Products Inc. v. Windsor*, 521 U.S. 591 (1997). The Court has also restricted the use of settlement class actions in *Ortiz v. Fibreboard Corp.*, 527 U.S.

815 (1999), and it is highly doubtful that the DES litigation could have been certified as a "limited fund" in the United States.

75. *See* Weber & Van Boom, *supra* note 68, at 77.

11. CONCLUSION

1. In particular, legal academics have much too facilely assumed that securities class actions directed at the issuer generate real deterrence (despite much evidence to the contrary) and have repressed the "circularity" problem. Little doubt exists that more deterrence is needed, but one must wear blinders to believe that the securities class action normally generates it, given the ubiquity of D&O insurance and settlements funded almost exclusively by the corporate issuer.

2. This tendency is context specific. For the conclusion that private enforcement does spur legal innovation, based on a study of 6,000 qui tam lawsuits since 1986 under the False Claims Act, see David Freeman Engstrom, "Private Enforcement's Pathway: Lessons from Qui Tam Litigation" (Working Paper 2014) (on file with author). Professor Engstrom does not accept the claim that these qui tam actions were disproportionately frivolous or nonmeritorious, but does find private enforcers more ambitious and aggressive in pushing the law's boundaries. Of course, one can debate whether this tendency is an advantage or disadvantage. Still, it must be understood that qui tam actions are not class actions and hence are not subject to all the limitations under Rule 23, which may inhibit this tendency to "push" the law.

3. *See* Bell Atlantic Corp v. Twombly, 550 U.S. 544 (2007); Ashcroft v. Iqbal, 556 U.S. 662 (2009).

4. *See* ATP Tour, Inc. v. Deutscher Tennis Bund, 2014 Del. LEXIS 209 (Del. May 8, 2014) (en banc) (upholding bylaw imposing a "loser pays" obligation on an unsuccessful shareholder who sued the corporation). This is a recent decision whose scope has not been fully explored, but it could easily chill shareholder litigation in Delaware, depending on how it is interpreted. Delaware also will clearly uphold a forum selection bylaw adopted by the board of directors. *See* Boilermakers Local 154 v. Chevron Corp., 73 A.2d 934 (Del. Ch. 2013) (upholding forum selection bylaw adopted by board of directors prior to filing of suit). Either "reform" could be overextended so as to curtail most plaintiff's shareholder litigation.

5. *See* section 21D(a)(6) of the Securities Exchange Act of 1934 (attorney's fees and expenses awarded by the court "shall not exceed a reasonable percentage of the amount of any damages and prejudgment interest actually paid to the class").

6. Indeed, the tobacco industry did make such payments to the plaintiff's attorneys who represented the state attorneys general in connection with their actions against the industry.

7. For representative statements of this position, see David Freeman Engstrom, *Agencies as Litigation Gatekeepers,* 123 Yale L.J. 616 (2013); Matthew C. Stephenson, *Public Regulation of Private Enforcement: The Case for Expanding the Role of Administrative Agencies,* 91 Va. L. Rev. 93 (2005); Daniel A. Crane, *Optimizing Private Antitrust Enforcement,* 63 Vand. L. Rev. 675 (2010).

8. *See* Joseph A. Grundfest, "Damages and Reliance under Section 10(b) of the Securities Exchange Act," Rock Center for Corporate Governance, Working Paper Series No. 150, at 1 (Aug. 28, 2013), *available at* http://ssrn.com/abstract =2317537.

9. *See* sources cited *supra* note 7.

10. *See* John C. Coffee, Jr., *Rescuing the Private Attorney General: Why the Model of the Lawyer as Bounty Hunter Is Not Working,* 42 Md. L. Rev. 215, 218 (1983); *see also* John C. Coffee, Jr., *Understanding the Plaintiff's Attorney: The Implications of Economic Theory for Private Enforcement of Law through Class and Derivative Action,* 86 Colum. L. Rev. 669 (1986).

11. When U.S. District Judge Jed Rakoff refused to approve the SEC's settlement with Citigroup Capital Markets in 2011 on the ground that the settlement was neither fair nor reasonable because it failed to explain what had happened or who was responsible, the SEC appealed—and won. *See* SEC v. Citigroup Capital Mkts., 2014 U.S. App. LEXIS 10516 (2d Cir. June 4, 2014). The impact is that public agencies can today settle in nearly as much silence as private litigants and can expect judges to rubber stamp their unexplained agreements. It is difficult to be content with this state of affairs, particularly if one believes that there are expressive values associated with law enforcement.

12. For an analysis of this experience with the "qui tam" action, see David Freeman Engstrom, *Harnessing the Private Attorney General: Evidence from Qui Tam Litigation,* 112 Colum. L. Rev. 1244 (2012); *see also* Engstrom, *supra* note 2.

13. The executive order, adopted in the Bush administration, banning the payment of contingent fees by federal agencies in most circumstances was discussed earlier in Chapter 9. The proposal made here does not assume that a classic contingent fee contract need be used, but that a variety of "success" fees could be designed and negotiated.

14. When the corporation is itself selling its securities, the circularity problem fades away, as the shareholders in the selling corporation are enriched by the sale at an inflated price. In the classic "stock drop" case, the corporation is sued for its failure to disclose material information, with the penalty falling on its current shareholders (and those who sold during the period of nondisclosure escaping any penalty).

15. *See* Tom Baker & Sean J. Griffith, ENSURING CORPORATE MISCONDUCT: HOW LIABILITY INSURANCE UNDERMINES SHAREHOLDER LITIGA-TION (2010). These authors elaborately document that D&O liability insurance

is not risk adjusted (and thus low-risk corporations subsidize high-risk ones). Nonetheless, the authors propose only disclosure reforms, in part because they consider substantive reforms politically infeasible. *Id.* at 200–234.

16. Such a reform would require the legislative overruling of *Central Bank of Denver v. First Interstate Bank of Denver,* 511 U.S. 164 (1994), which placed secondary participants generally beyond the reach of Rule 10b-5. In addition, in related decisions, the Court has also narrowed the scope of primary liability by construing who is the "maker" of a statement very restrictively. *See* Janus Capital Group, Inc. v. First Derivative Traders, 131 S. Ct. 2296 (2011).

17. Although private litigants are denied the ability to sue aiders and abettors under the federal securities laws, the SEC can sue such parties and based only on a standard of "recklessness." *See* section 20(e) of the Securities Exchange Act of 1934.

18. Indemnification of liabilities under the federal securities laws has been held to be inconsistent with the policies of the federal securities laws and therefore impermissible (at least when the violation was a more than negligent one). *See* Globus v. Law Research Serv., Inc., 418 F.2d 1276, 1287–1289 (2d Cir. 1969). In private litigation, this rule will seldom be a barrier because the plaintiffs (in order to negotiate a settlement) will agree that the violation was not a "knowing" one. Hence, the use of private counsel by a public agency can outflank the two problems that today most cripple private enforcement.

19. Other means may also be possible by which we could focus entrepreneurial litigation on senior executives. Section 954 of the Dodd-Frank Act mandated "clawbacks" for listed public companies so that incentive compensation received over a defined period would have to be returned to the company by its senior executives in the event of an accounting restatement that was "due to material noncompliance of the issuer" with reporting requirements under the securities laws. For an overview, see Jesse Fried & Nitzan Shilon, *Excess-Pay Clawbacks,* 36 J. Corp. L. 721 (2011). This is in effect a group sanction that could affect a number of executives, and the dollars involved could be sufficiently substantial to attract entrepreneurial plaintiffs. But Dodd-Frank did not establish any procedural mechanism by which this right could be enforced. This leaves plaintiffs dependent on the traditional derivative action, which is usually crippled by its "demand" rule. If a liberalized remedy were recognized so that demand on the board was not necessary, "clawbacks" would represent a very promising remedy because D&O insurance would not cover such amounts and indemnification would probably be unavailable.

20. *See* Wal-Mart Stores, Inc. v. Dukes, 131 S. Ct. 2541 (2011). In second place for the most constraining recent decision is *Comcast Corp. v. Behrend,* 133 S. Ct. 1426 (2013), which has largely precluded complex antitrust class actions. Both decisions are discussed earlier in Chapter 7.

FIGURE AND TABLE CREDITS

Figure 3.1

Source: Gordon, J. N. *Stanford Law Review,* Volume 59, Issue 6; p. 1474. Copyright © 2007 by the Board of Trustees of the Leland Stanford Junior University. See note 45, p. 247.

Figure 4.1

Source: Reprinted from SECURITIES CLASS ACTION SETTLEMENTS: 2012 REVIEW AND ANALYSIS by Ellen M. Ryan and Laura E. Simmons, Cornerstone Research; Figure 1, p. 2. Copyright © 2013 by Cornerstone Research, Inc. http://www.cornerstone.com/files/upload/Cornerstone_Research _2012_Settlements.pdf. All Rights Reserved.

Table 4.1

Source: Reprinted from REPORT OF THE PROCEEDINGS OF THE JUDICIAL CONFERENCE OF THE UNITED STATES 187 (1972); Table 52.

Table 4.2

Data source: Simplified from SECURITIES CLASS ACTION SETTLEMENTS: 2012 REVIEW AND ANALYSIS by Ellen M. Ryan and Laura E. Simmons, Cornerstone Research. Copyright © 2013 by Cornerstone Research, Inc. All Rights Reserved.

Table 5.1

Source: Reprinted from SHAREHOLDER LITIGATION INVOLVING MERGERS AND ACQUISITIONS: REVIEW OF 2012 M&A LITIGATION, SETTLEMENTS, PLAINTIFF ATTORNEY FEES, NEW LAWSUITS CHAL-LENGING ANNUAL PROXIES by Robert M. Daines and Olga Koumrian, Cornerstone Research; Figure 1, p. 1. Copyright © 2013 by Cornerstone Research, Inc. All Rights Reserved.
Data sources: Thomson Reuters' SDC; SEC filings; dockets.
Note: The data include shareholder lawsuits related to acquisitions of U.S. public companies valued at or over $100 million.

Table 5.3

Source: Adapted from SHAREHOLDER LITIGATION INVOLVING MERGERS AND ACQUISITIONS: REVIEW OF 2012 M&A LITIGATION, SETTLEMENTS, PLAINTIFF ATTORNEY FEES, NEW LAWSUITS CHAL-LENGING ANNUAL PROXIES by Robert M. Daines and Olga Koumrian, Cornerstone Research; Figure 3, p. 2. Copyright © 2013 by Cornerstone Research, Inc. All Rights Reserved.
Data sources: Thomson Reuters' SDC; SEC filings; dockets.
Note: The data include shareholder lawsuits related to acquisitions of U.S. public companies valued at or over $100 million.

Table 5.4

Source: Adapted from SHAREHOLDER LITIGATION INVOLVING MERGERS AND ACQUISITIONS: REVIEW OF 2012 M&A LITIGATION, SETTLEMENTS, PLAINTIFF ATTORNEY FEES, NEW LAWSUITS CHAL-LENGING ANNUAL PROXIES by Robert M. Daines and Olga Koumrian, Cornerstone Research; Figure 6, p. 5. Copyright © 2013 by Cornerstone Research, Inc. All Rights Reserved.
Data sources: Thomson Reuters' SDC; SEC filings; dockets.
Note: The data include shareholder lawsuits related to acquisitions of U.S. public companies valued at or over $100 million. Only lawsuits proceeding after consolidation and stay are included.

INDEX